Hear my Testimony: María Teresa Tula, Human Rights Activist of El Salvador

Translated and Edited by Lynn Stephen

South End Press
Boston, Massachusetts

Cover design by Linda Dalal Sawaya.
Front cover photo (and inside front cover) of María Teresa Tula
speaking in front of a CO-MADRES poster, © 1987 by Rick Reinhard.
Text design and production by the South End Press collective.
Printed in the U.S.A.

Library of Congress Cataloguing-in-Publication Data
Tula, María Teresa, 1951-
       Hear my testimony: María Teresa Tula, human rights activist of El
Salvador/ translated and edited by Lynn Stephen.
       p. cm.
Includes bibliographical references.
ISBN 0-89608-485-X (hard): $30.00. -- ISBN 0-89608-484-1 (paper):
$14.00
       1. Tula, María Teresa, 1951- 2. Human rights workers--El Salva-
dor--Biography. 3.Women in politics--El Salvador--Biography. 4. Human
rights--El Salvador--History. 5. El Salvador--Politics and government--
1979- 6. El Salvador--History--1979- I. Stephen, Lynn. II. Title
JC599.S22T85 1994
323'.092--dc20
[B]   93-48349
                                                                           CIP

South End Press, 7 Brookline Street #1, Cambridge, MA 02139-4146

07 06 05 04 03 02   3 4 5 6 7 8 9

Table of Contents

This book is dedicated with all of our love to our families,

especially to the next generation: Susi, Genevieve, and Gabriel

ACKNOWLEDGEMENTS

Because this book is a collaborative effort we would like to acknowledge some people individually and others jointly.

María Teresa Tula:

I would like to thank and acknowledge the importance of my children, my friends, the Salvadoran people, and my country. I remember and thank my parents in Izalco and all my relatives, my grandparents, and friends who were so much a part of the story that is this book. All of you brought me happiness, love, made me laugh and sometimes cry with all the pain we suffered. I thank all of you in my blessed family who shared so much happiness and pain with me. I would like to acknowledge the struggle of the courageous women who are my compañeras in CO-MA-DRES. They walked with me up the difficult road of confronting the horrible realities of war and the loss of loved ones. Thanks to them I was able to become a part of CO-MADRES. I will never forget all the affection and material and spiritual help they gave me. We will continue together in our struggle until there are no more disappeared and justice has been achieved in El Salvador.

I would like to thank all of my friends who helped with this book, and especially Lynn, who had the idea to turn my life story into a book.

Lynn Stephen:

This book has been a truly collaborative process that brought me many new friends and insights. My first appreciation goes to María, who had the inspiration, fortitude, and patience to follow this project through. Her wonderful ability to tell her story in an inspiring and powerful manner is the heart of this book. Martin Diskin first inspired my interest in El

Salvador while we worked together on a political asylum project. Todd Jailer encouraged this project early on and read large portions of it, providing critical insights into Salvadoran history and the ever-changing political situation. Fran Rothstein provided helpful criticism on the chapter on women's movements in El Salvador. Felix Padilla's and Neil Larsen's suggestions were important in helping me frame my discussion of the politics of testimonials. My colleagues in Women's Studies, the Department of Sociology and Anthropology, and in Latino, Latin American, and Caribbean Studies were very encouraging of this project and I thank them. Willie Rodríguez, my colleague in Latino, Latin American, and Caribbean Studies supported and encouraged the project, as did many of my students.

I gratefully acknowledge the collaboration of the following women in El Salvador whose willingness to be interviewed and to share their insights were critical to my understanding of changes in Salvadoran women's organizing and the evolution of the women's movement: Gudelia Abrego, Cecilia Masín, Pasita Rosales, Susana Rodríguez, Gloria Castañeda, Margarita Jiménez, Alba América Guirola Zelaya, Mercedes Cañas, Alicia Panameño de García, Sofía Alas Escamillas, and Oralía de Rivas. Interviews were carried out in September, 1991. Some of these women no longer work with the organizations they were associated with at the time of the interviews. Organizations interviewed in 1991 include: Centro de Estudios de la Mujer "Norma Virginia Guirola de Herrera" (CEMUJER), Asociación de Mujeres Salvadoreñas (AMS), Comité de Madres y Familiares de Presos Políticos, Detenidos, y Asesinados de El Salvador "Monseñor Romero" (CO-MADRES), Instituto para la Investigación, Capacitación, y Desarrollo de la Mujer (IMU), Asociación de Mujeres Salvadoreñas (ADEMUSA), Comité Femenino de la Federación Nacional de Trabajadores Salvadoreños (CO-FENESTRAS), Mujeres Por La Dignidad y La Vida, "Rompamos el Silencio" (DIGNAS), COUNADES, and Mujeres Universitarias de El Salvador (MUES)

My time in researching, translating, and editing this book was supported by the Research and Faculty Development Fund of Northeastern University, and the Young Faculty Fellowship of the Project on Governance of Nonprofit Organizations at the Indiana University Center on Philanthropy.

I want to acknowlege the love, support, and daily encouragement of Ellen Herman in the process of creating this book with María. This book developed in parallel with our son Gabriel, who was born in the middle of its production and grew from a tiny infant to a wonderful toddler as the project was completed. The joy my family gives me on a daily basis provided the energy to complete the book.

Joint Acknowledgments:

Many individuals contributed to the production of this book. First, we would like to thank Kelley Ready not only for her important chapter, but also for reading through the entire manuscript with us several times and providing critical feedback. She also provided help and guidance for research and interviews carried out in El Salvador. In many ways she is a third author of this book. We gratefully acknowledge the financial support of Genevieve Vaughn and the Foundation for a Compassionate Society that provided a secure foundation for this project.

Many thanks to the following individuals: Willie Rodríguez, Marielena Hincapie, Lornia Rivera, Jennifer Herriott, Sheila Kraybill, Stephanie Willman, and María Morelli for transcribing tapes; Sister Maureen Foltz in Washington, D.C. for providing important editorial help; Kenneth Berman for putting the glossary together.

The members of CO-MADRES in El Salvador provided ongoing support for this project. We gratefully acknowledge their contribution and the inspiration their work provided us while working on this project. The Washington Office of Friends of CO-MADRES also provided support and resources for the project, and we gratefully acknowledge their contribution.

Carlos Suárez-Boulangger and Cynthia Peters have provided encouragement and critical editing and feedback in the process of producing this book. We gratefully acknowledge all of their contributions and enthusiasm for the project.

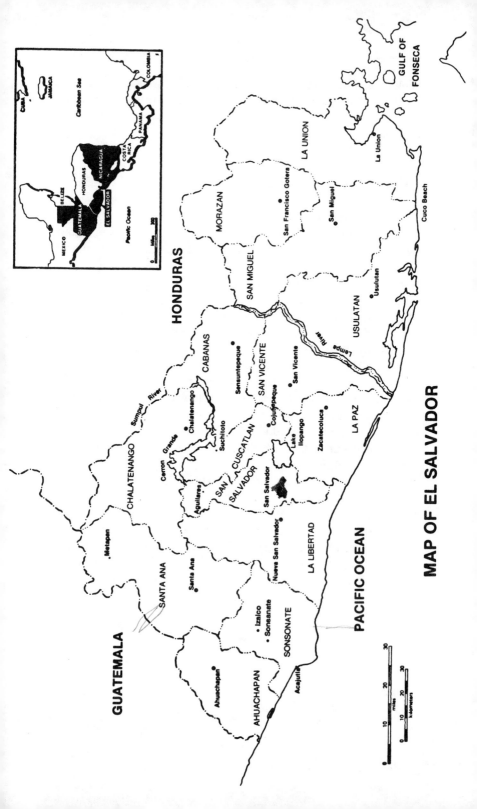

MAP OF EL SALVADOR

CHAPTER 1

INTRODUCTION

There are thousands of women in El Salvador with little formal education, no political experience, and extraordinarily difficult lives, who have participated in a wide range of struggles. This book documents the life of one such woman, 40-year-old María Teresa Tula, a working-class housewife who became an internationally known human rights organizer. María's story is both ordinary and truly exceptional. On the one hand, the trajectory of her life reflects that of many Salvadoran women who entered political life in an effort to move their country toward peace, equality, and democracy. On the other hand, María is a truly exceptional person who was transformed through her political struggles. Her work with CO-MADRES (The Mothers and Relatives of Political Prisoners, Disappeared, and Assassinated of El Salvador "Monseñor Romero") shaped her into a remarkable surveyor of political and economic events and a thoughtful feminist theorist. In María's story, we see the painful reality of life in El Salvador, beginning in the 1950s until the mid-1980s, when she left to reside in the United States. Through her eyes we experience the alienation and difficulties thousands of Salvadorans have as they struggle to "make it" in the promised land of the United States. We also see the transformative potential of political activism as María, who first acts as a responsible wife trying to protect her detained husband, becomes increasingly motivated by her own sense of justice to confront the military, government officials, and her own torturers in the battle for human rights. In the process, she also is awakened to her own oppression as a poor, Salvadoran woman and begins to see the world through gendered eyes.

María's story is full of transformations. We see not only the bloody evolution and beginning resolution of the civil war which raged in El Salvador from 1979-1992, but we also see the growth and stability of CO-MADRES, perhaps the most persistent popular organization to emerge in the past two decades. María joined CO-MADRES in 1978, shortly after it began as a small group of mothers searching for their disappeared relatives and imprisoned and assassinated family members. Unlike María, who had no political experience until she was rudely awakened to political reality when her husband was imprisoned for being a union activist, most of the first CO-MADRES members came out of Christian Base Communities. Following a philosophy that regarded poverty and exploitation as a sin, these women worked with priests and nuns to begin confronting the Salvadoran military and oligarchy to change the gross inequalities that characterized Salvadoran society in the late 1960s.

With their radical philosophy of justice, the CO-MADRES slowly peeled away the shroud of silence surrounding the repression that had become normal in El Salvador in the 1970s. Armed with a list of missing relatives they demanded to know who was in the jails, forced the excavation of clandestine cemeteries, and publicized the government's repressive tactics. Their first actions in 1978 included taking over the Salvadoran Red Cross Building, organizing a hunger strike, and planning the peaceful take-over of the United Nations building in San Salvador. They then moved on to occupying Catholic churches and holding public demonstrations in parks and plazas. Their 1979 invitation to Costa Rica launched an extremely effective campaign to build international solidarity for their work. In the 1980s, CO-MADRES activists, voicing their demands for justice, travelled around the world to Europe, Australia, Canada, the United States, and Latin America. They became one of the leading voices of FEDEFAM (Federación Latino Americana de Familiares de Detenidos y Desaparecidos, the Federation of the Relatives of the Disappeared and Detained in Latin America), which includes organizations from 17 Latin American and Caribbean countries. In 1984, CO-MADRES was the first recipient of the Robert F. Kennedy Human Rights Award. The Kennedy family has been a long-standing supporter of CO-MADRES, along with musician Bonnie Raitt. "Friends of CO-MADRES" organizations were established in the United States, Australia, Switzerland, Germany, Mexico, and Canada beginning in the mid-1980s to raise money and act as political watchdogs for human rights abuses in El Salvador. Nine chapters of Friends of CO-MADRES were established in the United States.

Soon after the members of CO-MADRES began organizing in the late 1970s, they became the victims of government repression. Their first office was bombed in 1980 and since then their offices have been bombed four additional times, most recently in 1989, shortly before the FMLN's (Farabundo Martí National Liberation Front) November offensive. Each time they have regrouped and kept on working. In 1989, the Women's Section of the Norwegian Social Democratic Party donated money that was used to purchase a permanent office site.

Many of the most active CO-MADRES members have been detained, tortured, and raped, as documented in María's story. Since 1977, forty-eight have been detained, five have been assassinated, and three have been "disappeared." Even after the peace accords were signed in January 1992, harassment and disappearances have continued. In February 1993, the son and nephew of one of the founders of CO-MADRES were assassinated in Usulután. This founder had already lived through her own detention, the detention and gang rape of her daughter, and the disappearance and assassination of other relatives. For many CO-MADRES members, their experience of torture and abuse has fortified their determination. The use of rape as a special instrument of terror for women led CO-MADRES to question the social and sexual roles assigned to Salvadoran women.

While the formal agenda of CO-MADRES members remained focused on confronting the sources of human rights abuses in El Salvador, in their private conversations and experience, they also began seriously questioning female gender roles. Many activists were not supported by their husbands at best, and beaten by them at worst. When members of CO-MADRES were raped, as a routine part of their torture, they would be rejected by their husbands and families as damaged goods. Private, internal discussions about what rights they had as women, as workers, and as mothers, slowly became part of their public agenda at the end of the 1980s. Support for this new aspect of their work came in part from a small feminist movement emerging in El Salvador at that time. As women's sections of other popular organizations began to question their subordinate position within their own organizations and homes, other Salvadoran women were beginning to take a public stand on such issues as rape, unequal work burdens in the home, the political marginalization of women, and women's lack of control over their own sexuality and bodies.

In the 1990s, CO-MADRES is focusing on unequal gender roles in the home, holding the state accountable for human rights violations committed during the war, and educating women about political participation. As the struggle to implement the terms of the January 1992 peace accords paves the way for the 1994 general elections, CO-MADRES is organizing participation in the upcoming electoral process. Grassroots democracy is now part of their programmatic list of priorities. New post-war programs also include working with children and adults to alleviate the psychological effects of the war, education, and literacy for women, changing the legal codes of El Salvador to ensure that human rights are protected within the framework of the peace accords, and legal training for women in the area of human rights.

The deepening and broadening of CO-MADRES' political agenda and ideology since 1977 is extraordinary. Because CO-MADRES members come from different ethnic, class, and regional backgrounds, the organization means something different to each of them. CO-MADRES has deepened and redefined both traditional gender roles and what is encompassed under the umbrella of human rights. The meaning of mothering has expanded to include not only taking care of one's family, but also of one's country, taking responsibility as a participating individual who stands up for the rights of all and demands adherence to democratic principles. Human rights now includes not only the right to free political expression, but also the right to a decent standard of living, to education and opportunity, and for women, self-determination and the right to be treated and valued equally to men.

The story of one woman in CO-MADRES cannot, of course, tell us the stories of all women in CO-MADRES. María Teresa Tula's experience as a woman who grew up in a poor rural community is different from that of women who grew up in the city or in the more marginal areas of the Salvadoran countryside. Her story does reflect, however, the significance of CO-MADRES in the lives of all the women involved.

From Conversation to Book

For the past eight years, I have been conducting research on Latin American women. From 1985 through 1987, I lived and worked in a Zapotec community in Oaxaca, Mexico exploring how economic development since the 1920s has affected women's political, economic, and social roles. During 1990 and 1991 I spent time in Brazil, Chile, Paraguay, and El Salvador looking at women's participation in grassroots peasant organizations and urban social movements. I did this work as an ethnographer, relying on participant observation, interviews, and life histories for my information. During this time, I developed many close relationships that were the basis for much of what I learned. They involved long hours of conversation, sharing important events and reflecting on the past and the present.

Without a doubt I gained the most insight from long conversations with some of my Zapotec friends, cultural intellectuals who shared detailed personal life histories and used them as a basis for reflecting on community history and culture. I came to know other such intellectuals in Brazil's rural women's movements, in a seasonal worker's union in Chile, and among leaders of El Salvador's grassroots women's organizations. From these experiences, I developed a deep respect for the insights to be gained from personal narrative.

The courageous struggle of the Salvadoran people in the face of a terrible civil war has been an important part of my teaching and political work over the past five years. As an anthropology professor, one of the hardest tasks I have is convincing U.S. students, whatever their background, of the reality of war, poverty, and people's resistance in other countries. In my courses on Latin America, I find that many students have unconsciously adopted the dominant ideological explanations for the miserable conditions found in many parts of the world. In their education, they had received either no information or disinformation. The voices of marginalized people around the world are seldom heard.

Many students have been taught that communist intervention is the reason for the wars in Central America, that people are poor because they have too many children, that women are oppressed because of inevitable machismo found among Third World men. Helping students to rethink their perceptions so they can better see the links between U.S. policy and the situation of people around the world is a major challenge, but a welcome one.

In trying to meet this challenge, I have found no tool more effective than the testimonial. Watching the change that comes over students after reading *I, Rigoberta Menchú* or listening to María Teresa Tula talk is truly inspiring. The opportunity to collaborate with María in producing a testimonial based on her life story meant that I would be able to combine one of my favorite aspects of anthropology with the creation of a powerful teaching tool for use both within and outside of the university.

My participation in testimonial writing began over my kitchen table. I first met María in the Fall of 1990 when she came to Boston to give a series of talks for CO-MADRES. I planned to interview her for an article on women activists in Latin America. We reserved about two and a half hours for the interview. After I had used up about two hours of tape and we only had half an hour remaining, I began to realize that what was happening was not an interview. I had originally asked María to summarize her life story for me. After two hours, we had made it to about age ten. At that moment it was clear that a new project was taking place.

I asked María if she'd be willing to return the next day to finish the interview. She agreed and we met again for two more hours the following day. At the end of those two hours we had made it to age fourteen. The previous night I had thought about the interview and concluded that I was witnessing a testimony in progress. It could be a testimonial. In retrospect, this was not something that I influenced alone. Around my bright blue kitchen table, María had also carefully chosen the words she spoke and had stretched the time to accommodate what she thought was important to convey.

She is a wonderful story-teller, and accustomed to telling "her story." María had given her testimony on many public occasions and in many interviews. She had testified for the Senate, for rock stars Sting and Bonnie Raitt, for delegations visiting El Salvador, for countless groups of people across the United States, and she had told her story on video. But usually the time was limited to one hour, one tape, or one meeting. The full detail and richness of her story had yet to come out.

After our second meeting, I proposed that she return and we spend about five days recording her story. She said that she would think seriously about it and discuss it with others in the CO-MADRES office in Washington, D.C. We agreed that it would be best to devote an entire trip to taping her story. We talked again in December and she enthusiastically endorsed the idea of turning her life story into a book.

She returned in January 1991, on the day that the United States began pounding Baghdad with "smart" bombs in what came to be called the Gulf War. We sat riveted to the television watching Fourth of July images of fireworks over Baghdad as journalists talked about clean surgical strikes. Periodically, the cameras cut to the Pentagon situation room where the war was explained with reference to neat, multicolored maps. Our work on the testimonial started at the beginning of a war with no people in it, or so we were told. By contrast, María's story was filled with the pain and anguish inflicted on people's daily lives by the civil war in El Salvador.

During the day, we would spend six to eight hours talking. Often María would speak for 15 minutes to half an hour uninterrupted. She would work with a question and then go on from there. Her life story came out in roughly chronological order, but was always mediated by comments on the civil war in El Salvador, the military, U.S. foreign policy, women's rights, or other topics that came to mind. She chose to tell her story beginning with her childhood and ending with the close of El Salvador's civil war. We would stop and eat and then talk again.

When we were not talking we made signs and took them to the daily anti-war demonstrations held in front of the Kennedy Federal Building in Boston. María always commented about how orderly and obedient U.S. protesters were. "Why don't people take over the street and the sidewalk? Why do they always move so nicely out of the way for the police? In my country we would never be so passive." We talked about children, sons, what it is like to have your kids in the military. We discussed what war does to families and to children. At one point, María gave an impromptu speech at a large gathering in Madison Park High School in Boston. It was a multiracial gathering of Boston youth who had come together to talk about the war. María described what war meant to her and to young people in her country. We then returned to the blue table in my kitchen to continue talking about the war in her country—torture, bombing, the maiming of innocent children, hatred, and the seemingly inexplicable nature of militarism. The testimonial took shape not only in response to the questions I asked and what María had to say, but also to what was going on around us.

The bulk of María's story was recorded during that visit in January 1991. We continued to work on it, however, until the manuscript was submitted in 1993. Every time María came to Boston to give a talk for CO-MADRES we would add to her story.

When the FMLN and the Salvadoran government signed official peace accords on New Year's Day 1992, and hundreds of thousands of Salvadorans flooded the square by the Cathedral in San Salvador, María had more to add to her story. Every time we see each other there is more. And there will always be more. A testimonial, like someone's life, is never complete. It is always in process and changing as is each individual's perspective on his or her own life and the way in which he or she wants to relate it to the outside world.

The text was put together in the same order María spoke it. It was edited for repetition and translated from transcriptions of the Spanish. In some cases parts of the spoken story were omitted, usually to avoid repetition and bring out what María felt were the most important parts. María helped to make those choices. The structure of her story, order, and details of events were all discussed several times, and the manuscript was read back to María to check for accuracy and her agreement.

María recognizes the limitations of personal narrative. Whenever I would tell María that we were working on her life story, she would always gently remind me that it was only part of it. "What you have on those pages is just part of my story—only part of it." When I gave her 500 pages of transcribed Spanish, she thanked me, smiled, and said, "Just imagine, how many pages it could be. This is only part of what I could tell."

This book was written as a collaborative effort to bring María's story to light, to provide a context for thinking about it, and a framework for looking critically at the process of testimonial collaboration, production, and consumption, represented in the creation of this book. Chapters 2 through 14 are the story of María's life as told on tape, recorded, transcribed, edited, translated, and discussed with her. Her testimony is followed by several descriptive chapters. Chapter 15 offers a brief political and economic history of El Salvador and women's place in it. Chapter 16 is an overview of women's grassroots organizing since 1970 and the relationship of CO-MADRES to other women's organizing. The final chapter raises critical questions about the genre of testimonials, what they represent, and how they are produced and consumed.

CHAPTER 2

FROM CHILDHOOD TO MOTHERHOOD

I was born on April 23, 1951 into a very poor family. I grew up with my mother, my grandmother, and part of my mother's family. My father was an irresponsible man. He had two women. My mother was really young when she decided to go with him, maybe 16 years old. Meanwhile, my father was involved with another woman, whom he later married when he learned she was having a baby. My mother had a baby boy before I was born.

My father was very mean to my mother. He dominated her and kept her shut up in a house. He even did all the shopping so that she wouldn't have to leave. My mother began to realize that he had another woman because sometimes he would come home and other times he wouldn't. When my mother realized that my father was also living with another woman, she left him.

She was three months pregnant with me when she left him and went to live in her mother's house. My grandmother was a very humble woman. She never went to school or learned how to read or write. Her work was to cook and to make chocolate to sell. She also washed and ironed clothing in order to survive.

She was a well known cook in the town of Izalco which is in the department of Sonsonate, about 78 kilometers from San Salvador. Izalco is a small town, but it is well known. My grandmother was a very elegant woman of Indian origin, as are all of the people of Izalco. She was tall with a pretty nose and she had long black hair. She was very traditional and never dressed in pants, never dressed outlandishly, and she never went to any dances. She did everything according to community traditions.

Grandmother was very Catholic and I remember that she taught me that during Holy Week we couldn't run around on Monday, Thursday or Good Friday because if we did, the earth would open and swallow us up. So I always was well behaved during Holy Week. She also taught us that we shouldn't bathe until Sunday during Holy Week because we were doing penance for Christ's crucifixion. My family was religious and we went to the processions for all the saints in the neighborhoods of Izalco. We believed in the saints like Santa Teresa, the Virgin of Dolores, and San Lazaro. Each month one of these saints had its own day of celebration, a *cofradía*.* The whole town would celebrate with flowers, fireworks, and a procession to honor the saints. We also had to go to mass.

My grandmother's house was very simple and made of adobe, just the earth. When she lived there, my mother made a living by harvesting coffee and by going to sell yucca and other things to tourists at a nearby resort called Atecozol. At that time, my grandmother worked in the home of some middle-class people for about 30 colones per month.**

My mother didn't know how to read or write because she never went to school. She always depended on doing domestic work or other work to support us. When I was very small, my mother decided to move to Santa Ana, to look for work. She wanted to take both me and my brother with her. I was one year old. My grandmother refused to let her take us. "What are you going to do with two small children in a city where you don't have any relatives? Anything could happen. Why don't you just take the older boy?"

I stayed with my grandmother. As a child, I couldn't remember if I was living with my real mother or my grandmother, because I grew up saying "mother" to my grandmother. Her name was Joaquina Isabel Tula. My grandmother had a hard time providing for me, but we had food and medicine, and we slept together in one bed. Later on, I remember that we went to live in another house made of wood in the neighborhood of Santa

---

* *Cofradías* are religious brotherhoods that are responsible for sponsoring festivities for the cult celebrations of community saints.

** In the 1950s, this would have been the equivalent of about $5-10 per month.

Teresa in Izalco. It wasn't made out of ordinary wood, but out of very cheap wood with lots of knot holes in it. We would have to fill the holes with paper to keep the wind from blowing through and making us cold. The whole house was about five square meters. We cooked with firewood because we didn't have electricity. We didn't have any water either. The house had one room that was everything—the kitchen and the bedroom. But this small house had a yard with mangos, guayabas, oranges, soursops, and cashews. I liked that yard very much.

My grandmother used to tell me things about being a girl. I could feel the difference between boys and girls. She used to tell me, "You are a girl. You have to be well behaved. You have to sit like this with your legs together and pull your dress down." The people I grew up around were very conservative. They took care of their bodies like they were important pieces of personal property. We wore dresses, long dresses. I can never remember wearing miniskirts. I never used tight clothing. We wore very simple clothing. I didn't wear shoes until I was eight years old and went to school. My grandmother couldn't afford the shoes and the uniforms that they require students to wear to school in El Salvador.

I didn't quite understand who my mother was until I was seven years old. After my mother went to Santa Ana, we didn't hear from her for a long time. She couldn't write and we didn't have any money to talk by telephone. Actually, I called my mother "aunt" like my cousins did, following their example. I didn't think of her as my mother.

When I was younger, I got very sick and had serious problems. I had asthma which is a very difficult disease. You need money to treat it, and to pay for all the hospital visits and the medicine. The hospitals in Izalco were not very good, so we had to go to San Salvador. But we didn't have the money for the bus fare to the city. Instead, my grandmother treated me with her love, and looked for ways to give me natural medicine.

I look like my father and my other two siblings. He had these children with other women, not my mother. We grew up in different towns. I remember visiting my brother and sister and noticing that they had shoes on and they were better dressed than I was. My father was also well dressed. I didn't have any shoes and my clothing was in worse shape than theirs, but I was clean. When I met my father he never asked me, "Are you in school? What do you want? What do you need? Can I help you with anything?" Instead, he just reached into his pocket and pulled out five cents. Five cents was nothing then. He said, "Take this and go buy some candy." I remember that it made me happy. Maybe it was because my father gave me a little bit of money and it was really rare for me and my grandmother to have any money. I bought a handful of candy at the store.

When I returned home, my grandmother asked me, "What do you have there? Candy? Who gave that to you?"

"My father," I said.

"Your father gave you candy?" she asked.

I didn't tell her that he gave me five cents and that I went to buy the candy.

She said, "How much did he give you? Five measly cents? What a jerk."

I didn't know what a jerk was. Then my grandmother added that he was irresponsible. That he should have known better since he had children. She said, "He should have bought you clothing and food."

Then my grandmother sat me down in her lap and told me, "Listen, he is your father, your real father, but he lives with another woman, and he has other children. He never came here to talk with me about what you need for school and other things." Then my grandmother began to cry.

"Why are you crying?" I asked.

"Because the whole situation is sad and I am just feeling it." She sat there and cried.

I finally was sent to school because someone in the house where my grandmother worked helped me. Grandmother was working in the house of a politician, a representative of the PCN (Partido de Conciliación Nacional, National Conciliation Party). My grandmother cooked for 10 people, and for the dogs and cats too. These people had huge dogs who guarded their houses. Dobermans. They were very expensive dogs and really big. And they ate very well.

This man had a daughter living with him, but she wasn't a daughter from his marriage. This politician was a real womanizer and usually nine months after he was with a woman, a child would appear. He was a real Don Juan as we say in our town. He had children in his house from humble women whom he had gotten pregnant while they worked for him. When these women got pregnant they would leave, but later when their children were bigger, he would recognize them, and they went to live with him, together with the children from his marriage. He had a lot of illegitimate children. This daughter was one of them. She was also my confirmation godmother.

One day she asked my grandmother why I didn't go to school. Grandmother said, "I don't have the money to pay for her uniforms. Neither her mother nor her father give me any assistance."

Although she was only about 17 years old, this young woman said to me, "Look, I want you to go to school."

"Me? I'm going to go to school?" I said.

"Yes. You are going to learn to write. You can get to know children your own age. It will be good for you in the future. I'm going to help you," she said.

She became good friends with me and my grandmother, and she helped us. She understood us because her mother was also a poor and humble woman. Some man had abused her and made her pregnant. That was why she went to live with her father.

So I went to school. It was called the Doctor Mario Calvo Marroquín school in Izalco. It was a school for children between first and sixth grade. All of the children wore blue and white uniforms. I thought that the school was beautiful and very large. It had fruit trees in the yard.

In the first grade, we would start at eight in the morning and get out at eleven. Then we would return at two in the afternoon and leave at four o'clock, with homework. We had classes Monday through Friday and sometimes on Saturday. They taught us Spanish, social science, mathematics, calligraphy, geography, and the history of El Salvador. They told us about the history of the rivers in each town, about the volcanoes and mountains, the number of people in each town, and about people's customs. That's when I realized that there were other towns and places in El Salvador. I had never thought about it before. I only thought about my own town of Izalco.

After I had been in school for about a year, my grandmother told me, "I want you to go visit an aunt who lives in San Salvador. I want you to go with me for a few months. I am very tired." My grandmother was also worried about something else.

There was the problem of the politician whose house we were working in. He always tried to take advantage of all the young women working in the house as they grew older. He would always try to seduce them with gifts or shoes or little presents of money. His sons would do the same.

I remember my godmother called me aside when I was eight or nine years old and she said to me, "I want to talk to you. When my father offers you money, don't take it. Don't ever go into his room when he is alone. Always be aware that the worst can happen."

I didn't know what could happen, but I was careful. One time I brought him his food and he began talking to me, and I felt him getting closer to me. I remembered what my godmother had told me. I backed away, saying, "I'm going now. I'm going to buy some ice cream."

I didn't even clean up the dishes or anything. He came back that afternoon very angry and asked me why I hadn't cleaned up the dishes. I just remembered what my godmother said about when he got close and offered me money.

Because of that, we left and went to San Salvador. After that I didn't ever go to school again. Instead, I sold bread and eggs in the market of San Carlos in San Salvador to help out my family. It wasn't easy for us poor people to sell a few things in the market. We didn't have a lot to sell, and people didn't have much money to buy things with. I remember all the people who lived in the market with their children. They had no houses, nowhere to go. They just lived there. I learned a lot about poverty by selling things in the market.

When I was 13 or 14 years old my grandmother died of a heart attack. I think it was in 1965. The death of my grandmother was the first big blow that life dealt to me. It was horrible. I didn't feel that my own father and mother loved me, and I didn't think that anyone else would accept me or be able to love me as much as my grandmother. She treated me like her only grandchild, even though she had a lot of grandchildren. When she died, my life changed completely.

Before my grandmother died, I remember visiting my father and getting to know the woman he was living with. Everyone used to say to me, "You are the daughter of Gregorio Pinto, right?" I think that this woman was jealous of me and my older brother because we looked a lot like my father, maybe more than her children.

On one of these visits, I said to him, "Papa, I need some new shoes. I saw some nice ones made of leather in the market that I would like to have." They were black shoes, the kind of shoes I needed for school.

He said, "Okay. That's fine. I'm going to buy you those shoes." He gave me a little piece of paper with a note on it for a woman who worked in the market. Her name was Toñita Artiga.

Soon I went to see her and said, "Doña Toñita, look, my father sent me with this piece of paper."

"Don Pinto? Of course. Come with me."

She took me to the shoes and clothing section of the market and I showed her the shoes I liked. But when she saw which ones I wanted, she said, "Oh, that's not what it says here. It says on the paper you are to get rubber shoes, not leather. The cheap shoes that cost 50 cents."

I knew that these shoes were uncomfortable, and they can burn your feet because they get very hot. I thought to myself, well, maybe I have to take these. I won't look at the shoes I like, maybe they are expensive. I sort of got used to the rubber shoes, but sometimes I couldn't put them on because they hurt too much. These are the shoes my father gave me. I didn't see my father very much and grew more distant from him. I never went to see him in his large house again and by the time my grandmother died, I felt very distant from him.

When my grandmother died, I went with my mother to live in Santa Ana. Her house was very small. It had one small place for making tortillas and there were neighbors all around. My mother was making a living by selling tortillas to people who would come to the house. It was crowded and there was no place to go outside. There was no yard like at my grandmother's house.

Shortly after I arrived, my mother's tortilla business went under. There was too much competition from other people and she couldn't sell enough tortillas to get by. That's when she took a job as a cook in an agronomy school. My mother worked there for a long time and she began to take me with her. She would leave at four in the morning every day.

She took me with her because she was afraid of what my stepfather would do to me if she left me alone with him. My mother never talked to me about what went on between her and my stepfather, but I could tell that my mother was afraid for her life. Sometimes he beat her horribly. He was a very jealous man, even though my mother never set eyes on another man. I could hear them arguing but I didn't know what they were fighting about. I would ask her, "What's wrong with you?" She would reply, "Nothing, I'm fine." Later I realized that my stepfather was beating her in their room. But we couldn't say anything because they were a couple living together. As children we didn't have the right to interfere.

I had an 18-year-old brother and other brothers and sisters from my stepfather who were much smaller. I had a lot of trouble getting along with them. We fought often. They would tell me, "You're not really our sister. You have a different mother. Our mother isn't your real mother." This confused me, because the person I really thought of as my mother, my grandmother, had died. I felt terrible and very depressed during this period. I felt no one loved me or cared about me.

I think that all of this influenced me when I met a boy where my mother worked. He was a bit older than me, maybe two years, and all he knew about me was that I also worked there every day. He asked my mother about me. "Señora, who is this young woman? Introduce her to me. I want to meet her."

My mother informed him, "She's my daughter and she just came here to live with me." He was very interested in me at that time. I didn't know anything about him, if he loved me or didn't love me. I got to know him and he began to speak to me about love. At first I was afraid of him, but I also felt I needed him. I needed someone.

He was very kind. He didn't talk dirty to me, or embrace me, or even touch me. I used to smile and ask myself, "Wow, what is going on?" We went out for some time without my mother realizing that we were seeing each other. After a while, he began to talk to me about love, and how he loved me. After this, I began to feel some affection for him, but I was also afraid of everything that my mother had told me about men. Also, I was frightened by the men in my family. My mother didn't trust my stepfather near me, and my brother also frightened me. He used to beat me just because he was a man. He would say, "I am your older brother and you have to do what I say."

Despite my fear, I loved this boy and I wanted him, but I was very afraid. One day he said to me, "I'm going to make you mine." I said, "Me? Okay. I will be yours." But I wasn't sure what it meant for him to "make me his."

He said, "Good. I want to make you mine but I don't want to hurt you. I want to be responsible for you."

During this period, it was very difficult for me to deal with sex. I never had any education about sex, and no one in my family ever talked about it in front of us. I never saw my mother caressing or kissing my stepfather. Everything was hidden. I started to stay with this young man on the sly, sleeping with him. Whenever I would see my mother, I would be afraid. What would she do if she knew? Would she beat me? Would she kill me? That's how I got pregnant with my first child at the age of

15. The problem was that ever since I first got my period when I was 13 years old, my mother kept track of it. Because I was the oldest daughter, they really watched me. I think my mother realized that I was sick during my first month of pregnancy. I wasn't worried during the first month, but my mother questioned me just the same.

"Why haven't you gotten your period?" she asked. She asked me again and again, "Why didn't you get your period?"

"I don't know, Mamá," I answered.

"We're going to talk about this," my mother said.

Then I went to tell this boy I was seeing.

"I didn't get my period," I told him.

"You're kidding," he said, very surprised. He didn't say anything else.

Then my period didn't come for a second month and I was starting to feel different inside. My mother looked at me and said, "You come here and talk to me." She grabbed me by my shirt. She knew all about pregnancy because she had six children.

"Sit down in this chair and tell me the truth," she said sitting down in front of me. My stepfather and my siblings all sat there in front of me like judges waiting to pass a sentence on me.

"You have been deceiving us," said my older brother. "We have been victimized by you. You are making fun of us."

"What have I done to you?" I asked. "I haven't done anything to you."

"You are going to tell us the truth," demanded my mother, and I remember that she hit me very hard.

"Tell the truth!" she yelled. "You are pregnant. Who is the man?"

For about five hours all of them—my mother, my stepfather, my brother, they were all questioning me. I didn't think it would ever stop. Finally, I confessed who I had been seeing. That night was terrible. Awful.

I had already talked with the boy I had been seeing about what happened. He knew I was pregnant. He said, "I'll go talk with your family. Don't you worry. I will take care of you. I want to take you to my house."

"I don't want to stay with my mother any more," I said.

"No, now you won't be able to," he said. "We are going to form a family now. You are going to have a child and I want to be there when it is born. It's my first child too."

The next day my mother spoke with him at work. She was very angry with him. She called him a lot of names and told him that he was irresponsible.

He told her, "It's true, Señora. I am responsible for getting your daughter pregnant. I love her and it's my first child. I want to start a home with her even if you don't want me to. I realize how hard it's been for her since she came to live with you."

Later when we talked, he told me everything that he had said to my mother. Then we made a plan for me to go away with him. We chose a specific time on a certain day when he was going to wait for me one block from my house.

I was frightened by this. I said, "Why are you going to take me to your house? You make it sound like I am a motorcycle or a chicken that you take home with you. If you don't want to live with me, then I don't want to come."

"It's your decision," he said. "I can't force you to come, but I want you to."

I waited for the appointed day we were to meet and I felt I wanted to go and live with him. I had decided I would, but my mother wouldn't let me out of the house. She told me that I wasn't going outside. It was terrible. The time we had said we would meet passed. Then one day passed, then another, and another. And I never saw him again. That's what happened. I just never saw him again, the father of my first child.

"Now you're pregnant," my mother told me, "you will have to work and make a living for yourself and your child." I began to work in a house where they paid me to cook and clean. I also sold tamales and other food. I used the money to buy clothing for my baby.

"You are not innocent anymore," my mother said. "You have to be prepared. You have to be strong. Children need a lot of care. They have to be fed, dressed, nursed."

I kept cleaning the house where I worked right up until my daughter was born. I was scrubbing the floors with a huge belly on all fours. I came home at four o'clock in the afternoon and I felt the contractions in my stomach. Sometimes they hurt a little and sometimes they hurt a lot. I spent a whole night this way with the contractions coming on stronger and stronger.

My mother asked me how I was doing. In the middle of the night, I said, "I can't take the pain anymore."

"Okay," she said, "Let's go to the hospital."

At one in the morning we walked for about 40 minutes to the hospital. There were no buses then, and my mother didn't have any money for a taxi. We walked until we reached the hospital in Santa Ana. They asked me my age and if there were any problems with the baby. I said no. They told me I could stay.

As my mother left she told me, "Since you were brave enough to be with a man, now you have to be brave enough to have your child." Then she walked out and I was alone.

The contractions came on stronger and stronger, and closer together. When I thought I couldn't bear it anymore, a nurse came and moved me onto the bed. She put me in position to give birth. Then the baby was born. It was a girl. She looked just like her father. And I never saw him again.

María's mother, Lidia Tula

María at age 15

CHAPTER 3

WORKING-CLASS HOUSEWIFE

When my baby was born, my mother asked, "Is it a girl? What is it?"

"It's a girl," I told her.

"Oh. So it's a girl," she said. I think she was disappointed because she already had four daughters and she wanted a grandson. This was my daughter, her first grandchild, but when I presented the baby to her, my mother just looked at her.

"She looks exactly like him," she said, referring to the father. Then we talked for a while.

"How did it go?" she asked, referring to the delivery.

"Fine, fine," I replied. I didn't have any problems. In fact, I had been in the hospital for two days and no one came to see me. I didn't even have enough money to get home from the hospital, so I walked. They discharged me from the hospital and I only had clothes for the baby. Nothing else. After they discharged me, I started walking toward the house. It took me about an hour and a half to walk with my two-day-old baby.

I arrived home sometime after lunch and my mother was surprised to see me.

"Oh, you're back already," she said.

"They discharged me," I replied.

"Well," she said, "Now you know what it is to be a woman. You have to work to support your child. You can rest for about eight days and then you'll have to work. I can't be responsible for supporting this child."

My mother helped me out for a few days, maybe because she felt bad that she hadn't been more sympathetic, or because she empathized, since she had gone through the same thing herself. Soon, she came to adore her granddaughter.

About 20 days after my daughter was born, I began to sell tamales, roasted corn, and other various foods on the street that I would carry in a big basket on top of my head. I would leave the baby for two hours and go selling, and then I would come back to nurse her. At first, she was only drinking my milk. Later on, I would buy her milk, little by little with what I earned.

When my daughter was a few months old, I started to have intense back pain and problems with the muscles and cartilage in my back. There was a time when I could hardly walk because of the pain. The muscles supporting my back hadn't gotten firm again like they were supposed to. In addition to this great pain, I also had really high fevers. I was very ill. My mother never even asked me about it.

"Mother, do you have any medicine?" I would ask her.

"No," she would say. "You are just like those old ladies. You are so young and taking medicine."

Sometimes my fevers would go up to 40 degrees (celsius) and I would be covered with sweat, even on my lips. It was terrible. I had such a bad fever and it would not go away. And my mother didn't believe I was sick.

My neighbors would say, "Tere, don't you feel well?" They asked this because I would sit down and then it would take 10 or 15 minutes before I could stand up. When I did stand up, I would cry because of the tremendous pain I was feeling. I could not even lie down or anything. I would plead, "Dear God, help me." I would think of my grandmother. I would see her face in front of me. I would ask, "Grandma, why did you go? Why did you leave me? Nobody loves me." As the years passed, I would still speak to her. I would dream about her.

My mother asked me, "Why didn't you tell me you were sick instead of complaining to the neighbors? I am going to send you to the hospital and there they can cure you of whatever you have." So I woke up at two in the morning and started to walk to the hospital at three o'clock.

I could hardly walk. I walked very slowly. Finally, I arrived at the hospital at about eight o'clock in the morning, but my mother had made an appointment for seven o'clock. I missed the appointment. I couldn't make it on time.

I tried to explain to the nurse, "Listen, I came from this far away place, and I have this problem…"

"No," she said cutting me off. "There are no more appointments. Everything is booked. Come back tomorrow."

Once again, I had to walk back because I had no money to take public transportation. I did not even have a glass of water before I left because in these hospitals, they did not have any water. When I arrived home at about two in the afternoon, there was no food. We were so poor.

"How was the appointment?" my mother asked.

"I didn't make it," I told her. "I couldn't get there on time." Life was hard for us then.

But later, things at home became even more difficult for me. My brother would beat me, and I could not say anything because in their eyes I was an undesirable woman. I had a daughter; I was not married; and the baby's father had left me. This was a disgrace to them. Also because I didn't make enough money to support my daughter and myself.

The time came when I could not take it anymore, and I found a way to defend myself. The next time my brother tried to beat me, I defended myself. I was 16 years old. We were having a discussion. When it got heated, I didn't answer him. I wanted to show my other siblings that I wouldn't fight with him because my mother and grandmother had taught me to respect the family. Then came the moment when he didn't want to give in to my silence. He came over and took off his belt.

At this moment, I don't know what came over me, but I said, "No, you're not going to hit me." And when he raised his arm with the belt to hit me, I pushed him with a strength so great that I threw him across the room. I was in front of a basin filling up a bowl with water. When he raised the belt in the air I grabbed the end of it and wrapped it around my hand and pulled on it. I pulled so hard that he crashed to the floor. Doing that let loose all the anger I felt toward him and everyone else. We fought fiercely. I was kicking him and beating him on the head so badly that the neighbors had to come to break it up.

After this happened, I felt nothing. My hands were numb and I couldn't even feel my body. I didn't even feel like I had beat him. From that moment on, my brother had a little more respect for me.

The anger I felt was so intense that I wouldn't have wanted to express it, even if I had time to think about it. At that moment I did not even recognize him as my brother. I couldn't feel who I was either. I felt like my body was a shadow. After that fight, my whole being changed. Everything about my life felt different. I knew that the way I was being treated was unjust.

"What you're doing to me isn't fair," I told my family. "If you don't love me, tell me to leave and I will. If you don't want me to be here, then I will leave."

"And where will you go?" said my mother.

"Maybe, I can go somewhere and stay with a friend," I replied.

"The doors are open," my mother answered. "You can leave whenever your want. You can stay or you can go."

Around that time, about seven months after my daughter was born, I saw a relative of my daughter's father. He was very friendly and asked me about my little girl. He asked me to forgive his family for everything that had happened. Then he invited me to visit the house where the father of my daughter lived.

After inquiring with some people, I figured out how to get there. They had moved and now lived in a very nice place. They were farmers and had planted corn, vegetables, and other things. The father of my daughter had a room in this house.

Although the parents and the siblings of my baby's father were very kind to me, I was afraid when I first arrived because I did not know whether or not he was there, or if he was with another woman.

The first time I visited, there was no one there except a woman with several small children. When I walked up to the door, I asked her if my daughter's grandfather was there because he had the same name as my baby's father. When I saw this woman with all her children I thought to myself, "Oh my God, is this his other wife?" All the children looked like him. I kept thinking, "She must be his other wife, but he never told me about her."

Then the woman approached me. "Come in, please sit down," she said. Mr. Ortíz is out, but he should be back in about an hour." She offered me a glass of water as I sat there with my baby daughter.

"No. No thank you," I said.

"Would you like some coffee or something to eat?" she offered.

"No. No thank you. I'm not hungry." My stomach was in knots. I was feeling scared. What if this woman knew that my baby was fathered by her husband? What would she do to me?

I didn't have to wait long. In came my baby's grandfather, and he looked at my baby girl. "She is my son's daughter, isn't she?" he asked.

"Yes, she is," I answered quietly. I turned around and saw the startled look on the other woman's face.

She walked over to me and gently put her hands on my arm and said, "Look, I know that you are afraid of me. I know you are scared because you would not talk to me and you were looking at me as if you were terrified. I think I know why. You have seen all these children and you probably think they are all his." I didn't say anything.

"My husband is his brother, and that is why all the children look alike. So don't worry. I am your sister-in-law," she said looking at me softly. At that moment I felt relieved.

Then the other brothers arrived and started to tell me all about him. "Here is the key to his room if you want to stay there," they offered.

I looked in the room. He had everything fixed up for a family home, but he didn't live there.

"Where did he go?" I asked the brothers.

"He went to Guatemala just eight days ago," they replied. "He was very sad because you didn't want to live with him, and because of the problems that he had with your mother. He went to Guatemala to work. We are going to visit him. We will tell him that you came to visit and that we met his daughter. We will tell him that she is really pretty and looks just like him."

I thanked them and then I went back to my house. They helped me out several times, sending money, and lots of vegetables. The second time they came to see me they told me that when they spoke with him about my visit he was very moved. He wanted me and the baby to go to Guatemala to be with him. He said that he would send money for the bus fares and that his brothers would take me to him.

When they told me this I felt sad, but I told them, "I really appreciate all of your help, but if he wants to meet his daughter and see me he can come and look for us. Tell him that he should keep working and that when he wants to visit us he knows where I live. I will be there waiting for him.

He is the one who has to come to look for me. I'm not going to go looking for him."

After that last conversation with the brothers I never saw the family again. I don't even know if this guy is dead or alive. I never saw him or his family again.

I had this illusion that if I waited long enough for him, he would come. I waited and waited and waited, always looking to see if he was coming down the street. After a lot of waiting, I met the man who became the father of my other children.

He turned out to be different from the other men I knew. I was only 17 years old and he was older. When I realized that he was falling in love with me, I began to feel afraid. I remembered everything my grandmother had told me about men.

She told me, "Watch out for men. They make fun of women, abuse women, get them pregnant, and then leave and the women get stuck with raising the kids." And it's true. A lot of women keep having kids because they don't have access to family planning or any education about how to avoid pregnancy. Anyway, I thought about what my grandmother said and I was really afraid when he talked to me.

When I started to get involved with him, I got sick again. I was so sick with colitis that I had to go into the hospital. My little girl had to stay with my brothers and my mother while I was in the hospital. I wasted away to nothing, weighing maybe 70 or 80 pounds. The thing I felt the worst about was what it did to my daughter. It put her in a difficult situation. Then my mother prohibited me from coming to her house for a while because she didn't want to see me. So I went to live with one of my uncles.

As I was recovering, I went to stay with an uncle in Izalco, who worked as a cook on a construction site at the Agronomy school. He thought that working would help me recuperate. My uncle was well known as a healer and a man of spiritual insight in Izalco. He was called Toñio Tula. In fact, he was the one who cured me of my disease. He had a center for white magic. There are also centers for black magic, where people go to inflict harm on others. The white magic centers are for people who are fed up with doctors or who want to communicate with the spirits. Sometimes people also go there if they think that they are ill because of witchcraft. In my uncle's white magic center he had a round table that had religious images, crystal shot glasses, herbs, and many other things. He would cure people with herbs, with eggs, and spiritually. My uncle would talk to me about my problems.

"Don't worry, my daughter," he would say. "We will work things out with your mother and get your daughter back. Everything will be fine."

With my uncle's reassurances, I began to see, more often, the man who became the father of my other children. He knew that I was still waiting for the father of my first daughter. This new, older man also made me afraid. Whenever he would come around I would flee.

"Look," he said, "I know you are waiting for another boy."

"Yes, I am," I affirmed, moving away.

But he kept coming back. He was very good friends with my uncle. I think it was my uncle who first told him about me, probably when they went to drink beer or something. He told him about my childhood, and that my grandmother had died, and how sick I was. Then he began to visit me at my uncle's house.

His name was José Rafael Canales Guevara. Rafael came to visit often. He tried to get me to go to the nearby city of Sonsonate so that I could get out of Izalco. There are more things to do in Sonsonate. There are movie theaters, parks, restaurants, and places to eat pupusas. It takes about 30 minutes to get there from Izalco. Rafael didn't make a lot of money working at a sugar mill, but he still tried to take me to nice places. That is really how we got to know each other.

He was nice, but the relationship was difficult for me. I was very afraid, and would start to tremble when he would get close to me. After my first experience of being attracted to a man, getting pregnant, and then being left utterly alone, the prospect of physical contact was difficult. Maybe this would turn out the same way. And then there were all the things that my grandmother told me about how poorly men treat women. All of this was running around in my head and it paralyzed me physically.

He treated me very respectfully, even calling me "Usted," but I was still afraid.* He was 12 years older than me.

I didn't even like it if he would put his hands on my arms. They felt like the hands of a giant to me. Whenever he would reach out to touch me

---

* "Usted" is the formal version of "you," used to connote distance or respect. It is contrasted with "tu," the familiar form.

I would pick his hands off my body. Whenever he would approach me to give me a hug or anything I would react negatively.

"Please don't touch me," I would say.

"Why? What are you afraid of?" he asked. "You are going to be my woman. Now that I've said that you are going to be my lover I can caress you and touch you where I want to."

"Not if I don't want you to," I replied. "I don't want you to touch me, so you are not going to." I wouldn't go near him.

I'm sure he wondered, "Why doesn't this woman want me?"

After that he was careful. He held my hand or touched me only if I consented. He was really very patient. He kept talking to me like we were two friends. "Look," he said, "I know what you are thinking. I am not going to force you to do whatever I want. I will listen to you." I don't know if I loved him or not at that moment. I just remember that it was really hard for me.

You have to understand what it is like. I was embarrassed if we went out on the street together. I thought that other people would see me on the street with this man and they would talk about me. I thought that people would look at us and say, "Oh there she goes...so and so's woman, *la mujer de fulano.*" * I would always hide my face when I thought that people were saying things like that about me. Where I lived, people always monitored what women did, and talked about them.

Finally, I began to get over my fear. Slowly, my feelings began to change. We talked a lot. Unlike most men, he never forced me to do anything I didn't want to do. He never said, "You are my woman, so you have to do what I want." He only said it that one time. He was very patient and I told him everything that I had been through, and he understood.

I was very frank with him, telling him, "I don't know if I love you, if I like you, or if I am in love with you. I really don't know. Frankly, all of these feelings scare me. It still frightens me that we are so close."

I couldn't take off my clothes in front of him. I always asked him to wait until we turned off the light to get undressed. And I would sleep with most of my clothes on. I guess a lot of couples need time to get used

---

* *Fulano* in Spanish is equivalent to the expression "Joe Schmo" in English—a generic anyone.

to sleeping with each other. It's hard for a lot of men to get used to the fact that sometimes you just want to go to sleep without having sex. I remember that I used to sleep close to the wall because I didn't want him to get too close to me. I would wrap myself up in the sheets and the blanket. He would talk to me in bed, sort of talking me to sleep. It felt nice when he was talking to me in bed, but when it would get more serious it wasn't as nice. I just didn't feel anything.

But then, little by little, I started to have a lot of feelings for him because he was so patient with me. He understood me. And he helped me to work out my problems with my daughter, and to get along better with my mother. So we started to live together, and for three years we had a nice time.

When our first son was born he was very happy. He used to help me with the housework. When we first lived together, I remember he used to say to me, "I am going to cook. Sit down and I will serve you." I thought this was quite strange. I was very surprised when I saw him cooking and he said to me, "Do you like this food I just made?"

"It's fine," I said. "You can cook. You are a man who can cook." I had never seen a man cook before. My father, my stepfather, my brothers, and my uncles had never cooked. He would cook for me and then he would say, "Why don't you sit down and rest. I will clean up and do everything. Relax." This was a huge change. That is how he won me over. He won my trust by treating me so well and I finally started to feel love for him.

Rafael was so happy when our first son was born. He told me, "Don't do anything." It was a very different experience from my first child. He took me to the hospital, he brought me back, and he cooked for me. He said, "I am going to wash all the baby's clothes and your clothes. Don't get up. I am going to do everything for a while." And he did. He truly took care of me.

Every once in a while he would look at me and joke, "You are still waiting for that other guy to come back, aren't you?" He would always kid me about waiting for that first boy. Now when I think about the love I had for this first boy, I realize that I loved him in a way, but what I felt for Rafael was the real thing. I loved him like nothing else. Of course we had problems, but he never beat me then and he always respected me.

He was an unusual man. I think one of the reasons he was able to cook and do things around the house was because of how he grew up. His parents were from Chalatenango and Guazapa. They were very humble people who suffered a lot. He started to work when he was seven years old because they were very poor. When he was 15, he left home to look for his fortune. He had to learn to do a lot of different jobs at the age of 15, and also to take care of himself. He had to learn to cook because there was no other option for him. He also went through a process of gaining class consciousness when he was a labor organizer. I didn't know about that, but it influenced him. Because he was always struggling to improve the conditions for workers, he was conscious of a lot of things in life.

I think that from this experience of being on his own and also working as a labor organizer, he learned to do a lot of things. He could cook, wash, and iron. So we divided all of the household chores. When I would go to wash the clothes, he would help me. This is how we started to have problems with the neighbors. They would see him washing clothes with me and they would say, "Look at that. He's a man who is acting like a woman. His wife must have him under a spell." People talk about women having men under a spell because sometimes women bewitch their husbands to get them to do what they want, sometimes in a positive way and sometimes in a negative way. Because of this belief and the fact that Rafael was washing clothes, they thought I had him under a spell. Even his own brothers would say, "Look at that poor guy, his wife has him under a spell." Rafael realized that it was bothering me. He told me, "Don't pay any attention to what they say. I will talk with these guys about their gossip." And he did.

During that time I didn't have an occupation that would allow me to work outside the house. What I did was to keep house; he would go to work and I would iron for people. I couldn't do washing for money because it was hard to go down to the river with my kids. So I ironed for working people who didn't have time to press their clothes. They would bring me clothes to iron at home. I would iron with a steam iron and I received 10 centavos for each piece of clothing. Sometimes I would iron from two o'clock in the afternoon until eleven o'clock at night just to earn the equivalent of about $2.00. It was hard work. I always had callouses on my hands from where I had grabbed the iron in the wrong place.

My compañero Rafael was first a construction worker. Then he got a job as a blacksmith in the sugar refinery. He did a lot of different things. We have this saying, "*siete oficios, catorce necesidades.*" That means we have so many different occupations because we have so many financial needs. He was always prepared to do a lot of different kinds of work to support his children.

Rafael took an interest in educating our children. He taught them how to clean up the table, to take their dishes to the sink, and to help me. He also taught them to help other people. He often told them, "Always look for ways to help people. If you see a stone that is in the road, pick it up and move it to one side. If you don't trip over it, then someone else will." He provided the children with some moral orientation.

We lived this way for quite some time. Sometimes we were very poor and we hardly had enough food, and other times we had enough. We got along well. One day I decided to tell him how I felt about some things.

I told him, "You are a man and you have a lot of other opportunities. You work with other women and you want to be able to talk to them. I'm not going to deny you that. But while I can put up with being poor and having a hard time, one thing I can't put up with is for you to have another woman in front of me like my father did with my mother. I won't tolerate it. If it happens, you have to go and I will stay with my children. If you want to have other women, have them far away from here. And the day that I realize that you have them, I don't know what is going to happen. So beware. I want you to keep respecting me. The day that you don't want to be with me, that you are bored with me, or you don't love me anymore, please tell me. And we will break up. And if you want to be with another woman the next day, it will be all right. Because we won't be together anymore." After I told him these things we continued to live well. We had some small problems, but he knew how I felt and things were good.

Salvadoran women confront the Treasury Police. Photo by Jacque Gharib. December 1987

CHAPTER 4

FIRST POLITICAL EXPERIENCE

Izalco

After I lived with Rafael a while, my mother and my brothers and sisters started to treat me differently because they saw how well we were getting along. When they came to visit us we got along. We were poor, but we were always good hosts to them. We would also go to visit my family and he won them over. He would joke around with my mother and my brothers and sisters but he was never disrespectful. They liked him.

First we lived in Izalco. Rafael was working as a blacksmith in the sugar mill in Sonsonate between 1976 and 1978. Our lives were very hard then. It seemed liked I was always ironing, ironing to earn money but we never had enough money. We rented a house where there was a kitchen and we paid about 70 colones per month.* We had two more children plus my daughter and I was always worried that the children wouldn't have enough to eat. We just didn't have enough money for bus fare for Rafael, medicine, food, clothing, and shoes for the children. In 1978, during the

---

* At that time, there were 2.5 colones to the dollar. The house rental of 70 colones was about $28 per month. María was making 10 centavos for every piece of laundry she took in, earning between four and seven colones per day or between $1.60 and $2.80 per day.

---

sugar mill strike, life became even more difficult. We didn't have any money. The strike changed everything. It changed my life.

At the time, it was difficult for me to understand what a strike was. I didn't even know what Rafael was doing. He never told me. Sometimes he would come home late, and sometimes he would not come home.

The next day I would say to him, "Why didn't you come home last night?"

"Oh, they kept me for work," he would reply.

"You were working all night long?" I would ask sympathetically.

"Yes," he would answer.

"Oh, you poor thing," I would say and then I wouldn't ask anything else.

Often I would keep his food warm for him, hoping that he would come home to eat. The children would always eat first. Then, whatever was left over we would eat. The children were really important to him.

"I'm not going to be like other men," he would often tell me. "They always say that they come first. Serve me first and then everyone else. In this house, the children should come first." So they did.

Often I would wait for him. I didn't eat because he had told me he was going to come home. Finally I told myself, "Don't be a fool. That man has already eaten, and here I am waiting for him all the time." After that, I saved food for him, and if he arrived he ate it. If not, I went ahead and ate anyway.

Sometimes when he came home late he would say, "I'm so tired, I don't feel like getting up. Serve me my supper."

After a while I started to say, "Look, I don't want to get up. Go serve yourself. I'm already resting in bed." And I wouldn't get up.

"Ah, then you don't love me anymore," he would say.

"Okay. Then I don't love you. Serve yourself." And he would get his own food. You learn things about domestic life, and I was slowly learning that I could assert myself. I was learning through my own experience.

I was just starting to get a little bit more independent when the strike happened. One day a worker from the mill knocked on the door and asked if I was Mrs. Canales.

"Yes, that's me. Why? What's going on? Why did you come to my house?"

"I'm here to deliver a message from Canales. He is not going to come home because a strike has broken out."

"What do you mean, a strike? What does that mean?" I asked, becoming slowly afraid.

"Well," he replied, "The workers at the sugar mill had a strike, and Canales was one of the supporters. That's why he sent me here to tell you not to worry about him if he doesn't come home."

"Thank you for telling me," I said. And he left. My brother-in-law was there with me so I asked him about it.

"Juan, they just told me that there is a strike where Rafael is working. I am really worried. What can I do?"

"My sister-in-law," he said, looking directly at me. "You should go there and see for yourself what is going on. That is the only way that you will understand."

I was very ignorant then. I didn't know what a strike was, or why people had made so many demands. I had no idea what I would find. I decided to leave right away. It was already five o'clock in the afternoon. I asked my brother-in-law if I could leave my kids with him and his wife and I went to wait for the six o'clock bus. We lived in Izalco then and I had to get to Sonsonate.

The workers chose to strike the sugar mill during the busy season, which runs from the beginning of October until March. During this time, there were many women who went to the factory to sell food. They built their little stalls out of cardboard and bamboo, and sold different kinds of foods to the men who worked in the mill. Most of the men are either low paid factory workers or drivers who bring in the cane. The drivers haul the cane in from the east, drop it at the mill, and then go back to get more. Rafael's sister was working down by the mill selling food. She was always an independent, fiery woman. She liked having her small business, but because of the oppressive economic system we lived under, she could never have the security she wanted. Even though she worked so hard, several of her small ventures had failed. I knew she would be there by the factory.

When I approached the sugar mill, I noticed that there were many workers gathered on one side of the mill grounds by the fence. There were a lot of banners there. I don't remember the name of the union leading the strike, but they had a lot of banners. I immediately began to ask questions.

"What's going on here? Why have they closed the main gate? How come there are signs and banners all over the place?" I asked some people next to me.

Some men in the group answered, "We are here demanding our rights as workers."

"I want to speak with Rafael Canales," I said.

"Who are you?" the men wanted to know.

"I am his compañera, his wife." I replied. "I want to talk to him."

"Give me your name," one of them said. I gave him my name and he wandered off inside.

It took 20 minutes to walk from the fence where I was to the main part of the mill where the workers were gathered. There were about 1,800 workers. There were mechanics, blacksmiths, secretaries, and even the supervisors. It was a general strike caused by the owner's terrible treatment of the workers.

My husband earned 125 colones every two weeks, about $25 per week. He was a blacksmith. He told me a lot about his working conditions. His job was to keep the fire going where they sharpened the blades that were used to cut the cane when it passed through the cane-cutting machine. He had two helpers working with him. Every time they used their hammers to sharpen the blades, sparks would fly at them. These sparks would often make their clothing catch fire and also fell on their bodies. They didn't even have gloves or any protective gear. It was a very difficult job. He would burn up about one shirt a week on that job because of all the sparks. Every week he had to get a new shirt. His pants were always burned too and sometimes his hands. He even had sparks fly in his eyes.

Everyone had difficult working conditions like his. There were many accidents in the factory. Sometimes workers would fall into the cane-cutting machines and get badly hurt. They didn't have any holidays. In El Salvador, we usually take off the 24th and 25th of December for Christmas and December 31st and New Year's day. But not here. There was no vacation for the workers. They were obliged to work even on holidays. They were also assigned extra hours. The owners didn't want the cane factory to ever stop, even during the holidays, because they knew that they would lose money. As a result, the striking workers were asking for improved working conditions—things like limiting their work schedule to eight-hour days, and better safety conditions. They were also asking for a raise in pay and for a bus that would take people to Izalco, where many of them lived. Often workers would leave the factory in the middle of the night and if they had just gotten paid they would get robbed. There was a whole series of things they were asking for when I arrived.

After I waited a while, Rafael appeared. I said to him, "What's going on? Why are you here?"

He told me about all of the workers' demands. We talked for quite a while and the night wore on. Finally I said, "Why didn't you ever tell me what you were doing? I don't know anything about strikes. Just imagine if something happened to you. What would I do? Who would I talk to?"

"Ah," he sighed. "Tomorrow I can tell you what to do if anything happens. Now I am very tired and we are trying to get all the people here to move. We have to change our security shift right now and I have a lot to do." He took me to the bus stop and I went home to Izalco with a lot to think about.

The next morning, I woke up at six to dress, feed, and get my children ready for school. One of the kids was nine, one was seven and the little girl who was in kindergarten was four years old. I also packed clean clothes for my compañero, his knapsack, and his bronchitis medicine. I knew he would need his medicine because of the cold and the dust.

After I took my children to school, I got back on the bus and returned to the sugar mill. I wanted to bring Rafael the things he needed. I didn't even stop by my sister-in-law's house to say hello. I went directly to the mill. I saw him standing there by the fence. We talked through the fence, me on one side, him on the other.

"Good morning," I said. "How did you sleep last night?"

"Fine," he answered. But I could see that he was really tired. His eyes were all red.

"Come on," I said. "You didn't sleep at all, did you?"

"No. We were working all night."

"Are you in any danger here?" I asked.

"No," he replied. "We are not in any danger. We are just workers asking for better working conditions."

"Look," I said. "Here is your medicine and some other things you might need. I brought you your favorite food. I know that you aren't going to leave soon. Why don't you come with me a little while to rest?"

"I was thinking about you after you left last night," he told me. "Are you sure you are all right? Nothing happened to you?"

Actually, on my way home the night before, three drunks had come after me thinking I was a prostitute. I was saved by some friends who were on the street. Otherwise who knows what might have happened. But I didn't tell Rafael.

"No. Nothing happened to me," I answered. "Here I am. Touch me. You can feel for yourself that nothing happened."

"And the children? Nothing happened to them?"

"No. They are fine. They are in school. Your brother says hello. Everyone is fine. Now come here." I reached out and grabbed him with my arms. "Come out here and sleep a while with me. I'm going to take care of you for a while."

"No," he said. "I am very tired, but I can't rest. I will just stay here a little while with you and talk. Then I am going to go back with the others. If I leave, my friends will say I have no will power and that I am abandoning them."

"So what? What is your big obligation to those people inside?" I asked him.

"You still don't understand what is going on, do you?" he answered.

"Why don't you just come out for a little while. We can go down to your sister's food shack and you can sleep in the hammock there and relax a little. Then you can go back to work. Come on." I tried to convince him to leave.

"I really can't leave," he said. "Please don't insist that I do something that I can't."

"So, you don't love me," I said.

"Of course I do," he replied. "But I have my work as well. I know you don't really understand what is going on."

"Are you sure that there is no danger for you here?" I asked again, alarmed.

"No," he answered.

It was about 11 o'clock in the morning as we sat there talking. I was on the outside and he was on the inside, two lovers talking through the fence. All of a sudden he pulled back from me and started to run as he looked past my shoulder.

"What happened?" I shouted.

I was looking at him, shouting, when I saw that all the men inside who had been standing in front of barrels filled with sand by the fence were suddenly running as well. Then I saw that a whole army unit had descended on the factory from behind me. They were jumping over the fence, tearing up the banners with their bayonets, and running after the strikers.

I just stood there watching all of this with my arms crossed wondering if Rafael had gotten away or if they had already grabbed him. Then I saw that they had detained a large group of workers and had them lying down on the ground. There were vehicles inside. The soldiers broke down the fence and pushed aside the barrels of sand the strikers had used to form a barricade.

There were two entrances to the mill. I was outside the main entrance gate on the side of the street that went toward San Salvador. This was the gate where the trucks went in and out. While I was standing there amazed at what I saw, a police sergeant from the National Guard came up.

"What are you doing here?" he asked me loudly.

"Nothing. I'm not doing anything," I said.

"Then why don't you leave?"

"Because I'm not doing anything wrong," I replied. I think I was in shock. I had never seen so many military men at one time in all of my life. In places I had lived there would be two, four, or maybe even six policemen out on patrol, but nothing like this. This was the National Guard. It was their job to round up criminals and assassins. They were not like the local police who arrest the drunks when they have had too much *chicha*—that is a drink that we make out of fermented corn with brown sugar. They arrested people who would go out on Sunday and have too much to drink. The next day, their relatives would realize that they were in jail and they would go pay a fine to get them out. If the drunks had no family they would have to stay for eight days in jail and sweep the streets and the parks, and work in the cemetery to pay their debt. But the National Guard? No, these men were up to more than just arresting drunks.

I thought about what I knew about the different police in El Salvador. There were also the National Police who took care of transit, the municipal police who arrested the drunks, and the local guards (*patrulla cantonal*)—also called the barefoot patrol because they were simple campesinos who didn't have shoes—who provided security for their communities. There were also neighborhood patrols in the city directed by some provisional commander.

The units that patrolled the smaller towns consisted of ten or fifteen men who were workers. This patrol unit would also recruit young men for the army, detaining them by force as they left school, the movies, or other places where they went to have fun. Once they caught them they would take the young men to the commander in Izalco. Sometimes their mothers would be lucky to know someone who could get their sons out of the military. Sometimes they would succeed and sometimes they wouldn't. Later this method changed and they started enlisting people by means of a letter. If the new recruits didn't report for duty then they would be taken to jail and persuaded to enlist "voluntarily."

All of this was going through my head as I watched the National Guard pouring into the sugar mill. I couldn't understand why the National Guard was there. There hadn't been any crimes committed. No robberies had occurred. I was surprised that they were there and I started to argue with the sergeant who had told me to leave.

"Get out of here," he told me as he pointed his rifle at my chest.

"Put down that stupid gun," I said. "I am not afraid of dying."

He said, "Careful, because if you defy me I can kill you."

"Then do it," I told him, "I am not afraid of you." All of his friends and other people were around us watching. After he threatened me I was furious.

"Listen," I told him. "I am not leaving this place. Stop this foolishness and let me through. I am not afraid of you. What are you waiting for?" Then he left. But he said, "If I come back and you are still here, you will be sorry."

"If I don't want to leave, I won't. You can't tell me what to do!" I replied. "Furthermore, you don't have to talk to me like that because I am not a soldier. You have no right to order me around. You can talk to your soldiers like that, but I am not one of your soldiers."

"Just move out of the way," he replied.

"But I am not doing anything to you," I said. "You are offending me. I'm just standing in the street."

"What are you doing here?"

"I came to see my husband."

"What do you think? You think we are going to kill him?"

"What do I know?" I told him. "I don't know who you are. Look at how you are keeping them in there." Then I went up to the fence to see if my husband was there. The sergeant stuck his rifle in my chest again.

"Stop this foolishness," I shouted. "Cut this shit out. Leave me alone." When I screamed at the sergeant I wasn't thinking about anyone or anything. My mind was blank during those moments. I waited and waited for the bullet. I was sure that he was going to shoot me. I raised my arms in the air, and I was sure that I felt the bullet in my chest. But instead, he turned and left. Maybe because people were getting closer and closer to us.

Then a soldier turned to me and said, "Look Ma'am, it's best that you leave now for your own good. That sergeant or the commanding officer are likely to do something."

"Well, then let him go ahead and do it," I replied. "I am not doing anything to him."

"Listen, lady, go. It's for your own good," he said. "This man is evil."

Then my sister-in-law arrived and she said, "Come on, let's go." She put her arm around my shoulder to steer me away.

"Leave me alone," I told her.

"No, come with me," she said. "Come on, we do not have to stand here in the middle of these disgusting beasts. Someday they will make you pay for this. Let's go."

"But I want to see Rafael," I told her. "I don't know where he is, maybe they took him away."

"We'll find out what happened. Don't worry," said my sister-in-law.

Then an older woman came over to me and put her arm around me. She said, "We will find out, don't worry about it. Calm down, things aren't that bad." She guided me to a cardboard and aluminum hut where she had a little restaurant with one or two tables.

"I never thought that this would happen," I said, referring to the hundreds of soldiers around the sugar mill.

"I didn't either. We are all very, very surprised and frightened. Everyone," commented my sister-in-law.

As I walked with my sister-in-law, people were following me, women and men who were in their cars, even campesinos. They asked me, "Weren't you scared?"

"No," I told them. "I am not afraid of them."

"How are we going to find out about Rafael?" I asked my sister-in-law.

"Don't worry" she said. "We will find out. Let's go."

There was another entrance to the sugar mill that was called Santa Marta. This was a smaller entrance for pedestrians only. It was about 20 minutes away from where we were. My sister-in-law wanted to take the bus because she was tired, but I told her that it was getting late and we should not stop. The bus was not going to arrive for a while. So we decided to walk.

To get to Santa Marta, we had to cross a river that we called River of Ashes. We had to go down a big hill before coming to the river. I remember I was wearing blue jeans. At the top of the riverbank we sat down and started to slide down the hill, like sledding. We would grab onto things as we slid down the hill to keep from toppling over.

"Be careful," my sister-in-law told me.

"Yes," I replied as we continued very slowly. When the soil crumbled underneath us from our weight, we would wait and search out another path down. We slid all the way down to the bottom this way. We crossed the wet river bed and then we had to climb up the other side, which was steep as well. That side of the river was used as a garbage dump. People would come there to harvest the garbage, to look for some old thing that was useful or something to sell. We worked our way up this steep hill, pulling ourselves up with our hands and sometimes crawling with our elbows on the ground. When we got to the top, we stood up. Then we had to cross a small coffee field, maybe 20 or 30 meters wide. Finally we reached the gate.

We ran toward the gate until a solider jumped up and yelled at us, "Stop, there! Raise your arms high in the air!" He had been hiding in the grass. Maybe he was waiting there to surprise the strikers who were able to run away. Maybe he was going to grab them or shoot them. Who knows?

"Where are you going, ladies?" he asked us as we stood there with our hands in the air.

"We're going to the neighborhood up there," we said. There was a working-class neighborhood beyond the factory entrance.

"You're not carrying anything?" he asked us.

"No, we don't have anything."

"Let me see," he said. He looked at our things and then said. "Okay. You can go now. Be careful."

We kept on walking and we ran into another soldier. But because we were already inside of the fence, he waved us on. Once inside, we saw that there were other women there who had come through the Santa Marta gate. A lot of them were carrying food. There were also big trucks loaded with sugar cane parked there. There were piles of cane scattered all around that the truck drivers had thrown off the trucks. The place was incredibly militarized. I had never seen anything like it. All of this was totally new to me. I had no idea that this could happen.

While we were walking, Rafael's sister turned to me and said, "My sister-in-law, you are going to have to be strong."

"Why?" I asked her.

"Because we don't know what is going to happen to my brother," she said.

"You think something is going to happen to him?" I said, feeling alarmed.

"I don't know," she answered. "But I have a feeling in my heart that something is going to happen. How do you feel?"

"I'm not afraid," I told her.

"Good. I'm not afraid either," she replied. "Let's go in there together."

As we were moving forward we heard a woman calling for help. All of the women around us were crying. They were saying things like, "They are going to kill my husband. They are going to take him prisoner. They are going to disappear him." They were all there holding their baskets of food and crying out about what would happen to their husbands. And they couldn't get any closer. The National Guard had them surrounded. They had put a fence up around the main part of the factory where the men were. It was an ugly scene.

The woman kept screaming, "Help me, help me." Then one of the soldiers grabbed her by the hair. She was sitting on the ground but he had grabbed her so that she couldn't move. She couldn't stand up. She was calling him all kinds of names. "You dog, you fool." People scream like this when they are grabbed by a soldier, but it is dangerous to insult them so.

I had a hard time watching this. It affected me. So then I turned to the group of women without knowing any of them and uttered the word "compañeras"—comrades—for the first time.

"Look, compañeras," I said. "We have to make that soldier let go of that woman or he will kill her."

"Yes," chimed in my sister-in-law. "Everyone grab a big piece of cane and we will surround him, that wretched beast."

So all the women put down their baskets of food and picked up pieces of cane and stones. We went over to the guard who had the woman by the hair, and we surrounded him.

He pulled a grenade out of his vest and said, "If you get any closer, I am going to throw this at you."

"Go ahead," we shouted. "This is going to end right now. If you don't let go of her, you are going to die too," we told him. Soon he realized that we were very serious and that we had him completely surrounded. He let the woman go. She was all covered with blood. She limped over and told us, "Thank you. If it weren't for all of you, I might have been disappeared."

I remember hearing that word from her lips. "Disappeared."

"But why?" we asked her.

"Because I insulted them and struggled. They might have done it just to get back at me. They are dogs." she said.

Just then the wives of the union leaders arrived. They gathered us all together and told us, "Listen, compañeras. We are going to go directly to the Electrical Workers Union in Sonsonate because they can help us. They will provide support for the families of the strikers. Who wants to go with us?"

"I do," I said before I knew what I had said. I had no idea what was going to happen.

We went to the house of the Secretary of the Electrical Workers Union. She didn't know about the strike and what had happened. We told her all about it. "Okay," she said. "Let's go." She left her house without even eating. We went with her to the union office and from there called the leadership of all the other unions in Sonsonate. We also called San Salvador and spoke with FENASTRAS, the Federation of Salvadoran Workers.

We spent the day going around to other unions in Sonsonate gathering food that we needed to bring to the sugar mill. At about four o'clock in the afternoon we returned with our supplies, but we couldn't get in.

The military wouldn't let anyone get in or bring in any food. They had some of the men standing up, some of them tied up, and some of them were face down lying on the ground. Guards wouldn't let you get any

After I tucked the book safely into my blouse, he said, "Take care of that little book for me. Don't ever lose it or give it to anyone. I might return home and it will be very useful to me."

This whole scene was devastating to me. I said again, "But Chato, what will I do without you?"

"I don't know," he responded. "You have to be strong. I know that you are a very strong woman and very brave. I'll leave you with those words. I know that you will be able to face life. Please have faith in me."

Then the soldiers started to move people out. They treated us like we were a bunch of potatoes. They picked up the 22 men and threw them into a big truck like they were baskets in the market place. There were soldiers everywhere and lots of different kinds of trucks—big trucks, the kind they use in war. It was terrible. I kept thinking, "What if they kill my compañero and I never see him again? Where will I go to look for him? What will I tell my children?" As they drove them away, I had no idea what I would do, absolutely no idea. All I felt was fear, fear, and more fear.

That night I slept in a hammock in one of the stalls where women sold food during the day. I lay there all night thinking and at five o'clock in the morning, I went back home. As soon as I arrived, I went to see my sister-in-law.

"Ah, cuñada" I said. "We're in trouble."

"What happened?" she asked.

"The National Guard took them away," I replied quietly.

"Oh, shit," she said. "With God's help, they won't harm my brother. I hope they don't do anything bad to him because those fools are terrible. Let's pray to God that nothing happens to him and he returns to us safely."

The next day a man from the union came to my house looking for me. I don't know how he knew where I lived.

"Good morning," he said. "Was anyone in your family arrested at the sugar mill?"

"Yes," I replied. "My compañero, Rafael Canales."

"Ah, hah. You are the person we have been looking for," he told me. "We are going to go to San Salvador to denounce what happened in the newspaper *La Prensa Gráfica*.* We are going to demand that they

* Salvadoran papers frequently ignored arrests and detentions. The only way to

release all of the prisoners. We will demand the release of your compañero and all of the men they took. Don't worry. We have already been investigating what happened. We know that they are in the National Guard headquarters. They deny that they are holding them, but we know that they are there."

I went with him and a group of 10 to 12 other men and women to San Salvador. The group included the secretary of the Electrical Workers, Silvia Olán, who had helped us the day before. She told us what to do. She is a great woman. She arranged for all of our bus fares and everything was paid for.

I sat next to her on the bus. The radio was playing a song by Camilo Sesto, who is well known in Central America. His music never goes out of style. I was staring out the window with my mind totally blank, not knowing what would come next. The song was called "Viento a Tu Favor"—With the Wind.

"Compañera," Silvia began. "You don't mind that I call you compañera, do you?"

"No," I said.

"Look, compañera," she continued. "Life can be very sad, but it is also beautiful. The life of a labor organizer is very hard to understand. And as the wife of an organizer you always suffer. I have a son who doesn't have a father anymore. I loved the father of my son very much. I was crazy about him. And this song reminds me of when I used to go out with him to the mountains, to run and be free."

She had a dreamy, sad look in her eyes as she listened to the song. Then she turned to me again.

"I'm going to ask you something," she said. "When I am gone will you remember me and this song?"

"Why do you say this?" I asked. "Do you think you are going to die soon?"

"I don't know, compañera," she replied. "When you are in this line of work you never expect to live long."

"But how can they just kill you for no reason?" I asked.

draw attention to arrests, such as those of the sugar mill organizers, was to arrive at the newspaper offices in person to demand the publication of a paid advertisement denouncing the arrests. Even paid advertisements were sometimes refused.

"The enemy is very strong and they can strike at any time," she said. "And the saddest part for me is that my son is still very small. He is only five years old and they killed his father."

I began to understand the meaning of the song for her and I turned to her with tenderness and asked, "Did you suffer a lot with your compañero?"

"Yes, I did," she said still listening to the music. After the song was over and its effect wore off on her, she turned to me again.

"I don't know why I am talking to you. I am really good friends with your husband. He is a great person. You can be sure of it. Canales is a great person. He is very intelligent. He told me a lot about you. He told me that he had a compañera and children, but that you had no idea what he was up to. He stayed with me a lot while we worked on making banners and producing leaflets. Sometimes he even slept over. I always told him and the other men that they were going to get a lot of grief by not returning home. But they assured me that they had told their wives and families they would probably not return."

She proceeded to tell me all about what Rafael had been doing and I thought, "Why didn't he tell me. Maybe I could have helped him."

When we arrived in San Salvador we went to the newspaper. We took out a paid advertisement in which we denounced the arrests and we all signed it. After that I returned home to Izalco. I had to be there for my children.

Shortly after my return, I was listening to the news on the radio when I heard the announcement: "The 22 terrorists from the sugar mill have been moved to the court jail house where they will stand trial for what did. If they are found guilty of terrorist acts then they will not be released." That is where my compañero is, I thought.

After five days in court, they went to the First Level Court (Primera Camara Ordenal). The appointed judge was a political reactionary. He was a real son of a bitch. They didn't allow the press to be present, and the whole affair was cloaked in secrecy. The only testimony permitted was from the National Guard officers who had invaded the factory. They used their testimony to determine what happened. But the National Guardsmen contradicted one another. The judge had to suspend the testimony and they had to take the 22 prisoners back to National Guard headquarters. The next day they were tried again and all 22 were convicted of having committed terrorist acts and of threatening national security.

After their conviction in February, I didn't know how to find them. All they told us was that they had been taken to jail, but they didn't say where. Finally, I decided to start my search at the nearest jail, which is in Santa Tecla.

At the gate, a guard asked me, "Who are you looking for? A political prisoner or a common criminal?"

I didn't know what the difference was. I said, "I am looking for those from the sugar mill."

"Oh," the guard replied. "They are political prisoners. Who are you?"

"I am the wife of one of them," I replied.

"Do you have identification?" he asked.

"Yes," I replied.

Then they started to search me and everything I had with me. Inside the jail there were two men and two women. The men searched the men and the women searched the women in a special room.

"Take off your shoes," ordered the woman searching me. She looked inside my shoes. Then she began feeling me all over, my breasts, everywhere on my body. This was really strange for me.

"Why are you touching me all over?" I asked her.

"We search everyone who comes in here," she replied. "We have to make sure visitors are not carrying drugs, arms, alcohol, or other things to the prisoners because they are forbidden."

These women appeared to have no feelings because they even touched the intimate parts of your body. They would look between your legs and even run their hands around your bra to make sure you didn't have anything hidden inside. It was demoralizing. Finally, they let me in.

I had no idea where to start looking for my compañero. There were so many prisoners that I just asked the first one, "Do you know Rafael Canales?"

"No," he said.

Then the prisoners began repeating Rafael's name down the halls. "Rafael Canales has a visitor" they repeated over and over again from one person to another. Finally, he came out and he looked very surprised to see me.

"What are you doing here?" he asked me.

"I came to find you," I said embracing him. "Thank God you are alive."

"I'm fine, I'm fine," he reassured me. "Don't worry about me, I'm fine. All of my compañeros are with me too. How are the children? Are you okay? How do you feel?"

As we talked, the other prisoners from the sugar mill came over. One of them was a neighbor of ours. He was arrested in the sugar mill and had given the military the address where his wife and children lived. Her name was Ana. Later the National Guard went to the house and accused them of concealing weapons. They arrested the woman after beating her and throwing everything from the house into the street. They took the children and sealed the doors. The woman was badly tortured at the National Guard headquarters.

He asked me, "Do you know anything about what happened to our house?"

"Yes, your aunt told me something about it," I said. "Three days after you were tortured, the National Guard arrived at your house and claimed that they had found arms stashed inside."

"I gave them my address, like a fool," he said. "They told me that nothing would happen to my family." He repeated to me what happened. When he got closer to me, I could see that many parts of his body were purple and that he was swollen all over. I could see where his hands had been tied. After I saw him, I wondered if anything had happened to Rafael.

I remembered that when I first embraced him he resisted a little bit. At first I thought that it was because he was embarrassed to hug me in front of all of these people. So I didn't insist on it. Then I noticed that a lot of the men were moving slowly. Some couldn't stand up straight. It was a difficult moment because I began to understand what went on inside the jail.

Another man, a friend and assistant of my compañero, came up to me. "Are you Canales' wife?"

"Yes," I said.

"I'm really glad to meet you," he told me. "Your poor husband. They really messed him up when they tortured him."

"Really?" I said.

"Yeah," he told me. "He was badly beaten. You have to understand that."

"Oh, pobrecito," I said.

After this, I slowly moved closer to Rafael, and I could see the signs of torture on his body. That was why he had resisted when I wanted to hug him. I didn't touch him, but I asked if there was anything I could do.

"I'm fine," he told me. "The only thing that would be helpful would be if a doctor could come. There is very little medical assistance here." I left the prison that day with a great sadness, but a new vision of reality.

CHAPTER 5

CO-MADRES ACTIVIST

I continued visiting Rafael in jail. Sundays and Thursdays were visitors' days. On Sundays, I noticed that some women arrived, maybe two, three, or four, to speak with the prisoners and to bring food and other little things they needed. I didn't know who they were, but on my second visit to the prison I found out.

Rafael said to me, "I got to know these women here in the prison. They are looking for some scrap of hope, for information about the whereabouts of their disappeared relatives. They are also helping us a lot. They bring us food and medicine. They have met with me and the other men arrested at the sugar mill, and asked us if we had any family members who wanted to meet with them, to work with them to denounce what is happening to us. They could help you if you want to work with them. They will give you bus fare so that you can meet with them and see what they are doing."

"It would be interesting to get to know them," I answered. "I would like to see what they can do for you and the other prisoners. I don't have any more money to put up for your defense."

"Yes, I know," he said. "It's hard to find money."

During my next visit I met the women in the prison. The first one I met was Alicia de Blandino. I will never forget her voice or her manner.

"Did you come to visit your compañero?" she asked.

"Yes," I responded.

"How are you feeling?" she asked warmly.

"Okay," I replied.

"Where do you live?" she inquired.

"I live in Izalco."

"Are you working?"

"No, I don't have a job right now."

"And how are you going to live, to take care of all of your problems without work?" she asked me.

"I really don't know," I said. "I have no idea what I am going to do."

"It's hard," she said. "My name is Alicia Nerio de Blandino. My son is in prison. He is a student accused of being a terrorist. Some of us have formed a Committee of Mothers and Relatives of Prisoners, Disappeared, and the Politically Assassinated of El Salvador." (That is what CO-MADRES was called back then).

"We are a group of women who are looking for our disappeared children. I can tell you how to get to our meetings. We meet every Saturday in San José de la Montaña, Monseñor Romero's seminary."

While she was talking, I was thinking about how difficult it would be for me to go. I said, "I don't know where this place is. I have gone to San Salvador, but only to visit my Aunt. I don't know how to get around the city."

"I could meet you at the terminal, if you want to go," she said. "Do you love your husband?"

"Yes, I do."

"Well, then we have to do something for him and the others. We have to take a stand. No one else will. A lot of the time all we do is cry, but this doesn't help the prisoners at all."

"Yes," I said. "I want to do something. When should I come?"

"Come this Saturday." She told me what time to meet her at the bus terminal and that she would take me back there as well so that I could find the bus to go home.

She was a nice woman, about 43 years old. She was very cheerful and optimistic. On Saturday she met me at the bus station and took me to the seminary where CO-MADRES met. When we arrived she told me, "I am going to go in first. Wait about 10 minutes and then come in."

I waited and then went inside. "Good afternoon," I said to everyone.

All of the women seated there turned around and greeted me; then they asked me who I was.

"My name is María Teresa Tula. I am the compañera of one of the prisoners from the sugar mill."

"Oh," they sighed. "Come on in. Sit down. Look, it isn't that we don't trust you, but we need to talk to you first."

They asked me a series of questions: my name, my age, where I was from, my husband's name, and the ages of my children. After I answered all their questions they seemed to open up more to me.

"Pull up a chair, compañera," they told me. They had checked me out and decided I was okay. From that moment on I called them compañeras and we entered into a relationship of trust. One of them began to talk to me.

"What we do here is try to figure out how we can get into the jails to look for our disappeared relatives. And in the case of the political prisoners from the sugar mill, we have to figure out how to get medicine to them. We all know that the situation inside the jails is dismal. They don't even have aspirin or bandages in there. We also need doctors to visit and examine the prisoners so they can testify about the torture and horrible treatment they are receiving. Do you agree with this?"

"Yes," I said. I didn't have the slightest idea how to go about doing any of these things.

They discussed their plans with me and told me that they knew about my situation and how difficult it was. Slowly, I began to get more involved. I went a second time, a third time, and then I began to go regularly to the seminary. What surprised me the most was seeing Monseñor Romero at the meetings. He helped us by making announcements on the radio. "Monseñor Romero announces the meeting of the Committee of Mothers and Family Members of Prisoners, the Disappeared and the Politically Assassinated." He said that we were suffering mothers looking for our children and pleaded with government authorities to free them.

The mothers had a dinner with Monseñor Romero. When I arrived, I greeted him. I just said hello. But I didn't know that when you greet a bishop you are supposed to kiss his hand. When they introduced Monseñor to me, he held out his hand for me to kiss. I didn't know what I was supposed to do. I just reached out and pumped his hand saying, "Good day, Monseñor."

Then one of the other mothers leaned over and whispered to me, "You are supposed to kiss his hand."

"What? I'm supposed to kiss his hand?" I whispered back.

"Yes," she said.

So I finally kissed his hand and he gave me his blessing. They introduced me as a new member of the Mothers' Committee.

"Welcome," he said with a smile. He seemed pleased.

After that, he talked with us and read passages from the Bible. He gave us suggestions about how to organize and what to do while looking for our relatives. He told us never to lose faith in our work. "Hope is the basis of bounty, of love, and of humanity." He promised to help and told us that the rest of the country needed the work we were doing. He told us that we had an important commitment to keep.

The mothers' group was very important to me and the others. The work we did and the conversations we had were a great support to us. We wanted to see our children and relatives alive, but we also provided one another with moral and spiritual help. Hearing the words of so many people, each with major problems, was beautiful. When you hear other people with so much hope who also have serious problems it helps you to put your own problems in perspective. You realize that as difficult as your life may be, many other people have an even harder time.

I began to realize more and more what was going on by listening to the testimonies of the other women. They told stories of their children taken away wounded, taken away from their jobs, disappeared. All of these stories entered my head and began to change the way I thought. "How can it be that all of this goes on?" I wondered. "What is happening around us?"

The women also helped me understand my own situation.

"Look," they would say. "Do you know why your husband was taken prisoner?"

"Well," I replied, "He was just a worker."

"How much did he make?" they asked.

"Not much."

"Your husband is in prison because he was conscious of what was going on in El Salvador," they told me. "He knew about the injustice and the exploitation of working people. He wasn't just working for himself, but for a lot of other people. He is a great person. Little by little, you will understand what he did and see the things that he saw." They explained to me exactly what my husband had done—all the things he never told me.

I began to realize that in spite of my situation I was still better off than a lot of women. I was free to go and see Rafael in prison when I wanted. The children of some of these women were taken away and they will probably never see them again. Some of them had to go recover the mutilated bodies of their children. These women who had so much pain still managed to face life.

I began to participate in the group's activities. Sometimes we would make flyers and pass them around. While I was participating in these activities I never thought that I was in any danger. People used to say, "We know what we are doing is right, but we have to be careful. Be careful when you are passing out flyers; don't let them grab you."

"Who?" I would ask. "Who is going to grab us?"

"Don't worry," they would tell me. "Just be careful."

I started to spend more and more time with the Committee. Sometimes I would take my youngest child with me and the other ones would stay with my family. Sometimes I would take all three of them with me. During that time we received a lot of help from some lawyers from FENASTRAS, (Federación Nacional Sindical de Trabajadores Salvadoreños, the National Federation of Salvadoran Workers). They took on the case of defending the 22 prisoners from the sugar mill.

After about three weeks, they moved the prisoners to the central prison in Santa Ana where they were mixed in with common criminals. The prison commander in this jail was a little kinder than most, and I think that he tried to make sure that those under his command treated the prisoners reasonably.

The first time I went to visit Rafael in the Santa Ana jail, they told me they didn't have any prisoners from the sugar mill there. Then they told me to go and speak with the commanding officer. I did.

"Good day, sir," I said to him.

"Hello," he said to me pleasantly. "How can I help you?"

"I have come to visit my husband who is from the sugar mill," I told him.

"Oh, yes." he said. They brought them here two days ago. They are here Ma'am. Don't worry. They are fine. They are good people. Please, come in."

He let me in and they searched me like they always do. I hated the searches, but this was the worst because I had my period. They even made me remove my Kotex pad to make sure I wasn't carrying anything in it. That is really embarrassing when it is all covered with blood and everything. This is the kind of humiliation we have to go through just to go and see our relatives.

Rafael was surprised to see me.

"Don't you want me to keep looking for you?" I asked him. "When you are tired of me, tell me."

"No, don't worry about me," he said. "Actually, I thought that you would get tired of coming to see me. I am not doing anything. I am in jail and I can't help you with anything."

While I was talking to him, some of the other men and their families came over. While visiting him in jail, I got to know the families of the other prisoners and I began to talk to them about CO-MADRES. I invited them to visit the CO-MADRES office and I talked to them about what we could do to get the men out of prison.

We also discussed what we could do to publicize the many people being disappeared in El Salvador. No one was paying attention to us in El Salvador so we needed to get some international publicity and support. We decided to send a group of eight women to the United Nations office in San Salvador to ask for their freedom. It was the first time that a group of mothers went to visit the U.N. It was one of our first big actions.

We went to the U.N. office in two groups. I was outside with one group while the other group entered to speak with whomever was in charge. At first, they didn't want to let us in, but we just kept trying to persuade them. Finally, we spoke with the man in charge and told him all about the disappeared, the prisoners, and all of our demands. At the end of an hour, he said, "Thank you very much ladies. It was my pleasure to have met you. I hope that you can come back and that we can help you." He was trying to usher us out.

Then one of the women stood up, blocking the doorway of his office, and another woman joined her, saying, "Sir, why don't you sit down? This is a peaceful occupation of your office by the mothers. We want you to send the list of our disappeared to your office in Geneva and demand that they do something about it." Then we stated all our demands.

"This is a joke, isn't it?" he asked. He couldn't believe that his office was being occupied by eight women, all seated on the floor. "This *is* a joke, right?"

"No," we said. "We are the mothers of the disappeared and we are asking you to telex all the information we have given you to Geneva. Once you can guarantee that they have received the names of all the disappeared, then we will leave."

"You have to understand," he said. "That is very difficult for me to do. I can't go meddling in the political problems of another country."

"Well, then tell them that it isn't you, but us who are sending the information," responded the mothers. "We take responsibility."

He called the local authorities instead. Soon, the place was crawling with the national police. They wouldn't let anyone through.

People were talking about what was going on and they wanted to know, who were these women inside the U.N. headquarters making demands? A lot of people were watching outside. The TV, radio, and press arrived while the whole area was cordoned off by the military. Outside we shouted, "Instead of committing another crime here, why don't you give these women their disappeared children?"

Finally, we had to ask the man in charge to intervene for the mothers so that they could leave safely. The military wanted to forcibly drag the mothers out. By this time, a lot of people had gathered ouside to show their support for the mothers. Finally, the man in charge spoke with the military officials: "These women don't mean any harm. They haven't done anything wrong, and I will take responsibility for all of this." Because of him, the compañeras got out without any problems.

After that, we began to occupy Catholic churches. That is how we started getting our message out to the Salvadoran people. They were interested in what we had to say, too. People started to talk about us and ask, "Who are these women anyway?" People used to tell us how brave we were because there was a lot of repression then under the military president Carlos Humberto Romero. He was a thug. People would see us on the street and tell us, "Ay, madrecita, we are so sorry about what happened.* We weren't aware of the atrocities the government and the armed forces are committing. But we are with you. We are citizens and mothers too and we identify with your struggle."

---

* Often members of CO-MADRES carried out public actions in which they would be looking for specific individuals who had disappeared or who were imprisoned. They carried posters with people's names and photographs on them. This gave people on the street an immediate personal connection with their cause. The signs allowed them to identify with CO-MADRES by putting a face on the name of a disappeared person.

The press began to pay a little more attention to us as well and to report on what we were doing. One of our biggest actions was to take over the Salvadoran Red Cross building for three months. We demanded the release of the 22 union workers from the sugar mill. We carried out the action with various groups of women. One group arrived to talk with the Red Cross workers about what we were going to do. They said, "This is a peaceful takeover of your office by the mothers and families of the disappeared. We intend to stay here and even if you call the police we aren't leaving." After the first group occupied the building, a second group arrived. We talked to the Red Cross employees and finally convinced them to leave: "Don't worry. We aren't going to break anything or steal anything. We are simply going to occupy the building and hold a hunger strike."

That was on the first day. We began the hunger strike on the second day with 10 people—mothers and other relatives of the disappeared. We discussed our objectives in public, explaining why we were there and how our children had been disappeared. Little by little, people started to come over to the front of the building and see what we were doing. We had banners that read, "Mothers' Committee" and we also played music. I had often heard this kind of music, but I had never really listened to the words or understood the message before. Protest music was prohibited. There were a lot of folk music groups that formed in El Salvador whose music was censored by the authorities. We played this protest music loudly. It attracted people and we got a lot of support. We received messages of solidarity from workers in different unions and factories, from people in the market, and others who were hearing about the mothers for the first time.

Soon after we started the hunger strike, political prisoners around the country started a hunger strike as well in solidarity with us. They put forward their own demands for unconditional freedom and general amnesty for all political prisoners. I had been participating in the hunger strike for two days when I decided to visit the jail where my compañero was. I brought the prisoners honey, sweets, lemons, limes, and other things they needed to maintain the strike. I was already feeling light-headed, as if I were walking on air. I wasn't too strong.

Little by little, workers from the sugar mill were joining the hunger strike. At this point, there were about 12. "We're not having any problems," they said. "We are raising prisoners' consciousness. We can show them that going on a hunger strike won't kill them, that it is a sacrifice. We give them milk, sugar water, or honey." I also spoke with Rafael. He was participating in the hunger strike as well.

Two days later, I read something alarming in the newspaper: "José Rafael Canales, Miguel Angel Villalobos, Nerio Blandino, and others attempted to escape from Santa Ana Prison. They had been planning their escape for months by digging holes below their cells to get out through the basketball court. However, they were discovered before they could escape."

This is impossible, I thought to myself. First of all, their cells weren't anywhere near the basketball court. They couldn't have been planning to escape as the newspaper described. It wasn't true.

I went to the jail and showed the paper to the comandante in charge. He told me that he hadn't given out the names to the press, that there had been some mistake. He told me that the people who had tried to escape had already been moved to another jail. Then I went inside to talk to some of the men on the hunger strike. I spoke with my compañero Rafael and told him what it said in the newspaper.

He was very surprised. "Those sons of bitches from the press. It was them."

"Why?" I asked. "What happened?"

"They came to cover the story of the escape while we were here with our banners from the strike. We told them to come on over and interview us. They didn't pay any attention to us. They thought the escape was a better story. So we called them names, telling them they were *cabrones,* sons of bitches who didn't care about what was going on in their country. Then they started to pay attention to us and they asked our names. They probably just named us as those responsible for the attempted jailbreak to pay us back for swearing at them."

I went to the newspaper to confront them. After I spoke with the director of the *Diario de Hoy de San Salvador,* they threw me out of the office. We had a lot of problems around the hunger strike. Talking about this makes me remember other things that were really difficult about going to visit Rafael in jail.

Like Saturdays, for example. Those were the days for "intimate" visits. I just happened to arrive on a Saturday to visit Rafael, and I noticed that there weren't any other men or children. It was just women.

When I went in and they frisked me, I noticed that all the men were joking. They were all in a group outside waiting. My husband's group was there too. They shouted to him, "Rafael Canales has a visitor," smiling broadly. I went in to visit Rafael; we talked for a little while and then he asked me to leave. As I was leaving, all the men in the prison looked at me and started teasing me, saying things like, "There she goes. She looks really satisfied. She had a good time." I turned around and gave them a dirty look. I was furious with those men.

The next day I came back to see him and I asked, "I have been worried about yesterday. Why did you ask me to leave so quickly?"

"Well," he said. "I don't want to hurt you; it's hard for me to say this. Here in jail, Saturdays are the days for intimate visits between husbands and wives. That's what people are doing in the dormitories. All the women come to visit their husbands. That's why everyone is waiting outside and why the visits have to be short."

"What?" I replied.

"I know that this is really difficult for you and it is a lot to ask. All of my friends' wives come to visit them for this," and he named everyone's names to show me that a lot of women came. "Please come to visit me," he asked.

I went back to the CO-MADRES office to talk with them about this. One of them asked me, "Aren't you going to visit your old man on Saturdays?"

"No," I said.

So she took me by the arm and said, "Come here, hija, come here and sit down. What a woman has to go through when she has a husband is very painful, but men have their needs too. Men can't live without women so we have to make certain sacrifices for them."

"Yes," I replied. "But I have never gone on that kind of visit."

"Well," she said. "There are some things that you have to do that you have never done before in your life."

"I will go for these visits if the group gives me permission," I said, "but it is really difficult. When you go in there everyone knows what it is for. They know you are going for an intimate visit. The truth is that it is a real *sisana* in there with everyone making hissing noises and calling attention to you.* The soldiers and guards are doing this too, making jokes,

* *Sisana* comes from the verb *sisear* meaning to make hissing sounds. In El

talking and making fun of the women. They are very rude. There are also a lot of prostitutes who go there for men who don't have wives or compañeras. Going on these visits is a real cross to bear."

During my visits with Rafael, we mostly talked to each other. One day he said to me, "You know, Chata, you have changed a lot in the three months I've been in jail. The work you do is very good," he said. We often talked about the problems of the hunger strikers and everything they had gone through.

Two days later, the National Guard arrived and removed Rafael and most of the other political prisoners. When I went to visit Rafael the next day and then the following two days, he wasn't there. His name wasn't on the list anymore. I started to worry. What had they done with him?

They had taken away all of the prisoners who were involved in the hunger strike. We worried that they had been disappeared. We got together and organized a protest. Then, a few days later, I received a telegram that didn't have Rafael's name on it, but just had the name of some pills that he took for his asthma. It was signed by a common prisoner, not him. It said, "I need these pills." It had been sent from inside the San Vicente jail.

That's how I learned he was in the San Vicente jail. Not all political prisoners were so lucky. We began looking for some of the men who had been disappeared. Some were found in different jails after they had been severely tortured. We spent a long time tracking people down, and we finally found most of them.

We received lots of positive publicity and international solidarity while we were looking for people. Because of all our activity we received an invitation from Costa Rica to attend the World Council of Peace. People came from all over the world—from Guatemala, Nicaragua, Haiti, people from places who would understand what we were going through. We started a process in CO-MADRES to elect the people who would represent the group in Costa Rica, and they chose me as one of the representatives. This was hard for me to think about because I didn't have any idea how I could leave. Who would I leave my children with? How would I find the money to go? How would I tell my compañero that I wanted to leave?

Salvador hissing is used to get someone to look at you. A *sisana* refers to a whole roomful of men making these noises to get a woman's attention.

But I got ready to go anyway. I got my travel documents and about eight days before I was supposed to leave, I went to visit Rafael in jail and we talked.

"The mothers have invited me to go to Costa Rica," I said, looking at him.

"So, go ahead," he replied. "If you want to go, what's the problem?"

"Do you want me to go?" I asked.

"It's fine with me if you want to go. Don't worry about me. I'm going to wait here for you," he said. "But what are you going to do with the kids?"

"That's a big problem," I replied.

"Speak to my family," he said. "Maybe they will take care of them."

I felt very good because he agreed that I should go. I found someone to watch the kids and in July 1978 we left for Costa Rica. I remember that Somoza was still in Nicaragua at that time.

We received a lot of publicity in Costa Rica. It was a turning point for us. We talked about what was going on in El Salvador and how we had been invited to the World Peace Council. We visited universities, unions, and community organizations looking for solidarity for our work in El Salvador. One thing I will never forget was our visit to the presidential palace. The president wasn't there, but his sister received us. When we arrived at the palace, we were amazed because there were no guards. There were no military authorities, civil police, or guns like in El Salvador. They were very friendly to us. Not like in El Salvador where they walk around with guns and bayonets and they put them in your face and demand, "What are you doing here?" In El Salvador, it is practically impossible to get to see the president unless you are from the same class as the president. Poor people don't go see the president. That's why the way we were treated in Costa Rica was quite amazing to us.

The president's sister told us that the president thought our work was important and he supported it. She said that he was concerned about what was going on in El Salvador. We used this opportunity to make a request. "We would like for you or the president to send a telegram to the president of El Salvador telling him that there are seven Salvadoran women in Costa Rica and that they should be allowed to return without any problems."

"Sure, why not," said the president's sister. And she signed the telegram "Presidential Palace, Costa Rica." Then she sent it to El Salvador. And we went home without any problem 17 days later.

Founding CO-MADRES member Antonia Sedosa takes part in a CO-MADRES action. Photo by Jacque Gharib. December 1988.

CHAPTER 6

PERSONAL AND POLITICAL STRUGGLES

When I returned to El Salvador from Costa Rica I was happy to be back home, to see my children and most of all to see Rafael, who was out of jail. I arrived at six o'clock in the afternoon. My youngest daughter was walking naked in the street, dirty with nothing on. I felt very bad seeing her in the street like that.

"Mami, Mami," she called to me.

"What happened?" I asked. "Where is your father? Isn't he here?"

"He's here Mamá," she answered, "but he is very sick."

I ran inside and found Rafael with a 104-degree fever and bronchitis. His fever was so bad he was babbling incoherently. I thought, my God, what will I do? I put cool towels on his head and did other things to lower the fever. Then I went out to find medicine for him. After a couple of days, he started to feel better and we began to talk. One of his uncles had gone to get him out of jail.

I had been living alone in the house with my children for six months while my compañero was in jail. I had no idea what his ideas were going to be when he came back or if he was going to let me leave the house to carry out my work. And it turned out to be a problem.

At first he agreed to let me go out. But at the same time he said, "Chata, you didn't tell me everything you were doing. I don't know what I am going to do when they grab you." Slowly, I told him everything that I had been through in the past six months.

"You poor thing," he said to me. "You have really put up with a lot. I never thought that you could endure all of these things." He seemed to understand, but two months later, things had changed.

"The truth is that I don't want you to keep working with CO-MA-DRES. I need you here at home. Sometimes I want to talk to you and you aren't here. Sometimes I get tired of taking care of the kids, and they need you to be here more than I do. And sometimes I ask myself, what is she really doing? What is she doing fooling around in San Salvador?"

"Really?" I sighed, surprised. "You think I go to San Salvador to fool around?" I was crying, embracing him, and kissing him. "You really think that I'm just wasting my time?"

"Yes," he said.

"Okay, then." I replied. "I will obey the man of the house. If you want me to stay home, then I will. But if they come from CO-MADRES and ask what happened to me then you will have to answer to them."

"No, they won't come here looking for you," he said. "They won't even remember you."

I felt very conflicted. I had an appointment that day and people were counting on me. But at the same time, I was still dominated by my love for my compañero more than by my love for my work. Two days went by and he was very happy because I stayed at home the whole time. Then at five o'clock in the morning on the third day there was a loud knock on the door.

"It is the abuela. That's what they call her," I said.

"They came looking for you," he said.

"No, they are looking for you." I answered and opened the door.

"What's going on? How come you haven't come to the CO-MA-DRES office?" she asked, staring at me.

"Well," I said, shouting so Rafael could hear. "You see, it seems that when I go I don't really do anything at all. I don't do anything in the office, and I'm just going into San Salvador to hang around on the streets. My beloved husband doesn't want me to leave anymore. He wants me to stay here to take care of him and the kids, to clean the house."

The abuela turned toward the bed where Rafael was lying down and raised her voice. "Mmmm. Compañero, I had pegged you for a more intelligent person. But look at the foolishness that has come out of your mouth."

Rafael got up. "Good morning, Abuela," he said sleepily.

"Good morning," she said to him. "Now, tell me what is going on."

"Look Abuela, it isn't like it seems. This woman is just fickle. I was just kidding when I said those things to her and she took me seriously. I don't keep her from going out."

"This woman has responsibilities," the abuela told him. "People are counting on her. When she isn't there it is a problem."

"Why didn't you tell me that?" Rafael asked.

That day, I changed clothes and left with the abuela to go off and do some work. But it was the beginning of a long struggle with Rafael about my work.

My compañero was a working-class man who was very class-conscious. He had a lot of political experience—more than I did. He was always working to change the situation of workers who had been exploited by people in power. It seemed so strange to me that a man who I thought had more political consciousness than I did would be telling me not to get involved in anything. He wanted me to stay at home and take care of the house and the children. I couldn't really understand why he was saying this to me.

It was difficult because he wasn't working. It is hard for an ex-political prisoner to get work. His name had been all over the press and television, and no one wanted to hire him. So he was stuck at home.

I think he was also jealous about me spending nights away from home. I didn't tell him what we were doing or where I was going. I didn't think I had to confess to him about my work. After all, he hadn't told me anything about his work. We mostly talked about the kids and what was going on at home.

In El Salvador, couples involved in political work can't really confide in each other. First, I didn't know if he could understand the kind of work I did with women. I also didn't want to tell him when and where I was going. He didn't discuss those things with me either.

Rafael and I only talked about very superficial things, things that would never cause a security problem for either one of us. The same thing was true with my compañeras in CO-MADRES. They taught me not to ask about things I didn't need to know about. What if the police captured and tortured me, and I couldn't resist? Any information I gave the police could be used to arrest, kill, and disappear all the people participating in union activities. All of these things were going through my head while I was on the bus going to San Salvador to CO-MADRES.

When I arrived at the CO-MADRES office after staying home for some time, they talked to me about what happened.

"Are you such a fool that you are going to let your old man push you around? Women have the right to do what they want, not just what their husbands tell them to do. You don't need his permission for everything you do."

"Yes, it's true," I would reply. But then I would ask myself, who is right? Are they right? Is my husband right? It was hard to understand because everything had changed so much from when we first started living together. Before, I never left the house. I was always there making the food, cleaning, and taking care of him and my children. Saturdays and Sundays he would say to me, "Let's go take a walk in the park." I would just follow him like a little puppy.

Then when I started to get politically involved, things changed. He didn't approve of the fact that I was making my own decisions. Often we would talk about it. Sometimes when he would raise his voice I would tell him, "You aren't my father so don't talk to me that way. I am your wife, but you have to respect me. If you respect me, I will respect you. I'm not your daughter."

I realized that I had changed. My perspectives on everything had changed from how we lived earlier. I no longer accepted that he could make all the decisions without consulting me. But whenever we talked about these things I became frightened.

One day he threatened me, saying, "I am going to leave you."

What would I do if he left? I was very young; I had children and no secure job. I could have gone to live with my family again, but I didn't want that. I would apologize to him for my work with CO-MADRES and promise I wasn't going to do it anymore.

All the women in CO-MADRES had problems at home just like me. In fact, many of their problems were worse than mine. They had macho husbands who beat them, slept around, drank, and spent the family's food money on liquor and other women. I don't know how they came to have a political consciousness given the situation they came from.

I liked talking to other women in CO-MADRES about their personal situations. We were women of different ages (from 26 to 50 and older), appearances, and ideas. We were a fantastic group of women. We had our own problems, but we would always help other people out with a smile. They encouraged me a lot with Rafael.

"Talk to him about your rights. He has to listen to you. Women have the same human rights as everyone else. He may go out and work and bring in money, but you work too. Washing, ironing, and cooking is work. You just don't get paid a salary for it. You have the same rights as he does."

But things were still very tense with Rafael. There was a period when I didn't do much work with CO-MADRES and stayed at home for almost a month. One day, Rafael came to me and asked, "Are you going to keep going out and working with CO-MADRES?"

"Yes," I said. "I am going to keep working with them."

"I don't want to tell you when to come and go, but I want you to think this over. I can return to work now. I can bring home everything we need for the house so you don't have to leave. We can have the same life we had before I was arrested. It's very difficult to have you leaving all the time. Furthermore, what you are doing is dangerous. Someday they could follow you home and arrest you. Something could happen to the children, something far worse than you have ever imagined. This is the reality of what you are doing. I'm not telling you this to scare you, but because it's true."

"Well, listen to you," I responded. "Here you are telling me all about what I am doing and how dangerous it is when you never spoke a word to me about what you were doing. You never even talked to me politically about what was going on in El Salvador. Who are you to tell me to stop doing my work because it is so dangerous?"

"I didn't tell you what I was doing before because I didn't trust you. You could have turned me in. I also didn't know if you would be able to put up with everything if something happened to me." He said this because it is something that happens a lot in El Salvador. Mothers turn in their children; children turn in their parents; husbands and wives turn in their spouses.

"Don't go," he begged me.

"Okay," I said. "I won't go today, but I'm going to go tomorrow.

The next day, while I was making lunch, we heard on the radio that several members of CO-MADRES had been arrested. They had taken over the Cathedral to demand that a judge exhume the body of a young man who had disappeared. We found out where he was buried after we showed his picture around. We found a lot of the disappeared that way. They were buried in unmarked graves. CO-MADRES, the non-governmental human rights commission, and the boy's family went to the site where the body was supposed to be exhumed, but the judge didn't show up.

After I heard this, I said to Rafael, "Look, you finish making the meal. I am going."

"Where are you going?" he asked.

"Weren't you listening to the news?" I said. "The compañeras are in the Cathedral and I am going to go." I didn't ask him if I could go; I just left.

"Goodbye," I said. "I don't know when I will be back, but you have to look after the kids."

When I reached the Cathedral several members of CO-MADRES wondered why I hadn't gotten there earlier. The next day, while we were occupying the Cathedral, we received a notice from a judge telling us to go to the cemetery to exhume the boy's body. I knew both the boy and his mother. It was horrible. We took responsibility for the exhumation of the body. We also bought a coffin for the boy, and secured a location to take the body once it was dug up. We took it to the office of the FUSS (Federación Unitaria Sindical Salvadoreña, Federation of Salvadoran Workers). We stayed there until the next day with the body and with the boy's family.

He had been kidnapped and then machine-gunned in Soyopango. We didn't know who did it, whether it was the National Guard or the treasury police. They buried him too. They called it an *enfrentamiento*. That means that he had a confrontation with the army. They said that he was armed. Part of the back of his head was missing and his back was all messed up. He was shot and then they threw him in the ground and buried him. Witnesses said that he wasn't armed. He was out walking.

The next day his family put him in a coffin. But problems continued at the burial. The police claimed people were carrying arms in the coffin. The boy was well known, well liked, and belonged to one of the Christian Base Communities. Many of his friends came to the burial and some of them were carrying the coffin. The police opened fire on them and a lot of people were injured. The police actually opened the coffin to see if it contained guns or a dead body. Violence was everywhere. Then violence came into my own house, but in a different way.

One day not too long after we exhumed this boy's body, I was coming home from working with CO-MADRES. It was about 8:30 p.m. and I had been away for three days. I got off in the little bus terminal in

Izalco and went past the *pupusa* stand owned by a local woman.* She sees everyone that comes and goes, and I always talk to her. Some other women I knew were there too, just hanging out.

"Hey, Tere," they called to me. My friends called me Tere. "Your husband was out walking around here feeling good."

"Oh, yeah," I answered. "What was he doing?"

"He wasn't doing anything. He came here with some friends. He ate and then left with a big carton of beer."

I didn't believe them, but my friend who ran the stand took me aside and told me, "Rafael was here and he was very drunk."

"Thanks," I replied running out the door toward my house.

When I got home, I could tell Rafael was drunk. He was lying down in our bed. I came in and put my things on the table. We had a very small house and we had put up a curtain to separate the bedroom from the other part of the house. Everything was dirty, there was old food, empty bottles everywhere and it smelled of stale beer. My son Juan Carlos was there.

"What happened here, son?" I asked.

"My father came home with some friends and they were drinking."

"And your father is here?" I asked loudly, even though I knew he was.

"Yes," said Juan Carlos. What I didn't know was that my sister-in-law was in the house too.

"So, you disgusting man," I shouted. "What kind of man are you? How many times have I told you not to bring your friends home? This is a tiny house and we have children. And you are drunk." I was afraid that something could happen. Our youngest daughter was just four years old and he was supposed to watch her. What if something happened to her? He would never know.

"I already asked you not to bring any of your asshole friends home with you," I shouted. "I never bring home strangers who make trouble. Can't you see I'm tired? I go to work and look at the shape the house is in. It's disgusting. And you are supposed to be looking after the children. How can you watch them? You are drunk and lying down. We can talk about this tomorrow. You aren't in any shape to talk now."

* The *pupusa* is one of the staples of the Salvadoran diet. It is a thick corn tortilla filled with meat, cheese, or vegetables. Pupusa stands are the fast-food restaurants of the poor and the working class.

I was very upset, hungry, and tired. I went out the back door to go to the bathroom. My sister-in-law still didn't say anything and I didn't see her. I opened up the back door when I felt his hand in my hair. My hair was long then and it was easy to grab. Rafael pulled my head back with a jerk and I was very surprised that he grabbed me so hard.

"Now I am going to kill you."

I jumped after he grabbed me and turned toward him, trying to pull away. "And why are you going to kill me?"

"Because no woman speaks to me that way," he yelled. "And in this house I am in charge. I'm going to do what I feel like doing for once, not what you want."

"That's what you think," I said. "But I have the same rights as you because I also bring in money for food and I take care of our children. You are not the only one. Now stop talking to me like that and let go of my hair. You are hurting me."

"No," he said. "I am going to kill you."

"Stop talking like an idiot and let go," I said.

"No way," he screamed. And he started to beat on me. This made me very angry. Then he called me and my mother names. "You *hija de puta.*" I couldn't stand this. He had me by the hair with my head pulled back and he was taller than me. I was trying to think about what I could do to defend myself. I wasn't going to put up with this treatment. I was looking for a way out when I felt the first blow to my head.

I started yelling back at him. "You want a war, then I am going to give you war. You asshole, no one beats me. If you want us to kill each other then we will, but you are not going to lay another hand on me." I looked around the room. We had a big heavy pine table and chairs from Guatemala. I grabbed one of the heavy chairs. I don't know how I picked it up, but I did.

"You are not going to beat me anymore," I yelled at him.

I lost control after that. I was so angry with him. I hit him over the head with that heavy chair and he fell down on the floor. Then I pinned him to the ground with the heel of my shoe and I grabbed him by the hair. I didn't feel anything while I was doing this, I was so angry. Then, while he was lying on the ground, he tried to kick me from the ground. He knocked me over and we fought. He was throwing punches at me and I was trying to protect my face. I hit him and kicked him too. That's when my sister-in-law stepped out of where she was hiding.

"No, cuñada," I said. "Leave him alone. I am going to kill him. Why don't you just leave? You are not like him. Just leave. I am going to kill him."

She got angry with me and said, "Think about your children and what you are saying!"

"Just get out of here," I answered.

While I was talking to my sister-in-law, Rafael got loose from me. He kicked me and I fell down again. It was terrible. Then he grabbed a machete and hit me with the flat of the machete. I tried to get it away from him.

"I don't deserve this treatment from you. Why are you doing this? This whole situation is impossible. We are going to kill each other." And I left. I went to stay with my family.

Later, he woke up and came looking for me. Nobody answered, so he went home. The next day I went back to our house and spoke to Rafael. I was still very angry.

"Yesterday you beat me. You are nothing to me now. I came to ask you to leave or else I will leave. I can't stand to live with you here anymore or even bear to hear your voice."

"Okay," he said. "What do you want?"

"I want you to leave. I want a separation," I said. "I don't deserve what you did to me, Rafael. I don't."

"But you came home already angry," he said.

"Oh, come on," I said. "Whose fault was that?"

"Well, maybe you are right," he said.

"Well, you either have to leave, or we will kill each other," I said. "I want this to end right now." I picked up a knife that was on the table.

"Are you serious?" he asked.

"Yes, I am serious," I said. I put the knife down and he left. He went to stay with some friends. Later, he came back to ask me to stay with my mother, and I agreed. I took the kids and went to my mother's house in Santa Ana.

The next day I went to the CO-MADRES office. The women all gathered around me. They could see I had a black eye.

"Tula, what happened to you?" they asked.

"I fell down," I answered.

"Hmmm," said the abuela. "I smell something funny here."

"No, it's nothing, Abuela," I told her. Then I looked in her eyes and said, "Well, what really happened is that I had a fight with my compañero last night."

"And what are you going to do?" the abuela asked me. "Have you spoken with him?"

"No." I answered. Then she and other people convinced Rafael and I that we should meet to talk with each other. We were supposed to meet at our house. He didn't show up at the time we had set. He went to his uncle's house instead. Finally, he came and we both sat down to talk. The first thing I asked him for was a separation. I just kept asking for that. He asked me to forgive him. He said he was sorry for everything that happened, for all of the problems and the big fight. He told me that he hadn't been thinking straight, and that he hadn't seen me for who I was.

"And if I hadn't been able to defend myself from you, what do you think would have happened to me?" I asked him. "What kind of shape would you have left me in?"

Fortunately, I had been taking self-defense classes for about three or four months. We were all preparing to protect ourselves. This had really helped me in defending myself against Rafael. I also went running with friends and spent a lot of time walking. If I wasn't in such good shape then he might have broken my nose or my whole face. As it was, my whole body, my legs, and my arms were purple from where he had beaten me.

"You know," I told him, "when we first got to know each other we said that there wouldn't be any fighting. You went over the limit last night. You treated me horribly. You beat me like a coward. You behaved like a wild animal, not a man. I can't be with you any more. I love you, but I can't be with you. I am not your property. I have my principles as a woman. If you beat me last night, you could do it again tomorrow. But I won't give you the chance." I took a deep breath and continued.

"When I met you, you didn't have any children. Now you have three. I gave you three children. Either you leave permanently or I will stay at my mother's house with the children. You can visit them when you like because they are your children, but I am not your wife anymore. I am not your private property."

Rafael looked right at me and said, "Are you serious about this?"

"Yes," I replied. "I have already made up my mind."

"Well, I haven't," he said.

"Why not?" I asked.

"Because I am sorry and I want you to forgive me for what I did so we can start again," he said.

"Saying you are sorry doesn't change what you did," I said.

Finally, we reached an agreement because of the children. We were worried about what would happen to them. I made a proposal to him.

"If you really think it is going to upset the children if one of us leaves, then you can stay in the house. We will live like two friends, not husband and wife. You are their father and I am their mother, but there isn't going to be any more relationship between the two of us. If there is a question that I have to answer for you, then ask it. Otherwise don't talk to me. If you can accept this, then you can stay. If not, then go."

"Well, I want to stay with my children," he said.

"Are you sure?" I asked. "You accept my conditions?"

"Yes," he said.

So he stayed at home and I went out. He never asked me where I was going, what I was going to do, or when I would be coming back. One day, however, he wanted to know.

"Chata," he said, "Are you going out?"

"Why do you ask?" I replied. "You don't have any right to ask me where I am going. That is what we agreed to. I am free to do what I want."

"I'm sorry," he said.

Sometimes he would ask me where his clothes were or what to wear, but he had to find them himself. We spent three months like this, not communicating, but being in the same house. It was really hard on him during this time and sometimes it felt terrible.

After three months he said to me one day, "Please, I am begging you to forgive me. You don't see how much I regret what I did and how sorry I am. I am going to go because I'm tired of this situation. I have put up with it for three months. I think your treatment of me has been just, ignoring me and not paying attention to me. If you want to be free of me, then fine. But I can't take any more of this."

"All right," I said. I did love him and I had been hard on him. "I want to see if you can change."

So we started living as a couple again. And he was different. He truly regretted what he did and he was always asking for forgiveness. Inside of me, I believed him. That was in January 1980. That was the last serious problem we had as a couple. From then on, we understood each other. We would each respect what the other wanted to do, and he never interfered with my work again. He started to support my work. He would bring me food or fruit or clean clothes, and the other women would point at him and say, "Here comes the old man again." Our life really felt different and when I think back on our relationship, we only had that one big fight in nine years.

CHAPTER 7

INCREASED REPRESSION AND THE DEATH OF SILVIA OLÁN AND MONSEÑOR ROMERO

In 1979 and 1980, there was a lot going on. There were student movements, peasant movements, labor movements, and all kinds of human rights organizations springing up to publicize human rights violations. During this time, many people had to leave El Salvador and go into exile in other countries. We were moving around too. In July 1979 we moved to Santa Ana to live in a house that was close to my mother.

Right around this time Silvia Olán was disappeared. I had met her in 1978 during the sugar mill strike. She was the secretary of the SLES (Sindicato de la Luz Electrica de Sonsonate, Electrical Workers Union of Sonsonate). Two members of a death squad arrived and abducted her from her office. I was devastated when I heard about her capture because she was such a wonderful woman and an important leader. CO-MADRES took up the search for her body along with those of two young men who had disappeared.

Their bodies appeared in a place known as "Las Cruces," on the way to Santa Ana. They had been captured in Sonsonate. One of them, Miguel Angel Osorio y Alballeros was a nice young worker. The security forces had burned both him and the other young man with acid. It was hard to tell what happened to them because both bodies were severely burned. They had burned their eyes with acid and had cut their hands into pieces. It was terrible to find them this way. Miguel Angel was the grandson of the woman we called Abuela, Rosalina Osorio Melgár. She had raised him like a son. She was so upset and stayed depressed for a long time.

Two days later, the body of Silvía Olán was found by a group of campesinos in a place called La Laguna in the town of Coatepeque. There was evidence that she had been raped before she died. They had cut off part of her genitals and stuffed them into her nose. They cut off her breasts and her fingers as well. They had burned her eyes with acid, pulled out her tongue, and strangled her. You can't imagine how terrible it is to find someone like that, especially someone you admired and cared for.

CO-MADRES took charge of her burial. We also paid her the honor and respect she was due as a great woman and fighter for human rights. We found a funeral home and had her prepared for burial. FUSS let us hold a wake for her in their building. Many union activists attended and we had an honor guard for her.

The wake lasted all night and into the next day. It made me think of the last time I had seen her. We were riding the bus together to Izalco. I remembered the romantic song she liked, "With the Wind." She asked me to remember her through this song when she died. At that moment, we had been passing the Izalco volcano. It was a majestic sight to see.

The next day we had a memorial mass for her in the Church of the Rosario. A lot of people came to pay their respects. She died such a horrible death, but in life she was a courageous fighter for democracy and justice in our country.

In October 1979, there was a coup d'étàt that brought in the junta of the Revolutionary Government. The junta had two military members and three civilians: Guillermo Ungo and Román Mayorga, and one other person whose name I can't remember. When they took power, they promised to carry out agrarian reform, create more employment, uphold democracy, and clarify what happened to the disappeared. They promised that the disappearances would end and that peace would come.

We thought we might be able to pressure this new government. Doctor Guillermo Ungo and Román Mayorga were social democrats who had a lot of popular support.* We made a list of the disappeared and went

---

* They were members of the social democratic MNR (Movimiento Nacional

to the presidential palace to ask if we could have a meeting with them to discuss their cases. All the names on the list were documented cases with testimony from their families. We had the names of 500 disappeared.

We sent the letter and the list to this revolutionary junta, but they never responded. We published the letter in the newspaper, but they still didn't respond. Finally, we decided that we would get their attention by occupying Parque Libertad in front of the Church of the Rosario in the center of San Salvador. We set ourselves up under the main statue in the park, and engaged in a hunger strike. We demanded that the government grant us an audience to deal with the cases of the disappeared. They had promised to resolve these cases and we were just holding them to their promises.

This was also the time that the LP-28 (Ligas Populares 28 de Febrero, Popular League of February 28) was occupying the Church of the Rosario.* So a lot of people came over to support us—workers, peasants, and students who were in the church occupation.

We were occupying the park, when José Napoleón Duarte came back from Venezuela supported by the Christian Democrats. He went to talk in front of the Central Theater and then went on a march with his supporters. They provoked a confrontation with us. We had a loudspeaker in the park, and the Christian Democrats cut off our sound. Duarte claimed that he supported the people, but he didn't come over to talk with us. He knew who we were, but he ignored us. That's when the people began to distrust the Christian Democrats.

We had to leave the park that night at midnight. The Red Cross came to pick us up, to protect us from further confrontations. The next day, at

Revolucionario, National Revolutionary Movement). Ungo had been elected Vice-President with Christian Democrat José Napoleón Duarte in 1972, but the military regime deposed them, installing instead PCN candidate Arturo Armando Molina. In January 1980, Ungo and Mayorga resigned from the junta. A second, short-lived junta was formed in January. In March 1980, José Napoleón Duarte joined the third Junta government that lasted until March 1982. Duarte represented the Christian Democrats in the third Junta.

* LP-28 was a popular revolutionary organization whose small membership was heavily influenced by student militants. The organization is named after the day in 1977 when the armed forces killed over 100 people demonstrating against the fraudulent election of General Romero, successor to Colonel Arturo Molina.

five in the morning, we walked back to the park on foot. We found a lot of junk there: whiskey bottles, broken glass, and a lot of garbage. We began sweeping the park clean with our feet. We had to clean up everything.

We had been in the park about seven days when there was a big peasant march demanding agrarian reform. The new government never carried out the agrarian reform in spite of all their promises.

I remember that we were on the other side of the park, in front of the *Gráfica* newspaper, when we began to hear shots, again and again. We saw people running and screaming. It was terrible. It was a massacre. Then we saw that people were pulling the bodies of men, women, and children into the Church of the Rosario. It was such a macabre thing. It was the first time I had seen such a slaughter up close. Other CO-MADRES members came running up.

"What happened? My God! So many people killed!" they shouted. Then we saw that the National Guard was throwing the bodies onto trucks. Only 28 of the dead were taken to the Church of the Rosario. The sight made us tremble and we felt sick from what we were witnessing. Then we saw tanks roll in and begin to surround the church.

We went into the church and saw the dead. Once we were inside we began to get nervous because the authorities would confuse us with the LP-28 members occupying the church. We were talking about this in the middle of a huge pile of bodies, people in pieces. I felt dizzy from the sight, like I was going to fall down. A young man who was part of the occupation told us to get out of there. We left with the help of a taxi driver and this young man.

At six o'clock that evening, we heard the news that some of the young people involved in the occupation were asking Monseñor Romero to intervene because the tanks were still in front of the church, and the military was getting ready to pull people out. There were a lot of people who had taken refuge in the church. When marches are attacked like that, people run into the churches for protection.

Monseñor Romero arrived at the church just in time, because the tanks were already breaking the windows. He stood in the doorway of the sanctuary and told them that they would have to run him over with a tank to get in. This held them off for a while. These people were barricaded inside the church for eight days. They wouldn't even let them out to bury the dead. So they buried them right there in the church. And they put a cross for each of the dead—28 altogether—in front of the church. The military threw away the crosses, but the dead are still buried in the Church of the Rosario.

In November 1979, we began to pressure the government again, demanding to know what happened to the disappeared. The junta announced, " The mothers and those who work in human rights say that there are clandestine cemeteries in El Salvador. But there are no such cemeteries. We want the people to live in peace and not be afraid of the military anymore. So we will provide judges so that they can go and find the bodies that the mothers are talking about."

So CO-MADRES, along with the non-governmental CDH (Comisión de Derechos Humanos del Salvador, Human Rights Commission) and FENASTRAS, initiated a campaign to expose the existence of clandestine cemeteries. We knew where they were. We went to El Playón. We found bodies and skeletons there. We found these cemeteries all over the country. People would find bodies and come and tell us. "Come and see," they would say. "Look in this canal. There are a lot of bodies in there." And people would show us where the bodies were and we would dig and dig and we would find two, three, four, or five bodies in one grave. Sometimes in a grave that was only a meter wide we would just find bones. Sometimes we would find a whole body. It was incredible. Every day we would dig up about 25-30 bodies that would be sent in plastic bags to the central cemetery. We found a lot of clandestine cemeteries that became famous as body dumps.

We would exhume the bodies, but we would always go with a judge. The judge would testify as to what was found. He would write down what happened to the body, where and in what condition it was found, and write a daily report about how many disappeared we had unburied. We did this all over El Salvador—in Sonsonate, San Miguel, Santa Ana, San Vicente. Many people found their disappeared relatives this way. Sometimes they identified them because of their belt buckle, their shoes, their socks or something they were wearing. Often, the bodies were decapitated or mutilated so badly that you couldn't tell who it was. Sometimes we would find a whole body intact so it was possible to identify. The media was paying a lot more attention to us. They would follow us all over and even to the cemetery when we would arrive carrying in plastic bags the bodies we had found. When the government saw that we were turning up lots of bodies, they tried to stop us by increasing the repression against us. They started to watch us and we had to be more careful.

In reality, there was much more violence in El Salvador under this supposedly "revolutionary" junta than before, under President Carlos Humberto Romero. Because of the repression, the people decided that they had to defend themselves from the government junta. As a result, in 1980, the five revolutionary organizations united.* People went out on the street and the government was frightened at the power the people showed. People chanted, "We don't want this government any more. We want a change. We want a real democracy not a fabricated one." That is how the five revolutionary groups came together, in opposition to the government.

When the FMLN (Frente Farabundo Martí de Liberación Nacional, Farabundo Martí National Liberation Front) was formed, people went to the mountains. The people who belonged to the armed revolutionary organizations couldn't stay in the city anymore because they were being pursued by the army and by the different security forces. Political assassinations increased in 1980. Students, workers, peasants, and a lot of different sectors realized the need to get involved with the opposition. Many people participated in the fight against the injustices committed by the military and by the oligarchy: factory owners, large coffee growers, and large landowners who supported the military. People got involved in struggle because they had to defend their class, their dispossessed class. This struggle resulted in massive repression.**

Even before that, there had already been repression. In 1978, 1979, and 1980 there were bodies turning up all over. There were 10 or 12 bodies of students found in Sonsonate and in Santa Ana. Whenever workers asked for a wage increase, they were killed, disappeared, machine-gunned, and assaulted in their factories, schools, and institutes. In Santa Ana at the National Institute of Students, 18-year-old students disappeared. Ten, twelve, or thirteen bodies appeared. All of this repression encouraged the

---

*   See page 203 for names.

** Between January of 1980 and January of 1982, 30,000 lives were lost in El Salvador. Most of them were in small attacks and massacres. Only the FMLN's general offensive of January 1981 involved large scale mobilizations and military confrontations.

unification of the FMLN and also pushed a lot of people to join the military forces of the five political organizations.

We, as the mothers of the disappeared, also got involved in a lot of political activity. Every day, more and more people would come to us telling us about people who were disappeared, assassinated, or imprisoned. They needed our help. People were even being tricked by funeral parlors. They came to us saying, "They told me that my son is buried in the cemetery, and it will cost me 300 colones to dig him up and to pay for the coffin."

All of these bodies were big business for the funeral parlors. Sometimes two bodies would appear and three different funeral parlors would show up to grab the body, load it into their car, fix it up, and document the death. Then they would find the families and charge them a lot of money for all their "services." Usually the families were poor people who didn't have a dime to spare. They would come to our office and ask for financial help. So we would have to help raise money for these people to bury their children. If people couldn't find their children, they would ask us to help them by taking out ads in the newspapers describing their disappeared.

Living through this time was incredible. We were living in constant crisis, repression, and tension. Then there was a change of government. Duarte, who was elected president, was supposed to be a big hero who was going to change everything. The truth is that he was full of shit. He lost all his human dignity when he sold the sovereignty of the Salvadoran people to the U.S. government. I really think that the situation we are in now is more his fault than any one else's. If he hadn't cut so many deals with the U.S. government, we would not have had so much war. He sold out completely.

Nineteen eighty was a dark year. Probably the most terrible thing that happened was the death of Monseñor Romero on March 24th. We used to see him often since we had regular meetings. We would read parts of the Bible with him in a beautiful place called Santa Teresa. We would sit outside under a big cottonwood tree and talk. Afterwards, we would drink soda and eat yuca and pupusas. It was a calm and serene place. We would talk with Monseñor, and give him updates on our list of the disappeared, and he would read the names in his sermons.

I heard about his death the day the Mothers' Committee held a meeting in the Basilica de la Providencia Divina in Sacamil, a working-class neighborhood of San Salvador. We all knew this church because we often went there with Monseñor Romero. He had a hospital there for people with cancer, the elderly, and people who didn't have any family. He and the nuns took care of them. That was his home. When we finished with the meeting, I went back to Santa Ana because I was tired. I had been away in San Salvador for three or four days without going home. It was about six o'clock in the afternoon.

I remember walking in the door and shouting hello. My compañero wasn't home, and the kids were next door at my mother's house watching television. Suddenly I heard on the radio: "News update, news update." When you hear that in El Salvador you know that something bad has happened.

"News update. We have just heard that Monseñor Romero was assassinated by a death squad. He was taken to the emergency room of the Clinica Salvadoreña, but it was impossible to save his life. Monseñor Romero is dead."

"This can't be. Oh, my God. Please don't let it be so. It can't be so!" I was shouting. My mother came over to see what was wrong.

"What is it? Why are you shouting? What happened?" she asked.

"Ay, Mamá," I answered. "They have killed Monseñor Romero." My mother heard me, but she didn't comprehend what I said.

I went out into the street. Everyone seemed to be doing the same. The streets filled up with people as the sun went down. Then the church bells started to ring. We heard the bells in the Cathedral of San Martín, then those in the Palmár, and finally those of San Francisco. All the churches in Santa Ana began to ring their bells at once. As the bells were ringing, again and again, I felt a terrible sadness. I felt so heavy and sad that I thought the earth would open up. I couldn't move. I couldn't talk. I thought, "What are the people of El Salvador going to do about this? What will people say?" I didn't know what to do. I was immobilized in the street. Should I run? Should I scream? Or do nothing?

Everyone was pouring out into the street. People just kept coming and coming. We walked around, looking at one another in disbelief. The churches announced all over the country that if people wanted to come see Monseñor Romero that they should come to San Salvador.

I waited until the next day to go. The people from CO-MADRES went together to see the body of Monseñor Romero. There was a huge line. We stood in line at eight in the morning and we entered the Cathedral where he was lying in state at two o'clock in the afternoon. All kinds of people had come to see him. There were international dignitaries too.

The people set up their own security system at the entrance of the Cathedral to protect themselves. We went in through the main door of the church and out the side door after we filed past his body. It was very painful for us when we got close to his coffin. We just stood there looking at him. He almost seemed to have a smile on his face and a look that said to me, "The man is gone, but his valor, his faith, and his force are with us forever." I will never forget that.

You might think we were masochists for wanting to see him when he was dead, but that wasn't the reason why we went. He was a very humble man. He was extremely sincere. He truly believed that there was no difference between the poorest peasant child and the richest city child. We were all equal in his eyes. He gave us this love and this way of looking at human beings with affection, love, and understanding. When someone gives you this insight into human life, you come to care about them a great deal. That is how we felt about him. A lot of us grew up without people understanding us or truly being able to love us. He gave that to us; we were like family. When someone offers you this kind of love and then they are gone, it's very hard.

When I looked at him there with what seemed like a smile on his face, I could hear him telling us to go on. That he was with us. I remember that he told us more than once, "One day they are going to kill me. But I have faith in you. I know that you will go on with your work and that you will find your children. You will find the disappeared." He understood our suffering and he knew the difference between the poorer classes and the dominant classes. He was an intermediary in many instances and he was accused of being a terrorist because he defended the poor. He used to go and talk to the military and to the government about the situation of the poor. I think the most difficult thing for Monseñor was when he wrote a letter to President Jimmy Carter in 1980, asking him, in the name of God, not to send any more military aid to El Salvador. That's when the trouble started for him. He got anonymous threats in the mail, and harassing phone calls. They targeted him.

When they realized how effective he was, they saw that he was a dangerous man. They took his life, just like they have taken the lives of so many others. They took his life because he was telling the truth. Telling the truth was his death sentence.

Top: Rafael Canales Guevara, María's husband.

Left: María with daughter Gisela, born shortly after Rafael died.

CHAPTER 8

BIRTH AND DEATH: UNEXPECTED PREGNANCY AND THE ASSASSINATION OF RAFAEL

After they killed Monseñor Romero, I didn't go to the CO-MADRES office very much because it was completely militarized. I was also five months pregnant because in November, I hadn't taken any precautions. It was very difficult because we didn't want to have another child; we already had enough children. But we didn't know how to avoid having any more once I was pregnant.

We didn't know anything about abortions. Sure, I had heard about abortions and sometimes I would see women in the hospitals who had tried to abort, but I didn't understand how it happened. All I remember is that it made me feel bad to see the terrible condition of these women who had attempted to have abortions.

When I was pregnant with my first son, I had two friends who had abortions because they didn't want to have the children. The men who had gotten them pregnant took off. They just used them, got them pregnant, and then said, "Adios." When my friends told these men they were pregnant, the men responded, "Too bad, that isn't my baby. You should know whose it is." My friends had a hard time understanding why these men would deny the existence of their own children.

One of them was someone who had suffered a lot. She grew up without parents. The first time she got pregnant, the child's father took the baby away from her and then left her for another woman. He threw her out of the house without her baby. After that, she went to live in a friend's house. Her friend's son took advantage of her and she got pregnant again. This time she was determined not to have her baby.

I saw the things she was taking to try and get rid of the baby. She started out drinking quinine. When this didn't work, she drank a tea made out of oregano. After that, she drank a potion with lots of cinnamon in it.

Nothing worked and the baby kept on growing inside her. That's when she decided to take some pills called *pergamanato*. I had never heard of these pills. She put these pills in her vagina in the morning, and about two or three o'clock in the afternoon she began aborting the baby. I was really frightened by all of the blood that was coming out of her. They took her to the hospital where they saved her life.

She is not the only woman who used these pills for abortions. In our discussions in CO-MADRES about our personal lives, I have heard other women mention these pills. Some women talked about having abortions with midwives who used surgeon's probes for aborting fetuses. All of this is illegal in El Salvador, but a lot of women use these methods.

I didn't know how a surgeon's probe was used to induce an abortion, but once I saw how it was done. A long rubber tube with a sharp point on the end is inserted through the woman's vagina into her womb. Many women have died from this type of abortion. Sometimes they get infected, sometimes their internal organs are hurt, and sometimes they are lucky and abort. Sometimes they just get injured and don't abort the baby.

At the time of my pregnancy, I didn't know about any of these methods. Besides, I think I felt protected by having a responsible compañero. I knew that it would be very difficult for us to have four children.

The truth is that my compañero didn't want me to use any kind of family planning. The doctor had talked to me about it after I had my second and third children. When I went to the doctor for my 40-day check-up after the birth of my last child, the doctor—a friend of mine—told me that I should start using family planning. She gave me some birth control pills. In El Salvador we have pills and also that device that you're supposed to put in your womb. And there are condoms for men.

When the nurse explained these things to me, I felt really embarrassed. She described how to use condoms, how to use the I.U.D. and the pills. I just clammed up and told her, "I don't want any of these." They just hand you these things and say, "Take this." It makes you feel embarrassed and guilty. They don't give you any education or preparation. If you don't know anything about birth control and have never discussed it, you just feel bad about it, like you did something wrong. I told them I didn't want the condoms or the I.U.D., but I took some birth control pills home with me.

That night, Rafael asked me where I had been. "Did you go to the clinic today? What did they tell you?" he asked.

"They told me that I was fine and they gave me these birth control pills," I answered.

"You are not going to take those," Rafael said.

"Why not?" I asked. He is older, I thought to myself; maybe he knows better. I didn't think about protecting myself.

After that we went together to see a doctor friend of ours. Rafael explained that he had doubts about the pills because they could interfere with the natural body system. Finally, I took the pills. I took them for a while, but then I decided to stop. They bothered me. They were giving me big headaches. Women have different reactions to these pills. Some don't have any side effects from them, but I did. So I stopped taking them, but I didn't mention it to him. Of course, he was surprised when I told him that I was pregnant. What we didn't know was that when this baby was born, she wouldn't have a father. About five months after I found out I was pregnant, we moved from Santa Ana to Sonsonate. We had already moved several times that year.

On Thursday, June 19, 1980, we were sitting around the dinner table when we heard a knock at the door.

"Does José Rafael Canales Guevara live here?" a voice shouted.

"Yes," answered Rafael. "That's me. What can I do for you? Come on in."

"No, we'll stay right here. We are municipal police agents and we came to get you because there was a robbery in this neighborhood, and someone said that you were a witness," the men answered. They were dressed as civilians.

"I don't know anything about a robbery," said Rafael.

"Don't worry," they said. "We just want you to cooperate with us and we will have you back here in no time."

But when they said that I had a terrible feeling inside, as if my heart was going to beat its way right out of my body. They were carrying machine guns and municipal police don't walk around with machine guns. They came in and put handcuffs on him. I didn't like the look on their faces. Rafael just looked at them with a sad face. He cocked his head at us and we just watched. When I got up to go toward him the men stopped me.

"Stay right there," they said. "Don't move another step." That was how we said goodbye. Handcuffed, that was our last glimpse of him. I kept thinking, "What will happen to him? Will they disappear him? Maybe they would put him in jail." I had this illusion that they were just going to put him back in jail and not kill him. After he left, I was so nervous I couldn't sleep at all that night.

Two days later, I went to the local market in Sonsonate with my oldest son. We didn't have anymore food. The market is huge on Saturdays, with people coming in from the countryside to sell all kinds of fruits, vegetables, chickens, and other animals.

I was in a daze when I got there. I was just wandering around looking at everything as if it was the first time I had ever seen something like that. It was almost as if I was sleepwalking. Suddenly, I saw a man, who was a friend of Rafael's, standing at a bus stop. He looked as though he wanted to talk to me. He was just shaking his head while he looked at me. As I approached him, I saw that he had tears in his eyes. I raised my hand and waved hello. He just kept shaking his head back and forth. After that, I felt terribly worried.

I kept on walking until I ran into a lady named Julia Morán and her daughter Margarita. They both lived in Izalco.

"Hi, how are you?" I said to her. I didn't want to stop and visit with her because she was a real talker. She could go on and on. Talking to her always takes a long time. She would tell you stories about everyone. So I was just going to say hi and keep on going.

But she called out my name, "Teresa." I didn't pay any attention because in small towns a lot of people have the same name. You know how you can be in a crowd and someone shouts and you think it is your name, but it turns out to be someone else? That's what I thought. So I kept going, pulling my son by the hand.

"Teresa," she said grabbing me by the arm. "I am talking to you." She looked at me very intensely.

"Hi," I said. "I am sorry that I didn't see you."

"How are you?" she asked.

"I'm fine," I answered. "How are you?"

I was feeling tired and weak. She had stepped out of her pick-up truck. I leaned on the side of it because I felt like I was going to fall over. The heat, the sun, the noise, and my pregnancy were all getting to me. I felt really weak and shut my eyes for a minute while I leaned on the truck.

"Don't you know what happened?" she asked, waving a newspaper in her hand.

"No," I said. "What happened? Did my father die?"

"No," she said.

"Is it someone in my family?" I asked.

"No," she said. "You mean you don't know anything about what happened?"

"I don't know," I said with a sinking feeling in my stomach.

"Look," she said. "Where is your husband?"

"Oh, God, no." I sighed to myself.

"Where is he?" she asked.

"He went to work last night," I mumbled.

"And exactly where is he?" she asked again.

"I don't know," I told her. I couldn't tell her that he had been detained so I told her he was at work.

"So you don't know anything about what has happened?" she insisted.

When she told me this, I knew it was bad.

"Look," she said pointing to the newspaper, "your husband is dead."

"No!" I screamed.

"He is," she said.

I felt like I was going to pass out. I just sat there in the pick-up truck with the door open.

"Just give me five minutes," I told her.

"Mami, what's wrong?" asked my son and he grabbed me tightly.

"Nothing, son," I mumbled.

When I felt a little better I told him, "Your father is wounded."

"What happened to my father?" he asked.

"He is wounded," I answered, "but I don't know how, where, or what happened."

Then I turned to Julia, who was listening to me talk to my son and said, "Please read me the paper." Julia started to read.

"The ex-director of the Policía Municipal,* José Rafael Canales Guevarra, member of a terrorist cell, was killed in a confrontation at 9 o'clock yesterday morning in the Colonia Cedán." Next to the article there was a picture of him from his national identity card.

"Oh, my God," I said. I wanted to get up and walk, but I couldn't move. We took a cab home. My aunt had already arrived there and had taken my daughter, who was six and a half years old with her to San Salvador where she lived. When I went into the house my youngest son was alone and crying.

"Son," I said, "your father has been hurt."

He just stared at me after I told him that.

"I know, they told me," he cried. Tears were streaming down his cheeks. "Tell me it isn't true, Mami. My daddy isn't hurt, is he?"

"I don't know. I don't know, son," I said. "Just leave me alone for a little while."

"No, Mamá," he told me. "I am going to help you."

We got out a suitcase and looked for some clothes for Rafael. I knew that when we found him he wouldn't have any clothes on. I knew this from all of the bodies I had seen. When they kill people they leave them almost naked. I wanted him to be dressed.

My idea was to find his body and bring it back to Izalco so that we could bury him with my family. I didn't realize then what we would have to go through. First, we had to go to the neighborhood where the newspaper claimed he had been killed. I knew that it was in a new neighborhood in Sonsonate. So I went with my two sons and asked where I could find the town hall, the alcaldía, for this new neighborhood. I knew I had to go there to find the local judges.

When we got to the town hall, I met a woman whom I had known for a long time. She came over and gave me a hug. "You are going to have to be strong," she told me.

"I know," I replied.

---

* Rafael had worked briefly as the director of the local municipal police before his death. Municipal police are volunteers doing public service, and are distinct from the national security forces. It is a great irony that he was doing police work shortly before he was killed.

I also knew the judge. His nickname was Rabanito, little radish. I also knew his niece, Refugio, who was a teacher. She had been seriously injured when she was machine-gunned by the army along with some other teachers who were killed. We had lived half a block from her in Izalco.

I stood in front of the judge with my two sons and introduced myself. "My name is María Teresa Tula," I said. "I have come to ask you if you know about the three bodies that appeared yesterday in the Colonia Cedán. I am looking for one of them who is my husband, José Rafael Canales Guevara."

"Why are you looking for him?" questioned the judge.

"Because I love him," I responded. "He is my husband."

"Don't be a fool," said the judge. "Don't look for him. This man is a terrorist. He is a guerrilla. I know. Yesterday the army killed him and the others, and I had to go identify them. But don't be stupid. You will be taking on the identity of your husband and you might not even know what he was involved in."

I just stood there as if I was still asleep. I didn't say anything.

Then he said, "I know you. You are from Izalco, from the Tula family. Don't be a fool. Just leave him. You will be better off if you just leave with your children. He was a bad man."

I started to wake up and realized what he was saying.

"Look," I said, "I didn't come here to ask you about whether or not my husband was good or bad. Did you or did you not identify and examine him? What kinds of signs did you find on his body?"

He took out a document that described his height, weight, and the color of his hair, etc. "Okay," he said. "His arms and legs were bound. He was found in his underwear with a .38-calibre bullet hole that entered from the left side of his head and exited out of the right side, and he had been dragged around by one of his arms. But the army took his body away."

"Where did they take him?" I asked.

"I don't know," he said. "Look, they found him with arms. He was part of a terrorist cell. They had lots of arms and bombs. You have no idea about the things your husband was doing. This is what the army reported to me. They had a confrontation with them in front of a house that resulted in three deaths. Just leave now. Take your children and don't look for him."

"Don't you understand," I said to him. "He is my husband and now he is dead because they killed him. They are dogs. They killed him when he was tied up. You have to respect me. I didn't come here to get advice from you, just to find out what happened. You know they shoot judges and their families too. Just like they shot your niece."

I was really angry and continued to talk to him. "I have come here looking for my husband because I want to. Nobody is going to keep me from looking for him. Not you or anyone else. Where is he? What did they do with him?"

The town hall secretary was sitting there while I was yelling, just writing away with his pen and listening.

"I don't know," said the judge. "The army came and took him away yesterday. I don't know if he is in the hospital, the morgue, or in the cemetery. But I do know that they are going to bury him, and the two others at 10 o'clock in the morning today if their families don't show up to claim them. If the families don't appear, they will be buried in a common grave."

"Then tell me where they are," I said pounding on the desk so hard that the pen practically jumped out of the secretary's hand. I put both hands firmly on the desk and faced the judge.

"You are going to tell me where they are," I said.

"Mami," whispered my oldest son tugging on my hand. "Be quiet." I heard my son's voice, but inside I also heard the voice of Rafael telling me to go on. I kept demanding that they take me to where the bodies were.

Finally the secretary said to the judge, "Take her. Take her to them."

"All right," said the judge. "I will take her, but don't tell anyone that I took her."

"He's afraid," said the secretary. "Afterwards things happen to people."

So the judge took us to the cemetery in Sonsonate, me, pregnant, and my two sons.

"They were here, but now they are gone. I think they are over there burying them," he said pointing in the distance.

I pulled out a 10-colones bill that I had and said, "Here, take this. I know you didn't bring me here out of the goodness of your heart so take this money."

Then my children ran in the direction he had pointed to see if their father was there. I started moving. I didn't feel like I was walking at all.

It was like being in a dream. I had about two more meters to go when I looked up and saw his family, his bothers and sisters, his aunts and uncles, and his nieces and nephews. My other children were there too.

It turned out that my sister-in-law, Rosa Canales, who lives in Sonsonate, had found out about Rafael's assassination from a friend who saw his body in the morgue. While I was out looking for Rafael's body, Rosa sent telegrams to all the relatives telling them about his death. The relatives had all arrived, including my sister-in-law from San Salvador, and were standing around the body. They had put him in a simple coffin.

"My daddy, my daddy," sobbed my oldest son. He just stood there quietly not doing anything. He was just looking, whining, and saying a few words. They were about to bury all three of the bodies. This part of the cemetery was occupied by the military. There were soldiers all around us. We weren't even going to be able to see Rafael's body. But my father-in-law stopped the men before they lowered him into the ground, "Wait, wait. Here are his children."

I was there, but I don't remember much. I didn't speak to anyone. I saw his body, but I didn't believe that it was him. I just remember falling down on my knees in front of his body. I whispered to him that we were going to take revenge for his death, one way or another. I told him that I wouldn't give up and that nothing would keep me down. I promised him that I would take care of our children and help them be prepared for the future. It was a horrible and difficult way to say good-bye to him.

They buried him even though I wanted to take him with me to Izalco. It would have been impossible to do so. I didn't even think about the problems I would have with the military if I had taken him back. They were looking for me in Izalco as well as in Sonsonate.

They buried him quickly. I don't remember what happened. I passed out. The next thing I knew they were putting alcohol on my face to try and wake me up. His family was all around me.

"What are you going to do?" they asked me. "Are you going to keep living in Sonsonate?"

"I don't know," I said turning to my children. "Let's go home."

When we got close to our house, the neighbors came out and warned us, "Don't go home. There are soldiers inside the house." We looked up toward the house from a block away and saw that there were soldiers in front of the house. We turned around and my sister-in-law told me, "I'm going to my sister's house. Where are you going? Can we talk tomorrow?"

"That's fine," I said. "I am going to Izalco where my family lives."
In Izalco, I saw an uncle of mine in the street, and greeted him.

"Good afternoon," he replied. Then I slowed down because I thought he would talk to me and offer some consolation.

Instead he put his hands up and said, "Don't talk to me. Your case is very dangerous. Don't even acknowledge that I am in your family. Just don't talk to me."

I just stood there looking at him. Friends passed me in the street and said, "Tere, we are really sorry about what happened. You have to be strong."

I went to my Tía Dolores' house. I had grown up with her. Her family was really sad; they couldn't believe what had happened. They didn't believe any of the accusations against Rafael. They had always known him as a working man, an honorable man who had been very affectionate with everyone. The next day, however, I went back to Sonsonate because I saw that more and more people in my family were afraid to talk to me.

I went to talk with my sister-in-law again. "What do you think I should do?" I asked her. "I don't have anywhere to go."

"I don't know," she said. "You can stay with us." I stayed with her for a few days in San Salvador, but after a while, she and then other people in my family began to tell me, "You are a fool. Why did you get involved with those terrorists? That is why Rafael was killed. Think about your children." I understood they were just as sad as I was about the death of Rafael. But after a while I just couldn't put up with it anymore.

"Listen," I told my sister-in-law, "I forbid you to mention your brother's name anymore. If you are going to say good things about him, then fine. But if you are going to say bad things about him, don't bother."

A few days later I went to the CO-MADRES office and to the Human Rights Commission to denounce what had happened. They had already heard about it. They asked me where I was staying. I told them that I was staying with my sister-in-law, but it was really hard. I stayed with my two sons and my daughter, and it was really hard. It was very crowded there and we were used to living alone. Then we stayed in several different houses because it was too hard to stay with my sister-in-law. We had to sleep on the floor. I didn't have any money for food or clothing and I didn't want to be a burden to her.

Probably the hardest thing right after Rafael's death was my daughter's reaction. She didn't really know he was gone because my aunt had taken her to San Salvador. They loved her very much. I came to see her with my two sons. She was so glad to see me.

"Mami, Mami," she said running to me. "How are you?"

"I'm fine, honey," I told her.

"And my daddy?" she asked.

"He isn't here," I said.

"Don't tell her anything," whispered my aunt. I heard what she said, but I wondered, how can I fool my daughter? She hasn't seen her father for five days and she is never going to see him again. I picked her up and held her in my lap.

"How come my daddy didn't come? Where is he? I want my father," she said.

She knew that something was going on. She could feel it.

"Where is he? Where is my daddy?" she screamed.

"Honey, your daddy isn't coming. He isn't here anymore." I told her.

"What do you mean? Where is he? Where is my daddy?" she screamed again.

"Ay, honey," I sighed. "Your daddy is dead."

"Why, Mommy? Why is he dead?" she yelled and jumped off of my lap.

"Why did my daddy die? Why? she said. "Maybe you didn't give him his medicine Mommy. Maybe he got sick and you didn't give it to him and that's why he died." She was breaking my heart.

"Yes, honey. He was sick and he didn't want to take his medicine and that is why he died."

My daughter was traumatized at this moment, and she said to me, "Mommy, it's your fault that I don't have my daddy any more. You let him die. It's your fault."

"Yes," I said. How was I going to tell her that they killed him, shot him in the head? She wouldn't understand that.

From that moment my daughter changed. She became a different person. She had severe problems. She lost weight and didn't want to eat. She would call out for her father every day and tell me, "Look, Mommy, here is Daddy. I see him. He came to talk with me."

We needed a psychologist. Families going through an experience like that are all wounded. My other sons were affected too. The oldest one just kept pursing his lips and blinking. He didn't say anything for the longest time. It affected all of us in a deep way.

We lost everything we had because we never went back to our house. We knew they were looking for us. I didn't have anything for the child I was carrying. All the baby clothes I had were in the house. Finally, CO-MADRES gave us some money to rent a house. We found a house near some of Rafael's relatives in San Salvador. We lived there for two years.

The house was absolutely empty because we had nothing. We slept on the floor and at first we had only one plate. Then we got another and another. We didn't have anything for the kitchen. My oldest son went out to do construction work because we didn't have any money. He was only twelve years old, and he would come home with cuts and blisters all over his hands from the work he was doing.

"Don't do this type of work," I would tell him.

"I have to, Mommy," he would answer. "We need the money." We lived through three very difficult months after Rafael died.

My daughter was born on August 21st. I remember the date because there were lots of general strikes in El Salvador then. There was no public transportation because of a strike. I didn't have any of my own family nearby and I was alone with my children. I told my aunt that I was going to leave the children alone. I took a taxi to the hospital. It was· very expensive. Because of the strike, there was no other way to get there.

At the hospital, they asked me, "Who came with you to take care of you?"

"No one," I said. "I came alone."

"Where is your husband?" they asked.

"He's not here," I answered. "He's working far away."

They put me in a waiting room with a lot of other pregnant women about to give birth. The hospital was a mess. There was no electricity and no water. This was common in 1980 because of the war. While I was in there I saw a doctor I knew from the Human Rights Commission. He examined me and I felt a little funny about it because I knew him. He sent me up to the delivery room.

My daughter was huge and the doctors were worried that they might have to operate. I was so thin and she was so big. But in the end, she came out normally. She weighed nine pounds and was really chubby. The nurses took care of me and then they gave me my daughter. They put her in my arms and took me to another room. The situation in the hospital was terrible. There were no sheets and they had two women in each bed with their babies.

The next day they discharged me from the hospital. I had three colones to my name. Nobody had come to see me. Nobody even knew that I had given birth to this baby. This little girl was born without anyone knowing. We lost Rafael and then my baby came into the world.

CO-MADRES members outside their office after a bombing.

CHAPTER 9

ANOTHER BOMBING AND MORE DISAPPEARANCES

The first time they bombed the CO-MADRES office was in 1980. They put the bomb in the garage below the building, and our office had the most damage. All the windows were shattered, our machinery was ruined from the explosion, and we were frightened. The director of the National Guard came and told us that he was investigating the extent of the damage caused by the bombing done by terrorists. We never found out who was responsible for the bombing. After they bombed our office, they placed a bomb in the main door of the non-governmental Human Rights Commission. We shared a building with them. They were on the first floor and we were on the second floor. After these two bombings we stopped going to the office very much. We stopped going completely when we found three decapitated bodies in front of the main entrance to the building.

It was horrible. We were sure that these bodies were meant as a signal that the same thing would happen to us if we didn't stop doing our work. After these mutilated corpses appeared on our doorstop, the situation got even worse.

The first person they captured was Delmi González, the daughter of a long time CO-MADRES member. She was a young woman, about 22 years old. One day she went with some friends to Planes de Renderos, a place just outside the city. It's well known in El Salvador as a place you can go to get a great view of the city and relax. It's nice and cool, very pleasant. There is a big wooded area you can walk around in. You can hear the birds there, smell flowers, and just feel a different kind of air than there is in the city. There is also a little market where you can go to eat pupusas and yuca, and drink sodas. There are all kinds of things to do there for fun.

She went there with her boyfriend and some other young people. They were running around, playing on the basketball court which is a natural thing for young people to do. The army, however, is always suspicious when people are running. Any time they see someone running in public, they say that they are guerrillas. This means that young people can't even go out on the street and play. If they do, then they can be accused of being "in training."

The civil defense patrol picked them up in the park. At least they said they were a civil defense patrol. They were men dressed as civilians. Witnesses told us that they grabbed all of them, threw them down onto the ground, and bound their hands behind their backs. Delmi, like her mother, was a member of CO-MADRES.

They killed them and dumped their bodies in a place called Panchimalco that is near the Planes de Renderos. They raped Delmi. They tortured her by pulling out her tongue and her fingernails. After she was dead they cut off her head. She had a lot of wounds on her body where she had been cut. When Delmi didn't come home, her mother went to look for her. And this is how she found her.

After that they captured the secretary of the Human Rights Commission, María Elena Henriquez. Another member of the Commission was captured by the National Guard or the National Police. She was also brutally tortured. Then there were the three people from the Human Rights Commission who were abducted from their office, right below ours.

With all of this going on, we didn't go near our office. We met in the parks while we played with our children. In 1981 and 1982, the authorities were suspicious of everyone. It was a state of siege. We had to talk to each other at bus stops to try to coordinate our work. We couldn't look like we were having a meeting. Sometimes we would have meetings in three or four different places. We could never stay in one place. We were always moving around.

Finally, about halfway through 1981 we got an office through the Archbishop, Monseñor Rivera y Damas, together with the Human Rights Commission. Behind the archbishops' offices, there was a little storehouse surrounded by some mango trees. We used to go there to meet because we had nowhere else to go. We had enough room to set up a desk. We used to have press conferences there to denounce the bombings of civilian populations.

During this time, there was a curfew that caused us many problems. If people were out on the street after the curfew, they could be legally killed. At first the curfew was from twelve o'clock at night until five in the morning. Then they made it from six o'clock in the afternoon until six o'clock in the morning. I remember it as a very hard time for me because I was very depressed about the loss of my compañero. I did the best I could to participate in CO-MADRES activities. Wherever I went, I took my little daughter with me. She was still breastfeeding. She always reminded me of her father.

We were involved in many different projects. We distributed food to the families of the disappeared. The archbishop received international food aid, and we proposed that the rice, beans, corn, oil, milk, and flour he received should go to the people who came to us. We also received visits from international delegations. They would interview us about what was going on in El Salvador. Sometimes journalists would show up and they would want us to take them to the body dumps. They wanted to film the clandestine cemeteries because people would not otherwise believe the kinds of macabre things going on in El Salvador. They also wanted us to take them to the marginal zones where the really poor people lived. We would take these journalists to the body dumps in spite of the risk to our lives. In turn, they would support us by filming the meetings we requested with government officials.

We also were doing work with the embassies. We visited many European and Latin American embassies, and left them updated bulletins about the human rights situation in El Salvador. Most of the ambassadors we met with were quite friendly with us and would invite us to receptions or call us up when they wanted us to meet someone new. The Mexican embassy was especially friendly.

In April 1981, CO-MADRES lost someone who was like family to us all. Rosalina Osorio Melgar, the original Abuela, died of cancer. Perhaps cancer wasn't the real cause of her death, but sorrow. Her grandson died as a result of torture in 1979. She had raised him like a son and she never recovered from his death. She just couldn't get over this disease and her grief. We lost a dedicated, sincere woman who fought very hard for human rights. In spite of her age—she was 55 years old, older than most of us—she was an energy source for all of us. She was eternally optimistic and she always shared her experiences with us, and watched out for us. We were all like her grandchildren. It was a very difficult death for all of us. Forty days after she died, we all went to her house and held a day of mourning for her.* We also took out an ad in the newspaper in her memory. We always commemorate her death in April.

Right after her death, on the first of May, we participated in celebrations for international worker's day, what we call "Día del trabajo." We were always invited to participate in marches on this day. We would dress up in black and mingle with the workers and students in the march. The authorities usually respected us a little more than the young people and our presence could help keep them from being harassed. Often the police would grab people participating in the march and we would intervene. Also, whenever we saw someone taking pictures of the demonstrators, and we recognized that person as being from the police, we would take away their camera, remove the film, and destroy it. When we asked to see their journalism identification cards, they would always pull out their military IDs. We took away their film for security reasons.

We are more militant with the police than people are in North America. In the United States, the police control the streets during a demonstration. In El Salvador we control the streets. They are ours. If the police put up a barricade, we remove it. They can't tell us where to go in our own streets.

On the eighth of October 1981, my father died. He was living in Izalco. I was in San Salvador when my sister called me at the CO-MADRES office right before he died to tell me that he was extremely ill. I told the CO-MADRES about it and they gave me 150 colones to cover the cost of the bus fare to Izalco and other expenses. In reality, I didn't want to go and see my father. I had such mixed feelings about him. But my sister-in-law convinced me to go. She said, "Go on. He's your father."

When we got to the house, my father wasn't there. Only my oldest sister and her daughter were there. She told me that one of my brothers had taken my father to the emergency room in San Salvador. I had my

---

*   Central American Catholicism calls for remembering the dead not only with a funeral, but also 40 days after the date of death and on the first anniversary.

little daughter and my son Raúl with me. At about 11 o'clock that night they called and told us that our father had died.

As soon as we heard this, we started cleaning the house so that they could bring him home. The next day at about 10 o'clock my brother brought my father's body into the house. He had a lot of whiskers on his face and he needed a shave. Nobody wanted to shave him and clean him up so I did it. We had to put clean clothes on him, and a tie so that he would look good.

I had started to shave him and get him ready when I remembered that my daughter was still breastfeeding. She nursed until she was almost three years old. We have a belief that when when you are sick, have a cold, or are pregnant or nursing a child, you shouldn't go near a dead body because of *hijillo*. It's like some kind of bad air or bad karma that is around the body, and it can infect you if you are vulnerable in any way.

Because I had been exposed to *hijillo,* the women told me to take off my clothing and to bathe myself with lemon and orange leaves to get rid of it. They told me to squeeze out some of the milk in my breasts and throw it away before I let my daughter nurse again. So I did everything they said. I bathed, I squeezed out the milk, and they even fumigated me with incense to get rid of the *hijillo.* Then I nursed my daughter.

I don't know if it was a coincidence or if it was because of the *hijillo,* but at about three o'clock in the afternoon after she nursed, my daughter got really sick. She had nursed at 11 o'clock in the morning and at three o'clock she was in agony.

Soon after this, my sister called us all together to discuss what would happen with the house my father had left and where we were going to bury him. One of my brothers suggested that we bury him with his mother. Then one of my sisters started shouting at us, "None of you has any right to talk about this. I am the only legitimate daughter he has. I have a legitimate opinion and so does my mother whom he married." Her mother was the only woman my father actually married.

"But your mother knew about the rest of us," I responded. "Just treat us with respect."

I didn't want anything or expect anything from my father's inheritance. This daughter and her mother had refused to help me when I needed a place to live even though my father had agreed to it. Things weren't any easier now.

The next day my daughter woke up with bronchial pneumonia. I went with her and my son Raúl to the hospital, and my sister came to stay with my other two children. She was really sick. First, doctors had her under observation and then they moved her up to the fourth floor and put her under a respirator. I was up for almost 10 days straight with her while she was unconscious. I would lean over the cradle giving her oxygen. At night the nurses would tell me, "Don't you know it is forbidden to spend the night in the hospital?" I would tell them, "Well, the doctor gave me permission to stay. My daughter is very ill and she is still nursing. I don't want her to drink formula."

My sister-in-law finally realized where I was. When she came to see me, my eyes were open and I saw her, but I didn't recognize her. I had been awake so long that my eyes didn't really see. "Sit down and rest," she told me. I remember thinking, "How nice that this woman came to help me." But I didn't recognize her. I hadn't eaten, I had just been drinking water.

I sat down on a chair, crossed my arms and went to sleep. I stayed in that chair asleep from Wednesday until Sunday, just drinking water without fully waking up. When it was time for my sister-in-law to go, I woke up and recognized her. I spent about 12 days in the hospital with my daughter. I had to be right there watching her because she could have stopped breathing at any time. The nurses don't have time to look after every patient all of the time.

Being in the hospital for 12 days with my daughter was difficult for many reasons. First of all, I kept thinking about what the mothers were doing. What kind of activities were they up to? Our work never ends. We don't have a fixed schedule. We work Saturdays, Sundays, night and day. That is what you have to do when you are fighting for democracy.

In 1981 and 1982, we were living under a state of siege. We couldn't take out ads in the newspapers. We couldn't announce anything on the radio because it was forbidden. The army owned the streets. Nevertheless, we still kept visiting the embassies and having meetings with international human rights organizations. At one point, we couldn't even go inside to visit the archbishop's residence. The army had surrounded the residency and wouldn't let us in. Finally Monseñor Rivera y Damas intervened and demanded that the army stop surrounding his offices. We were finally able to return to our tiny office at the back of his residence.

We set up a small business selling food out of the office. People showed up there to tell us about bodies they were finding or to ask for help. Many of them were campesinos. It was hard for them to come and go because there were soldiers everywhere. So we would give them something to eat or sell it to them at a reduced price. We would sell a plate of food for three colones and a bowl of soup for 1.25 colones. We sold tortillas and vegetables, fish or chicken. We made enough money this way to pay for our bus fares and other small expenses. It also was a way for people to learn how to run a small business. The most we made was about 50 colones per month, but it was something. Later we started selling sandwiches as well. We organized ourselves around selling food.

At the same time, we would visit sites where bodies were turning up. Often we would go secretly because it was very dangerous. Sometimes five, ten, fifteen bodies would turn up in different places. We would go and take pictures of them. Some of the compañeras would wear sunglasses and scarves to hide their identity. We took pictures and showed them to people who were looking for disappeared relatives. This was very dangerous work. It was even more dangerous for families to reclaim the bodies once we found them. Sometimes, mothers knew where the bodies of their children were, but they couldn't go get them or even acknowledge their grief. The tactic of the military during this time was to kill off the whole family of people they considered dangerous. They would leave enough evidence for the families to identify the bodies, like personal documents or national identity cards. When the family came to look for their relatives' bodies, the military would exterminate the whole family. Sometimes they would shoot them with machine guns or disappear all of those who came to claim a body.

We had many visits from international delegations. They wanted to hear the testimonies of people who were victims of aerial bombings carried out by the army. The army started bombing in 1980 and continued until 1991. After the bombings, the army would come in and burn everything they found that wasn't already destroyed. A lot of people were hurt by the bombs or by shrapnel from the bombs. These delegations wanted us to take them to meet refugees who had come into the city after they were displaced from their homes in the countryside. We also arranged for them to visit with students, labor leaders, and people from the Human Rights Commission. These delegations always wanted us to go with them everywhere. It put us in a lot of danger, but we did it.

In 1982, we were in constant danger. That was the year that the first member of CO-MADRES was picked up and thrown in jail. Her name was Ofelia. Right before she was detained, we received lots of threats. We had a press conference denouncing the death squads and the constant human rights violations. The next day, *Diario de Hoy* carried an ad ordering us to stop having press conferences. It threatened us with decapitation if we did not obey this command. The ad was signed by the "Maximiliano Hernández" Death Squad. When we read this, we were really frightened. We knew they were quite capable of carrying out their threats at any moment.

Ofelia was in charge of visiting the central jail of Mariona. She would bring food to the prisoners and take out the folk art they made to sell. On the day she was captured, she was coming to the CO-MADRES office from Soyapango, on the outskirts of the city. A white minibus pulled up and she was grabbed by several unknown men. We immediately started to protest her disappearance. After three days, the National Police took responsibility for her abduction, claiming they were in the process of investigating her. We started a campaign to free her and carried out a series of protests even though we were under a state of siege and weren't allowed out on the streets.

They set her free after 18 days, in a place called Sitio del Niño that is on the way to Santa Ana. She was left on the railroad tracks with her hands tied behind her back and a gag in her mouth so that she couldn't scream for help. She was the mother of five children; she was very young and thin. Some campesinos found her at four o'clock in the morning. In the countryside, people get up early. They heard muffled cries, so they took their lanterns and went to see what was going on. They found her all tied up and thought she was dead. Then she tried to talk and they saw that she was alive. They untied her and took the gag out of her mouth, and she asked them to bring her to the CO-MADRES office.

These peasants were terrified of taking responsibility for bringing her to the office, but they did. They brought her to the doorway and took off. When we arrived at the office we saw a woman crouching in the doorway. She was exhausted and her hair was a mess. We thought, "Who is this woman? She is probably some poor thing who had to sleep in the street last night." There are so many people like that in this city.

"Who are you? What are you doing here? Who are you looking for?" we asked her.

She stood up, but we still didn't recognize her. She was a mess. Her face was completely swollen and her teeth were broken where they had smashed her mouth in with the butt of a rifle. She just stood there staring at us and crying.

Then she whispered to me with all the strength she had, "Ofelia. I am Ofelia."

As soon as I knew that it was her, I embraced her and all of the women surrounded us, saying, "Here is Ofelia. Here she is." All kinds of people came to see what had happened. We took her to the archbishop's office to get help because there was a clinic there and medicine.

First we bathed her with warm water. They had burned her body with cigarette butts. We took turns caring for her for several days. We fed her the food that the doctor recommended so that she would improve. It was almost impossible for her to talk at first. She was so nervous and tense. Any little noise would make her jump and put her into a crisis. After a while she was able to talk to us and she gave us her testimony.

She was captured by men from the National Police who were dressed in civilian clothing. They took her to their general headquarters and put her in a room where they had pictures of most of us all over the walls. They collected all the ads we had taken out in newspapers and other printed material.

They would point to a picture of one of us and say, "Who is this?" She would tell them that she didn't know. Then they would try again. "What is this person's name?" "I don't know," she would say.

"Of course you do," they would answer. Then they beat her. They rammed their rifle butts into her breasts and burned her. They took off all her clothes and she was raped by seven men. Then they burned her body some more. What they did to her was horrible. Horrible. She told us everything.

After she recovered she went back to her family. As she was leaving, she took me aside and warned me, "Be careful. Be careful because they were asking about you, but I didn't tell them anything."

And I believed her, because 18 days passed and I didn't have any problems. If she had told them anything about me, or that she knew me, they would have come and grabbed me. But I am sure she didn't tell them anything.

After this, we could see that they were really out to get us. It was dangerous for us. Fifteen days after they detained Ofelia, they captured three more women who were on their way to the Mariona Jail. Doña Carmen Ruano was going to visit her 16-year-old son. She had already lost her husband and two sons who were disappeared. Now she is exiled in Canada. The second woman was named Idé Morán. She lives in Los Angeles now. They were poor people. Carmen sold refrescos in the market and Idé walked around the market selling fruit from a basket. The third woman was Blanca, whose last name I don't remember.

They were captured in the neighborhood called Mexicanos by men dressed in civilian clothing. They picked them up one after another. I don't know if someone told these men who these three women were, or if they already knew who they were. They were captured by the National Police. They let Blanca go after 18 days. But they took the other two women to Puerto del Diablo, a place where bodies were dumped. They held one of them over the edge of a cliff and held up a machete to her. They said that they were going to cut her in half if she didn't answer their questions. The other woman was watching. They were trying to terrorize her. They told her, "If you don't tell us everything you know, the same thing will happen to you too. But if you tell us what you know, nothing will happen to you. Just to her."

They were both tortured. They let Idé go after about 15 days. Carmen Ruano was transferred to the Women's Prison. She had two daughters, one was seven years old and the other was 19. They were the only children she had left because all of the others had been disappeared. About two or three days after she was transferred to the Women's Prison, they captured her oldest daughter. Again, it was done by men dressed in civilian clothing. They took the oldest daughter and left the little girl. She was traumatized by what she had seen. This little girl knew that her father had disappeared, her brother and mother were in prison, and now they came and took her sister. She had heart problems and there was no one to take care of her.

They let Idé out of prison in 1983 as a part of an amnesty. When she got out, she also told me, "Be careful. The police are looking for you. I didn't tell them anything. I didn't tell them that I knew you."

"Why? Why are they looking for me?" I asked her. "I'm not doing anything."

"I don't know," she said. "But they have pictures of you. They have pictures of you from the front, from the side, wearing different clothes, with long hair, with short hair, with sunglasses. All kinds of photos."

This news made me nervous. I didn't like the idea that they were looking for me. This period was very difficult for me. I was still recovering from my husband's death. I thought I would be able to get over it. But I couldn't. It hit me really hard and I wasn't following through with my responsibilities. Finally, the women in CO-MADRES told me that I had to stay home until I felt better.

"We have decided," they told me, "that you need to stay home for at least three months."

"Okay," I said. "If that is what you want, I will stay home."

One day passed, then two, and then three. I couldn't resist going to the office anymore. I would hear about what they were doing on the radio and I felt that I had to be there. I tried to return to work, but they took away all my responsibilities. Looking back on it, this probably helped me recover. I changed, little by little. There were times I couldn't sleep and even though it was very dangerous to go out at night, I would go outside down to the corner where there was a streetlight and I would stand there and think. Sometimes I would get the idea that my compañero was going to come back any time. Then I would tell myself that this was ridiculous. I knew that he was dead and that we had buried him. I had this idea that he was still alive.

During this time, I realized that I was being watched. People I didn't know were always following me. Often, I would have to lose them in downtown San Salvador. So we decided that it would be better for me to go Mexico. If I didn't leave, they would probably kill me.

María with her children in Mexico City, 1982 (clockwise from left: Juan Carlos, Gisela, María, Tanya, Raúl).

CHAPTER 10

LIVING AND WORKING ABROAD: MEXICO AND EUROPE

In order to go to Mexico, I had to get passports for my family. I didn't go to the immigration office for the passports. Instead, I used these people we call coyotes, who are connected to people in the immigration office. They charge you a fee and they get your passport for you. Legally the passports cost 80 colones, but these coyotes charge 150 colones. If I had gone directly to immigration, I would have had to hire a lawyer to help me because my children were minors and needed special permission for them to leave. My oldest son was 13; the next son was 12; the daughters who were leaving with me were 9 and 2 years old.

When we were all in the taxicab ready to go to the airport my family still couldn't believe I was going. My oldest daughter, who I had when I was 14, was still living with my mother. We went to say good bye to them.

My mother told me, "It's fine that you are going. Just take care of your children. You have to be both mother and father to them because you are all they have. Frankly, I wish you weren't leaving, but you have already decided to go. I just want you to know that when you return I won't be here. I am going to die sometime soon. You will receive a telegram there in Mexico and when you return you will visit my grave."

My mother said this to me so seriously. I was worried because my grandmother had told me the same thing the day before she died in 1965.

At the same time I said to myself, it's not true. My mother is healthy and full of life. She'll be fine.

When we got to Mexico City, the immigration officers detained me. First they asked, "What are you going to do in Mexico?"

"I've just come for a vacation," I told them. "Is it a problem for me to come and visit your country? I have brought my children and my suitcases, and I have money to spend here." My idea was to stay in Mexico for three or four months and then go back to El Salvador after the situation improved.

They held me for about two hours without saying anything. Finally, I asked one of them, "What do you want then?"

He said, "Come here. Give me $50 for each one of you and you can come in without any problems."

"Why didn't you tell me that before?" I asked. I was getting nervous. So I took our passports, put $50 in each of them, and gave them to him. I had only brought 400 dollars with me. So I had to spend more than half of it just to get into the country. After I gave them the money, they stamped our passports and said, "Have a good day."

In Mexico City, I met three other women from CO-MADRES. They didn't have an office, but they were working with different Mexican organizations. We had a hard time in Mexico. The weather was much colder than we were used to and my children kept getting sick. All four of them got bad fevers and had continual problems. We didn't have a house to live in so we slept on the floor of a place where the compañeras lived. We pulled all the cushions off the couches and chairs and slept on them. We didn't have sheets or anything. We hadn't brought anything with us either except our clothes. All the other things we had worked so hard to get—a bed, a television, a radio, dishes, chairs, and a table—we had left behind.

After we left El Salvador, we had someone stay in our house. They told us that there were strange men watching the house all the time. One day, they came looking for me. "Does María Teresa Tula live here?" they asked the person living there. "No," he said. "I don't know her. I just moved in, and I never heard of her." They came back to the house two or three times to look for me. If I had stayed they would have abducted me. So I could never go back there again. About two weeks after we arrived in Mexico, we also heard that two women from CO-MADRES, María Adela Cornejo de Recinos and Ana Yanira, had been disappeared, along with another woman, América Fernanda Perdomo, who worked with the Human Rights Commission. So the repression was coming down heavily on the CO-MADRES and the Human Rights Commission.

CO-MADRES opened an office in Mexico City at the beginning of 1983. We worked with different people including Rosario Ibarra Piedra from the mother's committee in Mexico. We visited a lot of unions and shantytown neighborhoods that we call *barrios marginales*. Our idea was to go out a lot and talk to ordinary Mexicans so that they would understand what was going on in El Salvador. We would speak after films, to students, academics, peasants, workers, everyone. We were not trying to intervene in Mexican politics, but we wanted to build solidarity for El Salvador.

While I was working in Mexico, I was invited to go to Canada as a representative of CO-MADRES. At the embassy, where I went to request a visa, they asked me if I wanted political asylum in Canada. I told them no, that I was just going there to work. They offered again because there were not very many political exiles then. I said no. Then they told me that they were glad to grant me a visa because I was working for the people of El Salvador. They had a high level of consciousness in the embassy. I didn't have any problems getting into Canada. I didn't understand anything they said because I don't speak English. I showed them my letters of invitation and my visa, and they let me through without any problems.

I went to Canada in April 1983. It was the first time that I had gone to another country like this. Mexico is different from El Salvador, but Canada is *really* different. We went all over Canada—to Vancouver, Victoria, Rascatun, Winnipeg, Toronto, Montréal, Windsor. I couldn't believe how cold it was. It was April and they told me that it was going to get warmer in May and June. It always seemed cold to me. I met with many solidarity groups, especially church groups. There seemed to be a lot of Chileans who had political asylum in Canada. I got to know several Chileans there, especially intellectuals. The last thing we did in Canada was a big press conference with 10 Chilean exiles. In June, after a three-month visit, I returned to Mexico. I had some problems again with immigration. Finally, with help from Amnesty International and some churches, they let me back into the country.

Two issues took up most of my time in Canada. One was testifying to the Canadian Congress about why they should offer political asylum to 11 workers from the STECEL (Sindicato de Trabajadores Electricistas de la Comisión Ejecutiva del Río Lempa, or the Río Lempa Electrical

Company Workers' Trade Union). They had been captured in 1980 and put in jail. We campaigned for their freedom and tried to help them find political asylum.

We learned other things while we were in Canada. The Salvadoran government had contacted the Canadian government and told them they were going to send 400 Salvadoran children to Canada for adoption. They were children of the disappeared. Before sending them to Canada, the government was going to take them to a concentration camp to clean them up and educate them. We had never heard anything about this in El Salvador and we were shocked. People asked us if we agreed with this idea. We said we weren't opposed to helping the children, but the idea of taking them out of El Salvador and sending them to another country where nothing was familiar was not a good thing. We thought that the resources should be made available in El Salvador for them to be taken care of there. We had wanted to set up day care centers for these children in El Salvador, but we didn't have enough money to do it adequately. The Canadian government backed out of its agreement to accept these children because of us. We convinced them that the Salvadoran government should be held accountable for these children and that it would be better to send aid for the children to El Salvador so they could stay in their own country.

Many Salvadorans I knew came to Mexico. I got to know the daughter of the abuela Rosalina Osorio Melgar, who died of cancer in 1981. I was surprised at how many people I knew there. Some of these people helped me realize how close to danger i had been in El Salvador.

For example, before I left El Salvador, a man named Mario approached me saying that my husband Rafael was alive and he knew where to find him. I wanted to believe this because I was still dreaming that Rafael would return. It turned out that he was a secret agent of the National Police. People told me about him in Mexico.

"Oh," they would say, "you knew that nasty Mario. How did you escape from him?"

He would help set people up so that they could be abducted. One person told me that Mario had gone to the factory where he worked and later they had come to his house to abduct him. He had to leave everything behind and flee. I guess I got away from him by telling him that I didn't have anything to do with my compañero any more.

I told Mario, "My compañero left me for another woman. I don't have anything to do with him anymore."

He asked me for my phone number so that he could tell me where to find Rafael.

Other people had similar experiences. Sometimes, Mario acted like a friend and told people that he was going to help them find work. "Oh, yeah," he would say. "I have a friend who needs someone like you. Tell me where you live and I will get back to you." People who weren't on guard against him would fall for it and then the police would come to their house and abduct them. If he targeted them, they were marked as terrorists. Because I didn't give him my phone number or tell him where I lived, I was saved.

But when I heard from all of these people that he was a police agent I had to let go of the dream I still had that Rafael would return. I was not going to see my compañero again. I guess I was still holding onto the possibility that he was alive, even when I was in Mexico.

Something else happened in 1982 that made me realize how dangerous it was in El Salvador. I got a telegram from my mother informing me that my brother was found dead on August 22. Nobody ever knew how or why he died. I still think about that.

In 1983 and 1984, CO-MADRES began to do their work in a more public way in El Salvador. Even though there was still a state of siege, the presidential elections in 1984 allowed a little more room for public protest. This was the election that made Duarte president. Even though it was still difficult to have public protests, the mothers decided to dress themselves in black with white scarves and march from the archbishop's residence to the U.S. embassy. This was a very important march because it broke the silence that prevailed in public. The mothers took to the streets to proclaim that the streets belong to the people, not to the government and military authorities. The mothers went to the U.S. embassy to demand an end to U.S. military aid and intervention. After this they initiated a series of sit-ins for peace in a lot of churches in the city. They always wore black. By their example, other people began marching in the streets again. This was how the silence of public protest from a wide range of sectors was broken. No one had been in the streets for years. The only things in the streets were tanks and the military.

The mothers combined this more open militancy in the streets with international work as well. In Mexico, I kept on working. We received delegations, visited popular organizations, tried to get resolutions passed, and collected material to send to El Salvador. In 1984, I was invited to

San Antonio, Texas to commemorate the anniversary of the death of Monseñor Romero.

I had asked for political asylum in Mexico. I provided testimony about what had happened to my compañero. I never received a response. Living in Mexico without a well defined legal status was difficult. For a while, I received some helped from the UNHCR (United Nations High Commissioner for Refugees) for my children.

I never went to San Antonio. I got as far as the U.S. border, but they wouldn't let me through. First they were going to deport me back to El Salvador, but I had them call the UNHCR and they had to send me back to Mexico City. It was an omen; 1984 was a very hard year for me.

I didn't want to stay in Mexico. I had thought about returning to El Salvador even before 1984 because of the change of government. We thought that with Duarte in the presidency, and with the international pressure for democracy, there would be a political opening favorable for human rights work.

In June 1984, I received a telegram from El Salvador saying that my mother had died. It was horrible to hear this news and even worse because I didn't have the money to leave right then. I felt awful that I had lost my mother and I hadn't even been able to see her again. The last time I saw her was in the airport in El Salvador when she told me she was going to die. Then I thought about my oldest daughter staying with my stepfather and my mother's children. She was only 18 years old and a heavy burden was going to fall on her. It was mostly thinking about helping her out that pushed me to go back. Finally, I saved enough money to go back with my youngest daughter. My three other children stayed in Mexico.

Because I had been in Mexico illegally, I had to get permission from the Mexican government to return to El Salvador. We went to the airport to have my documents checked. I just told them, "I'll pay." They didn't tell me I had to, I just did. I paid them for being there illegally.

I was so happy to be going back to El Salvador. It had been very hard to leave all my friends behind. In El Salvador, the airport was under military control. The guards examined everything I had brought with me. While they were doing that, my daughter slipped out of the line. She wandered over to a guard with a machine gun slung over his shoulder. "Why do you have this?" She asked him.

"Oh, I just carry it for decoration," he answered.

"Is it to kill birds?" my daughter asked.

"Yes," he replied.

"You shouldn't kill birds because they are so beautiful," she replied.

"What a pretty little girl you are," responded the guard. Then he shouted, "Whose little girl is this?"

"She's mine," I shouted.

"Let her through," he said, motioning to the guard who was pulling apart my luggage. Thank God for my daughter. She helped me to get back into the country. Usually they ask you where you have been, why you are here, what you were doing in another country.

As soon as I moved past the guards, I called the CO-MADRES office. "Here I am," I said.

"Get in a taxicab," they told me. "We don't have time to come and get you."

I went straight to the office. I didn't have anywhere else to go. I couldn't go back to where I used to live. My daughter and I went to stay for a while with one of the CO-MADRES members.

The next day I went to my mother's house in Santa Ana. I felt so sad seeing the house. It seemed so empty. My sister came out and said, "Mama isn't here any more; she's gone." The only thing left of her was her picture in the house.

"And my daughter? Where is my daughter Tita?" I asked her.

"She left yesterday for the United States. Carmen sent for her," she answered. My sister Carmen lived in Los Angeles. "She left yesterday afternoon at four o'clock. I think she had to go to Mexico first to cross the border."

I arrived in El Salvador at two o'clock in the afternoon and she had left at four o'clock. We had just missed each other. I was sorry not to see her, but relieved that she wasn't staying to take care of my stepfather and his children. She could start a new life in the United States. I hadn't seen her for two years and I didn't see her again until 1987.

Little by little, I re-integrated myself into the work of CO-MADRES in El Salvador. I had gained a lot of experience in the two years I was gone and the compañeras put me in charge of internal organization. There were always new people joining CO-MADRES and I would orient them about the international and national situation.

In November 1984, one of the mothers, Alicia García, went to Argentina for the international meeting of the human rights organization,

FEDEFAM.* Patricio Ray, the General Secretary of FEDEFAM, received a notice from the Kennedy family in the United States asking FEDEFAM to nominate one human rights organization for a prize. FEDEFAM members had a discussion and decided to nominate CO-MADRES because all the other committees of the disappeared in Latin America admired the work we did. The Kennedy family accepted the nomination of CO-MADRES and invited us to send four women to receive the prize and to hold press conferences.

CO-MADRES decided that I should be one of the people to go receive the prize. The Kennedy family sent us an official invitation and also said that we were going to speak to the United States Congress. They spelled out very specifically what we would be doing. We went to the U.S. embassy in El Salvador to try to get our visas. We went again and again and again to the embassy, but they wouldn't give us an answer. We held a protest march in front of the embassy saying, "We want our visas. We want our visas." We had asked to receive the visas on November 19th so that we could receive the prize on the 22nd. On November 19th, *La Prensa Gráfica* carried a big story about me. It said, "The U.S. State Department denies visas to four terrorist women. One of them is named María Teresa Tula with the pseudonym Laura Pinto." They didn't let us go.

Alicia García went to receive the prize. She was in Argentina and the U.S. embassy staff there was a little more flexible than the people here in El Salvador. So she accepted the Robert F. Kennedy Prize for Human Rights in the name of CO-MADRES.

Something positive did come out of the denial of our visas, however. Because of all the publicity, a woman in the United States organized an international tour for us in Europe so that we could bring our story to the public. The CO-MADRES office in Washington, D.C. was created out of the process of organizing this tour. A woman named Isabel Letelier, who worked at the Institute for Policy Studies in Washington, D.C., and others who were aware of our visa difficulties, helped us organize the tour. They provided the translators for the trip. Once again, we started getting ready to leave El Salvador.

---

*   FEDEFAM has member organizations of "relatives of the disappeared" from 17 countries.

Right before we left, there was an intense attack on the women's prison in Ilopango where the political prisoners were organizing. This women's prison was full of what we called common criminals as well as political prisoners. There were big conflicts between these two groups of women. The common prisoners would rob the political prisoners of everything they had, including their clothing, radios, and the food their families had brought them. They would threaten to kill them if they told anyone. These were terrible living conditions for the political prisoners. Many of them arrived in jail after having been severely tortured by the security forces. Then they would have problems with the common prisoners. Some of the political prisoners even testified that they had been raped inside the prison. The authorities would let anyone have access to the political prisoners. Sometimes, political prisoners were taken out and tortured again or just killed.

Because of this situation, the women inside the prison started to organize themselves. They denounced what was going on inside the prison and resisted their poor treatment. They created a women's committee of political prisoners as part of COPPES (Comité de Presos Políticos de El Salvador, Comittee of Political Prisoners of El Salvador). They demanded an end to massive searches of their quarters and asked to be treated with respect. At one point, they chained the door of the jail so that no one could get in. The army arrived and opened fire. Three women were wounded. One of them was María Ofelia López Marroquín. A bullet entered her leg and destroyed her knee. She was pregnant at the time.

I wasn't there. We were in the Panamanian embassy trying to get permission to go to Europe through Panama. But news travels fast. As soon as we heard about it we went to the prison to see what we could do for the women there. We negotiated to get some of them to a hospital because they hadn't received any medical attention and they were bleeding severely from bullet wounds.

The negotiations between the prisoners and the authorities were at a standstill so we intervened and tried to move things along. We were able to get an agreement that there would be two sections to the prison, one for common criminals and another for political prisoners. We also got them to agree that no police could get in to visit the political prisoners, that they would be allowed to cook their own food, and that family members visiting the prison would not have to submit to strip searches.

We left for Europe on January 20, 1985. There were three of us. We went through Panama and from there to Amsterdam. Two American women were waiting there for us. Ellen was the coordinator for the trip and Donna was the translator. At the airport, a group of Salvadorans were there to greet us. They were the political prisoners from STECEL who ended up getting asylum in Amsterdam and not in Canada. When we got off the plane, they were shouting, "Here come the mothers. Here come the mothers." It made us feel really good to hear that. We were also glad to see them because we hadn't heard from them for a long time. First, we went to say hello to Ellen and Donna, and then we went over and embraced these compañeros. They immediately asked us questions about their families. The two American women had no idea who they were. Ellen got really angry and criticized us for immediately taking up with these men. She said we didn't have any right to talk to them without her permission because, she said, she was responsible for us.

This whole situation was new to me. Ellen only spoke English and German and so we had to communicate with her and everyone else through the translator. As soon as we got to Amsterdam we started working. Later, the Salvadoran compañeros came to see us again at the hotel. Ellen and Donna got angry with us again. We tried to explain that we weren't doing anything devious, but just wanted to hang out with them because they were like our brothers; we had a common link through our class consciousness and understanding of Salvadoran politics. I don't think that these women ever really understood.

We worked really hard while we were in Amsterdam. We spent seven days visiting people non-stop. We went to the parliament, visited women's groups, churches, and unions. We had to work out many details with the women running the tour. Ellen accused us of excluding her at one point because we were always talking in Spanish with each other and with the translator. We weren't trying to discriminate against her, it was just that we didn't speak the same language. So we started to teach her some Spanish and communicated with her through a kind of sign language.

We then spent seven days in Geneva, Switzerland with the president of the Human Rights Commission. We were there on International Women's Day, which the Swiss celebrate with a big march. We participated in a lot of marches. We met Genevieve, the American woman who put up the money for us to go to Europe. We also met feminists and pacifists who were against the use of missiles. They were very famous and did the same kind of work we did talking with the press, going on television, and speaking with solidarity groups. From there, we went to Barcelona and to another part of Spain called Andalucía where people looked a lot like us and talked like us too. We went to Italy as well for eight days where we visited the parliament and various solidarity groups.

On this trip, several women talked to us about the way they made decisions and the kinds of issues they were organizing around. They discussed feminism. I had a bit of experience hearing about this from my visit to Canada. In El Salvador, we don't run around calling ourselves feminists, but we are feminists because we are fighting for our rights. The difference for us in El Salvador is that our struggle as women comes together with our struggle for change in El Salvador. Our feminism doesn't just involve fighting for ourselves, but for a change for all of us. We can't forget about the system that oppresses all of us. So we are doing two things at once. We are fighting for our rights as women and we are also fighting for social change in our country. If there isn't drastic social change in our country, then we will always be oppressed, even if we win our rights as women. For us, our struggle as women includes many things. I think it's fine for the women in the groups we met to be talking about feminism and discussing the oppression that women have suffered for centuries, and to be working for change through a women's movement. Everyone has the right to wage their struggle as they see fit. I have heard a lot about the abortion debate. I believe that I or any woman should have the right to decide what she wants to do. I am the mother of six children and I'm not going to criticize anyone's choice.

Women do share some common history. We are all different colors, but I think that we share some common sentiments and our blood is all the same color. We all have red blood, not yellow or orange. I think the suffering that women have gone through everywhere helps to build international solidarity among us.

But the system that we live under in El Salvador gives feminism a different meaning. We see all women as feminists, whether they are workers, peasants, or professionals. In El Salvador and other Latin American countries, there are big differences between bourgeois women, who call themselves feminists, and other women. Sometimes we meet with these feminists, but all they do is talk, roaring like lions, but not doing anything. They go on marches, but they don't really do anything, just march around in the name of feminism. To be that kind of feminist in El

Salvador means that you are a member of the bourgeoisie, not an ordinary woman like a peasant or a housewife, who has always been oppressed. These women don't call themselves feminists, but they are more oppressed than someone who is the wife of the president or a businessman. These humble women have demonstrated that they have the political, ideological, and military capacity to make changes in El Salvador. Being united for women's rights won't do us any good unless we change our government.

You know, being a woman doesn't necessarily make for change. There are women in positions of power, even presidents or prime ministers, who have the bodies of women, but the minds and hearts of oppressive men. It's a shame. It just goes to show that it isn't enough to have women in power; we have to change the whole system—in El salvador, the United States, and Europe. If we don't, then we could die and another generation of feminists would be born with more ideas, but we would all continue to be repressed.

In El Salvador and other countries, we don't even know what our rights are as people, as humans, and as women. In El Salvador women have always earned less money than men. If a woman is working in the countryside with a man and is as good a worker as the man, cutting down things with a machete, planting crops, or harvesting coffee, she never earns the same. She gets half of what the man earns. If he earns 30 colones, she will get 15, even if she works the same hours and does exactly the same amount of work. We have been working on this for a long time in El Salvador. Labor unions, peasant unions, and students have all been fighting around this issue. But we have to have an overall change for these rights to become reality. After all of our experience in the war and in the repression, Salvadoran women want to be equal to men. We don't want to be treated better than men, just equally. We want men and women to have the same rights.

I explained all these things to the women I met on this tour. I remember a discussion I had with Ellen that showed me how different we were. We were in England and I was looking out the window of the hotel. The sky was intensely blue and sparkling, like it often is in El Salvador.

"Look how beautiful the sky is," I said to Ellen as she walked into the room. "It looks like the sky in El Salvador. I really miss it."

She turned around and said, "You are a nationalist, aren't you?"

"Yes, I am," I replied.

In this conversation and in other ones, we talked about armed struggle. She was a pacifist and thought that women should never take up arms under any circumstances.

"How can women take up arms?" she asked. "If they do that then they are putting themselves at the same low level as men."

"But what would you do," I asked, "if you had a weapon in your hands and someone tried to kill you? If you had something to defend yourself with then you would use it."

"No, I wouldn't," she said.

"Well, how about if I come and hit you. Wouldn't you react in some way?" I replied. "That is how it is for women in El Salvador. Women have the capacity to defend ourselves just like men. Not everyone who takes up arms does it because they like to kill. A lot of people take up arms to defend themselves."

This time and every time we talked about Salvadoran politics we ended up shouting. Sometimes she would reproach me for what I said. I understood that she was a pacifist and wouldn't kill a fly. For her, hearing me talk about armed conflict was terrible. She couldn't accept it. I didn't understand her and she didn't understand me.

What was interesting to me was getting to know her partner, her compañera. She was a very nice woman who had suffered a lot in her life. She was a black German. Her father was African and her mother was a German woman with blond hair and blue eyes. When this woman was a little girl she was captured by the Nazis and they conducted chemical experiments on her. She had a sad life, and she could identify with the women from CO-MADRES even though she didn't speak Spanish.

While we were in Europe, América went to the United States and set up the first CO-MADRES office in Washington, D.C. The Lombardo Church gave her sanctuary as a refugee. There was a bilingual volunteer helping her and she did a lot of work building regional solidarity for CO-MADRES. She also went to the U.S. Congress to testify.

When we got back to El Salvador from Europe in 1985, the situation had changed. There were almost 2,000 political prisoners in the jails. Instead of disappearing people, they were putting them in jail. That year we worked for prisoners' rights. Many had been held in jail for over two years and never charged with anything.

In 1986, a German woman came to see us and urged us to visit her country. She organized a tour for us and told us that German solidarity groups had raised funds for the trip. So I went back to Europe on January 20th with another woman.

Our first stop again was Amsterdam. Then we went to Germany and on to Austria, where they gave us the Bruno Gracey Human Rights Award. We also went to Italy. On both trips, we worked hard. I could never bring my children with me because of the cost and because they put us on a killer schedule. Sometimes we would do five or six interviews a day, each lasting one or two hours, and we would speak to different groups. When it was nighttime I would fall dead asleep from exhaustion.

Talking to different groups of people is a lot of work. If you speak to a religious group then you have to talk about religion and relate what you say to parts of the Bible. If you are talking to a group of workers then you have to talk about exploitation and the living conditions in El Salvador. If you address a group of students then you have to talk about students. Peasants, housewives, feminists—they are all different. Sometimes people agree with you and sometimes they don't. A lot of times we didn't even have time to eat. We had to eat while we were talking because it was the only time available. It's hard to talk with your mouth full of food. It takes a lot of personal discipline to do this work and you have to be able to adapt to a lot of different situations. We needed to take advantage of all the potential that different solidarity groups offered.

The more I travelled, the more differences I would see. One of the things that surprised me the most was the first time that I saw two women hug and kiss each other. This happened on my first trip to Europe. I said to myself, "Well, they must be sisters, or something." In El Salvador two women who aren't sisters can never do that. It's prohibited. It's a sin. It's condemned by the Catholic Church and by society and by machismo on the part of our compañeros. We were in Germany and I knew that the Europeans were a lot more liberal than we were. I didn't say anything about it. I just kept thinking that maybe they were sisters or mother and daughter. There is always a lot of affection between mothers and daughters. Then Donna, the translator, asked me, "What do you think of those two women who are hugging and kissing over there?"

"Nothing," I said.

"Really?" she said.

"I'm not going to say anything because I don't know about it. Maybe they are doing it because they are friends."

Then Donna told me what they were doing. She explained their relationship and added that she was like that too. She was very candid about it. I had never talked about it before.

The second time I was in Europe, I went with a woman named Carmen. She was a peasant woman who had six children and lived with her husband. It was the first time we had ever travelled together. On this trip to Germany, we visited a women's university. While we were getting something to eat in the cafeteria Carmen and I noticed that there were pairs of women around us tenderly feeding one another. Carmen was looking around the room straining her neck so much that it looked like it was going to snap. She couldn't stop staring.

"Oh, no," she said. "I can't watch this."

"Well then don't look at it," I said. "Just sit down and eat."

"No, I can't eat," she said.

I don't know what she was feeling, but she was having some kind of crisis.

"Look," I told her, "Just clean whatever thoughts you have out of your mind. Just forget about it. This is their world and they have a right to be in it. You have your world, I have mine, and they have theirs. You know, as a woman, it's good for you to know about all of the things that exist in the world for women. This is a part of life."

Seeing women together seems very common to me now. But for us, the first time we see it, it's a conflict. Just like when anyone sees anything new. I learned many new things on these trips about other people and about El Salvador as well. I realized that there is so much about the life of people in my country that I don't even know. The work that I do takes me to certain places but I don't know everything that goes on. Even now that I have been doing solidarity work, I can get disconnected from what the daily life of most people is like.

María with her son Oscar (born in prison), denouncing her torture and imprisonment after her release.

CHAPTER 11

TORTURE AND DETENTION

We used to get a lot of visitors at the CO-MADRES office when it was on Second Avenue. My job was to receive them and talk to them about our organization. That's what I was going to do on May 6, 1986 when I was abducted.

I got off the bus four blocks from the office. (We always tried to vary our routine to avoid being followed.) All of a sudden, I felt someone come near me and grab my shoulder like they were going to turn me around and hug me. I was surprised because there was no one around whom I expected to be hugging me. I stopped and turned around to see who it was. I thought that maybe it was someone I hadn't seen for a long time, someone who was grabbing me very hard out of happiness. But when I turned around, I saw it wasn't a friend. I felt a pistol in my ribs, and it was in the hands of a large man.

He said, "Keep on walking and don't make any noise. We are going to make you talk. If you don't talk, we'll kill you." Then I felt a stinging slap, like a whip across my face. Then I saw a car.

"Come here," the man said, "and don't dare to make any noise." He wrapped his arm around me tightly with the pistol in my back. He held me as if he knew me, pretending he was being friendly.

"Get into the car, into the back seat," he growled. He pushed me in and blindfolded me. "Take away this driveling fool," he said. Then I felt the car speed up and zoom away. I couldn't see or hear anybody. The only thing I could feel was the movement of the car as it careened down the street. I felt frustrated because I couldn't tell where we were going. I couldn't see anything. I have no idea how many times we went around in circles or in which direction we were going. I only know I felt completely disoriented. Finally the car stopped. We ended up in a room but I couldn't tell if it was in an office or a house.

I was still blindfolded. They handcuffed me to a chair and they grabbed my feet and tied them together so that I was bound and sitting very straight.

Then a man asked me, "What is your name, señora, and where do you work?"

"I don't live in San Salvador," I said. "I live in Santa Ana. I work washing clothes and ironing."

"So what were you doing downtown?" he asked.

"I came downtown to catch a bus to visit my aunt," I replied.

"No, you are lying," he said. "We know who you really are."

"I'm telling the truth," I said. "I don't know who you are."

"It doesn't matter who we are," he said. "Look, we want to be nice to you. We don't want to hurt you. If you answer our questions then we can help you. We will even give you money. You could even marry one of us. We are looking for wives. Just answer our questions."

I didn't say anything. I just began to breathe deeply. Then they started to beat me on the back.

"We have the names of some people here and we know that you know who they are. Don't be a fool. Tell us who they are. If you turn in all the people we tell you to, nothing will happen to you. We will set you free."

I didn't say yes or no. I said nothing. They gave me names of people. They asked me if I knew who they were.

Within CO-MADRES, a lot of us didn't know each other's legal names. We all had pseudonyms to protect ourselves and our families. If they ever get hold of you and find out the last names of the people you work with, they will go and look for their families. So we didn't use our real names. They weren't false names in the sense that people had documents with false names on them. They were just work names.

So they went on asking me the names of people. "No," I would say. "I don't know who that is."

"Sure you do," they would say. "How about this person?"

"No, I don't know who that is either," I would answer. This went on and on.

Then they started to call me names. "You're a fool," they said. "Do you want to leave? Then collaborate with us."

"Come on. You know who these loud-mouth women are. Admit it."

"No. I don't know," I said. I still denied that I was in CO-MADRES because they didn't know that I was a member.

"Don't get mixed up with those crazy women," they said. "They are dangerous."

"Oh, really," I said.

When they were interrogating me they didn't let me have any water or food. They said it was a way to punish me until I talked. Until I said, "Yes, señores. I accept everything you have said."

They pushed me down on my knees while I was still handcuffed. They offered me money again, but I didn't say a word. Then they got rougher. One of them started to beat me and choked me around the neck with his hands squeezing very tight.

One started to say, "Don't grab her like that. Don't be so mean to her. She's going to talk to us."

They changed the tone of their voices between the two of them to confuse me. Each of them would use two different voices, and they asked me a ton of questions. Then they also started to beat me hard, very hard. They beat me with their fists on the head and in the chest. They would pull my hair hard also. They wanted me to say yes to them.

They told me, "We're not going to stop until you beg us by saying, 'please, please stop beating me.'" They kept this up. When they realize that someone is going to be stubborn, they start to torture them even more. A lot of people give in to this treatment. After the first blows, they say, "Please forgive me. Don't hurt me and I'll tell you everything you want to know."

"Where do you live?" they asked.

"I live in Santa Ana," I replied. I gave them my sister's name and address. She always said that I could use her name and address if anything ever happened to me. She and her husband don't get involved in anything. They didn't know what I was doing.

They put me back in the car and we drove to Santa Ana so that I could show them where I lived. But when we got there, I just pointed to any old house and said I lived there. I don't know if it was the house where my sister lived or not. Anyway, they never went to her house to ask about me.

When we got back, they asked me, "Where are your children?"

"I don't know where they are now," I said.

"Oh, you old bitch," they said, "We are going to kill you." Then they put a gun to my temple. I felt like I was going to lose all of my senses.

They kept putting guns to my temple and then they would play tapes of my children and say, "Here are your children. You say you don't know where they are and they are right here. If you don't want us to hurt them then you have to give in to us."

Then they would ask me questions again. And they said, "We are going to torture your children in front of you."

"No," I replied. "They are innocent." They just kept asking the same questions and I kept saying I didn't know anything. This just made them more and more angry.

This went on for three days and three nights. After they administer all of these psychological tortures, you get to a difficult point. They tell you they are going to kill your whole family. They told me that they had my sister and my children and they were going to kill them all. When they tell you that, you prefer that they kill you instead of your whole family because you have already been living through torture. These are the kinds of moments you don't wish on anyone, not even your worst enemy. It's terrible to endure the methods of torture that they use on men, women, and on children too. They even rape people. They raped me. That's how they get information. If one person knows something and reveals it, then a long chain of people can be affected. That's why we never know where people live. So we can't tell.

Later they came back to me. "How do you feel?" they asked. I couldn't get up from the ground because they had beaten me so badly. I ached all over. They held a knife to me and said, "Now we are going to kill you." That's when I felt the first cuts in my stomach—lines with blood coming from them. I was pregnant.

I was lying on the ground. They cut me across the stomach several times, just to frighten me. I didn't say anything else to them. I couldn't. I thought the time had arrived when they were going to kill me. I couldn't take any more. So I said, "Kill me. Do it. Go ahead and kill me. What are you waiting for?"

I felt the point of the knife on me and then I felt the baby. At that point I could only think of the baby. They put the point of the knife into me again.

"Yes, now I am going to kill you," one of them spat out.

Then another man came in. He said, "Don't hurt her like that. Why are you treating her like that?" He was trying to act like he was going to be nice to me. But then they threw me on the floor and the other one said, "No, no. We can't let women like her just leave. We have to take them and just fuck them." And then they both raped me.

I think this was probably the worst thing that happened to me. I'll never forget it. At that moment, I wanted to die. I had never wanted to take my own life, but I couldn't take the humiliation I had suffered at their hands. "Please kill me now," I begged. "I don't want to live."

Then suddenly, they told me that they were going to let me go because they were mistaken. I wasn't the person that they were looking for. They told me that they had gotten new information and found out that I was not who they thought I was.

"We are going to let you go," they told me, "but don't you ever go talking about the rape. Don't ever tell anyone about any of this or you will be very sorry."

They said this because I was a mess. My clothing was torn and full of blood from where they had cut me with the knife.

They let me go in Cuscatlán Park. When they dropped me off, they told me not to turn around and watch them leave or they would shoot me. They pushed me out and I fell on the ground. I couldn't see very well at all. I couldn't distinguish people around me. I could only hear noises. My head was going around and around. I said to myself, "My god, where am I? Where am I?" I almost felt like I was very drunk.

While I was lying there on the ground someone stole my purse. Boy, I'm free for two minutes and someone takes my purse. It had a little bit of money in it and a watch that some people had given to me in Europe, a ring, and just small things. It also had all my identification in it. So there I was with nothing.

I asked a woman waiting at the bus stop to help me. I think that she was frightened by me when I approached her.

"Excuse me," I said. "Can you tell me where I am? Somebody robbed me."

"That's terrible," she replied. "Should I call the police?"

"No, No," I said. "Just please do me the favor of loaning me five colones so that I can take the bus." She didn't know me so I wasn't at all sure she would loan me the money.

"Just loan me five colones and I'll pay you back tomorrow. You can come to the CO-MADRES office."

The woman looked at me and at first told me that she didn't have any money. Then maybe her own kindness got the best of her and she took out ten colones and said, "Here. Take this and go to the hospital."

I flagged down a taxicab and got in. I couldn't figure out where I was or in which direction I needed to go.

"What happened to you?" asked the taxi driver turning around.

"Nothing, nothing, " I replied in a hushed voice.

"Oh, so your husband beat you?" he asked.

I didn't want to talk to him. I needed to be left alone. So I said, "Yes."

"What a shame, " he commented. I just said, "Yes, yes."

Eventually, I got to the CO-MADRES office.

I got out of the cab a couple of blocks from the office. We never go directly there. I felt like I was going to faint before I even got there. My head was spinning. Just then I saw two of the CO-MADRES women walking toward me. They hadn't seen me for three days. They didn't know anything about what I had been through.

"Where have you been?" they asked. "What's wrong with you? What happened to you?"

"Nothing, nothing," I said softly.

They helped me climb up the stairs. I walked up to the second floor where our offices were. I remember giving them my hands and they got me up the stairs. I think I fainted on the way up. They called the doctor for me. There are some doctors in El Salvador who are part of a network of doctors called "Doctors of the World" and "Doctors without Borders." They work with the Human Rights Commission.

One of these doctors came to see me. I didn't have any huge wounds, but I had small cuts on my stomach that left scars that I still have. I was still passed out while the doctor was examining me. When I came to, people were calling other human rights organizations. I got up gradually and could see people. I don't know where they found me clean clothing, but they did. Then I began to give my testimony. Finally one of the mothers took me home.

My sister-in-law was very worried about me because I hadn't come home for three days. Nobody had said anything to her at all, nothing. She was in the dark. It was terrible because I couldn't tell her what had happened, even though we were close. I couldn't tell my children and I couldn't even hold them because I still hurt so much. That made me feel very bad.

Imagine not being able to hug your children because your body is still so sore from being beaten. The physical pain of not being able to hold my children added a new dimension to my suffering. My sister-in-law came in, gave me a big hug, smiled, and asked me how I was.

"I'm fine," I said.

"What happened to you?" she asked.

"Nothing, nothing. I'm fine. Shit, just fine cuñada." I kidded with her for a while.

I always play and joke with her because she is the sister of my husband. I lived in her house but she didn't know about my work. She still doesn't know. No one in my family knows about the work I did for CO-MADRES. Once, when I went to Europe for the first time for CO-MADRES, I had to leave my children with her. I told her that my sister was bringing me to the United States and that I was going to work and make some money. I said I was going to send for my children from the United States.

I had to return to El Salvador from Europe after three months. When I came back, she asked me, "Jesus, what happened?"

"Well, cuñada," I said, "Shit, the immigration officials wouldn't let me into the United States. I tried and tried and got so fed up that I finally came back."

"Really?" my cuñada asked.

"Yes, it was messed up."

And she believed me.

After I was detained and tortured, I would give my testimony to the international delegations that came to visit us from North America and Europe. I would tell them what happened to me, and they would say things like, "That's incredible. How could this be?" Sometimes they couldn't believe it. Some people even suggested that maybe I was dreaming—that it didn't really happen to me or to other people.

I always wondered if they believed us. Did the Americans believe us? Or the Europeans? I was never completely sure. Things like this don't happen very much in their countries. Maybe the fact that we survived was suspicious. We always explain how human beings have managed to survive all kinds of horrible tortures.

Shortly after my capture, several more people were captured. First, they got Michele. The police came to her house to tell her sisters that she had been detained. The sisters pleaded with them not to harm her, saying that she would confess to whatever they wanted if they didn't harm her. The Hacienda Police got information from Michele and afterwards more people were detained. The following day they detained a woman who was on her way to the legal aid office. Then the next day they picked up someone else, a woman named Reina. She was accused of being a terrorist. That meant that they were going to get names of other "terrorists" from her. In the next three days, they picked up two other people. They were getting names from those they had arrested and were torturing.

Right after this happened, I was walking with another CO-MADRES member whom we called the second abuela, after the first one died. Her name was Antonia Mendoza, and she was elderly. We went outside the main door of the Central Market. It was busy with people bustling around selling things from their baskets. They were selling outdoors because late in the day the market gets dark inside and no one can see. Everyone comes out onto the street to sell. We were getting ready to cross the street when we turned around and saw a blue Ford Bronco with dark windows that was moving very slowly. It was following us.

"Here come those animals," I said. My friend was very surprised to see the Ford Bronco jeep. Everyone knows that it is the car used by the death squads.

"Hurry up," I shouted.

"Hurry up yourself," she replied. For some reason I just stood there for a moment and looked. "It can't be. It can't be," I whispered to myself. When I stopped to look at the vehicle, I heard the sound of it accelerating...vrrrrmmm. It was heading for the sidewalk where we were standing. We were trying to pass by the right side of the vehicle as quickly as we could. "Go, go, go." Then I heard the sound of tires screeching, as the Bronco swerved in front of us. The vehicle jumped up on the sidewalk in front of us and came to a screaming halt. I was about to turn and run into the market. I noticed there was a bridge nearby and a dumpster I could maybe hide behind. I was thinking that. My feet were ready to run when I remembered that I was with a compañera and that I was responsible for her safety and for our work as well. After these thoughts settled in my brain, I stopped thinking of running.

I turned around and looked at my friend. She was old and couldn't run. I said to her, "I won't let them take you and not me. They will have to take us both."

While I was saying this, two men grabbed me by the arms on both sides from behind. Pow! I could feel them grab my wallet. I twisted around to see who they were. As I turned around, one of them put a pistol to my head. Then they pushed me toward the car. My friend fell down while they grabbed me and she called out, "Help me. Help me."

They sat me on the seat of the Bronco and held me with my arms crossed in front and blindfolded me. I could hear them talking to each other in some kind of code and they were speaking on a radio to other people: "We have her. What should we do with her?" A voice on the radio answered back to them, "Bring her to the big house." "Okay, that's what we will do. The orders will be carried out."

Then they began: "What is your name?"

"My name is María Teresa Tula."

"No, your name isn't María Teresa Tula. Your name is Laura Pinto."

"My name is María Teresa Tula."

I could tell that they were some kind of police, but I didn't know which one. The car went around and around in circles so that I wouldn't know where I was being taken. They took away my purse, which had in it money, cigarettes, matches, my documents, and a watch that a Canadian friend had given me. I also kept a little radio in it. You could hear all of the radio stations from San Salvador on it. I used it to hear what was happening. I also had a little cross made by a political prisoner. This was all the treasure I had. They took all of this from me because they said I was using my purse to smuggle arms. I told them I never carried guns, that I didn't have any.

"Yes, you do." They kept up these accusations the whole time we were riding around in circles.

When we stopped, they grabbed me by the arms again and told me where all the steps were. "Step up," they told me as my toes came up against each step. We got up the steps and they pounded on a door. We went in and they left me.

As soon as I entered, someone shouted to me, "Take off your clothes."

"Why?" I asked.

"Because it is an order," the voice boomed. "Take off your clothes."

I remember I had on a blue canvas skirt. I can see it so well. I started to take off my clothes very slowly, peeling them away a little at a time.

"Hurry up," they shouted.

"Yes," I said. But I continued to do it very slowly as a delaying tactic.

Then they hit me in the back. "Hurry up, now."

Then I hurried more and took off my clothes.

I was standing there just in my underwear when they began to touch me all over, my hair, between my legs, my elbows, my hands, everywhere.

"What are you looking for?" I asked.

"You are a guerrilla fighter. The guerrillas always carry pieces of bombs on their bodies," they explained.

"But, I'm not a guerrilla. I've never been to the mountains."

They found the scars from the cuts made when I was detained before.

"Yes. Here is the evidence, they said, touching the fresh scars. You certainly are a guerrilla. You have a wound."

The place was very narrow. Much later, after they took off the blindfold I saw that I was in a narrow room, like a hallway. But I was still blindfolded when they started to beat me against the wall, very hard. Sometimes, when their superiors came in, they would beat me too. They hit me in the face, on my body, and on the skull.

After a while, they look at us prisoners as if we are animals. They think that we are dangerous and that we are the worst thing possible. The military are trained to lose their human sensibilities and to become beasts. They are taught to ignore human suffering.

When they finished my initial beating, they brought me in front of the two people who were going to interrogate me.

"What is your name?"

"María Teresa Tula."

"Hmmm. Who do you work with?"

"I work with the Mothers' Committee."

"Sure. You won't tell us your real name."

Then they pushed me against the wall with my hands above my head.

"Aren't you afraid? You are going to die for nothing. Do you know where you are?"

"No. I don't know."

"We are the Hacienda Police. Watch out."

Then they began to beat me from all sides and to shout at me from all different directions. "Stand up." "Sit down." "Walk here." "Walk there." It all whirled together.

The next day, on May 29th, I found out that they had captured other compañeros and compañeras. They had Gregoria Paica, Miguel Angel Rojas, Renaldo Blanco from the non-governmental Human Rights Commission, and Dora Alicia Campos Segovia from CO-MADRES, who was known as Violeta. I saw them come in. They had captured them at five or six in the afternoon.

I was blindfolded but the blindfold was a little bit crooked so that I could see out of one side. I turned my head sideways to see better. Someone approached me and shouted, "She can see." He gave me a kick.

"No, I can't see a thing, I swear."

"Are you sure you can't see?" one man asked me.

"No, I can't see a thing," I responded. But I could see. I could see the two compañeros. They had them backed against a wall and they were beating them.

"What is your name?" they said to Renaldo.

"Renaldo."

"What is your name?" they said to Miguel.

"Miguel Angel Rojas."

"Well, Miguel, both of you. Who do you work with?"

"The Human Rights Commission."

"Really, sure you do."

Wham! They smacked them both across the face so hard that their heads hit against the wall.

"Look who is here, it's Laurita," referring to what they claimed was my alias, Laura Pinto. "We have her here."

I was right next to them.

"I want to see these two men," I said.

"No. Take her away."

The last thing I saw from the corner of my eye was that they were taking off Miguel's and Renaldo's clothes, and taking them away to a cell. I didn't see them again.

They grabbed me by the hair and dragged me into the interrogation room next door. They sat me down on a narrow bench in front of a desk. I was still blindfolded. There were two men in there. They always work in pairs. The torturer was behind my back and the one who was interrogating me was in front of me seated behind the desk. One was skinny and one was fat. The fat one was called Afro.

They sat me down and took off the blindfold and the handcuffs.

"How are you Ma'am?" one of them inquired politely.

"I'm fine. Just fine," I replied.

"Do you know where you are?" Afro asked.

"No, and I don't want to know."

"You are with the Armed Forces."

"This doesn't matter to me."

Then they began to question me about Violeta. "Do you know where Violeta lives?"

"No. I don't know where she lives," I replied. But I did know where she lived. She was the secretary of CO-MADRES. I knew that she had two small children and had been the wife of a comandante in one of the revolutionary organizations. I knew that he had supposedly died in an accident in Nicaragua but his body was never found. That was the reason she was in CO-MADRES. Because they never found his body.

After I denied knowing where she lived, they stood me up and moved me toward a window at the end of the room. Through it, you could see that there were two other small rooms. One was about three meters long and the other about two and a half. In each of them, there was a desk, a bench and a chair—the set-up for torturing. The walls and the doors were covered with thick foam. Thick enough to sleep on. They started again.

"You know Violeta, don't you?"

"Yes. I do," I answered.

"Where does she live?"

"I don't know."

Then they turned out the lights in the room I was in. In the next little room they turned on a spotlight. Then I could see someone, a woman, in the other little room with her back turned toward me at first. She couldn't see me.

They asked me again. "Do you know where she lives?"

"No." I responded. "Listen, if you want to talk to her, go see her at the CO-MADRES office. I don't know where she lives so I can't help you."

"Well, don't worry," they said. "We already have her here."

Oh! I was surprised when they turned her around and I saw that the woman in the next room was Violeta. Poor thing. She was sensitive. Sometimes people don't know how sensitive they are to the pain of torture. I felt bad for her. I knew it was a problem for me that they had arrested her.

They questioned me again. "Where is your husband?"

"I don't have one."

"Why not? What happened?"

"He died."

"Why did he die?"

"I don't know why. You all killed him," I responded feeling the sadness of his death.

"He was a terrorist. Did you know he was a terrorist?" they asked me.

"Don't talk to me that way and don't talk about my husband that way," I said.

"Well, you know, your case is a real problem," they said facing me. "We haven't decided what we are going to do with you yet. We don't know yet if we are going to kill you, mess you up for the rest of your life, or have you disappeared."

When they said this, I felt cold. Goosebumps spread all over my body like one long wave. I couldn't even imagine everything they could do to me. All the horrible things. When they said this, it terrified me. Then, with time, I began to think that it was just talk and they were just trying to intimidate me. Slowly, I learned how to read their tactics like a book. I learned to anticipate where they were going.

They showed me a picture of myself. In the picture I had on a white shirt and a black skirt with stripes. I was walking out of the market with a bag of food in my hands. CO-MADRES members were afraid to all go into the market to eat because we could be grabbed by the security forces. Because of this fear, one of the daily jobs was to go to the market to get food. The photograph was taken in front of the Pizzeria Bunt which is right in front of the market and close to the office.

"Do you recognize this photograph?" they asked me.

"Yes," I said. "It's me."

"You are carrying a bomb," they accused.

"A bomb? Anyone can see that I am carrying a bag of food."

"No, no, no honey. We can see that there are bombs in that bag."

"Whatever you say," I said.

They turned to me again. "Look, your case is a mess." They pulled out a file. "The first accusation against you is that you killed four national policemen."

"I didn't do that," I replied.

"Oh, you didn't?" they laughed. "It says here in this report that you also burned buses."

"Look," I responded, "I never did any of that. It's a mistake."

They repeated these accusations and added some others. "Finally," they said, reading from the end of the document, "it says here that you are looking for your disappeared children."

"Well, I do look for disappeared children, but my own children have not disappeared. I help other people look for their children because I have suffered a loss too. You killed my husband."

"We didn't kill him," they said. "But it's a good thing that he was killed because he was a terrorist. You are looking for your children but they are in Cuba and Nicaragua. All of the people who claim that their children have disappeared are full of it. There are no disappeared. They are all in Cuba. Your whole family is in Cuba because you know that something might happen to them here."

My head was spinning with all these accusations. My family in Cuba! Why were they accusing me of all these things? What was I going to do? They began to pressure me again.

"Listen, what harm does it do to confess, to admit to these things? If you cooperate, nothing will happen to you," they assured me.

"Why should I confess to things that I didn't do?"

"You say you are part of a mothers' committee that looks for the disappeared. Well, you never consider the fact that we have lost a lot of people too. The armed forces have disappeared people as well. We've lost a lot of compañeros."

"Okay," I said. "Why don't you form a committee for disappeared soldiers? Make a police committee if you like."

"Very funny. You think you are very clever. A committee for disappeared soldiers and police!" he yelled at me. He was getting angry.

He hit me as hard as he could across the face, again and again. I was seeing little flashing lights from the force of the blow and my ears began to hurt. He turned to me and spoke tersely.

"You are a criminal. You've been in the mountains delivering medicine. We know that you have taken care of the wounded and that you have contact with a comandante from the FMLN. In 1985, you entered the country with a large shipment of medicine. You are a terrorist."

"Listen," I said, still seeing little lights around my head, "Do you think that if I had brought in a large shipment of medicine for the FMLN through the airport that I would still be alive? You would know who I was. You check every detail. You check on everything down to the number of teeth people have when they come through the airport."

I continued to deny everything. "Look here. Let me show you something," I said, reaching for one of my torturer's hands. "Let's compare our hands. I have never touched any guns or killed anyone. Now let's look at your hand. Your hands are all hard compared to mine. They are stained and marked by all of the people you have killed. Not mine." This made them very angry and they began to repeat all of their accusations, backwards and forwards, forwards and backwards.

Finally, they tried a different tactic. One of them turned to me and said in a low quiet voice, "Listen, we are good people and we would like to help you. Why don't you work with us? We need women like you. You can choose a place in Europe to live, some place you visited. We'll send you there. Or we can provide you with security here in El Salvador. We will pay you well. But you have to accept the conditions that we impose. You have to say that CO-MADRES and all the humanitarian organizations here in El Salvador are fronts for the FMLN."

When they finished with this little speech they grabbed an attaché case from under the table, put it down, and clicked it open. It was stuffed full of money.

"This is all yours if you want it," they said. I didn't respond.

"We are offering you a huge pile of money here. Don't you want it?" I still said nothing. Then they changed tactics again.

"She doesn't want it. We don't understand assholes like you. You don't know how to take advantage of opportunities like this. You are turning down all this money. We'll see about you. Boy, are they well indoctrinated. They don't even take money."

I never responded. Their accusations continued. From the time I was picked up to this point, I had been detained at least 24 hours. They asked me if I was thirsty. Had I had anything to drink? Imagine standing up for 24 hours exposed, practically naked, blindfolded, and without anything to drink. But I hadn't even felt like going to the bathroom. My stomach was empty. Sometimes I felt like I had to go and other times I didn't feel like it at all.

Finally, I asked the torturer behind me for some water. They brought me a tiny glass of water. Then they said, "Do you want this glass of water? You should ration this water. The only reason we brought it to you is because we are nice. Most people here don't get any water at all. We felt sorry for you so we have brought you water."

I knew that they were trying something new to get me to talk. The beating and the money hadn't worked so far. They left, and then a young boy who was more or less a servant threw me a plate of rice, beans, and tortillas.

But I didn't know if I should eat the food. I had heard about people being given food laced with drugs. These drugs make them lose their heads. They start agreeing to everything they are accused of and even inventing things that aren't true.

It was tempting to eat. I was very hungry, but I resisted. Then I felt my baby move inside of me. Remember, I was pregnant. My throat was very dry and I was thirsty. I decided not to drink the water, but I thought if I don't eat something my baby might die. The baby needed food. I ate a tortilla with some beans, but I was very afraid.

Five minutes later I felt my eyes close. My eyelids were very heavy. I tried to keep my eyes open, but I couldn't. Every time I would close them I would start to see things like big animals and dinosaurs that I had seen in a movie. I imagined that I was thrown into the middle of them or that I was falling off a cliff. I was still conscious, but it was difficult to keep my eyes open. Then I saw someone I knew. It was Herbert Anaya,* a human rights worker who had been detained before me. I could see him through

---

* Herbert Anaya of the non-governmental Human Rights Commission was detained two days before María. CO-MADRES began denouncing his capture On May 27th, after they received a telegram saying Herbert Anaya and Reina Isabel Hernández de Castro were under investigation by the Hacienda Police.

the glass in the next room, where Violeta had been. It made me very happy to see him.

He looked through and tapped on the glass. Once he understood that someone was in the room next to his he put his hand on the glass. We couldn't hear each other, but we could see each other's hand signals. I tried to tell him through hand signals that I was drugged. He signalled back to me to walk, to keep moving, keep pacing. We were afraid we would get caught communicating like that. Our torturers had left, but there was a guard. I kept walking and walking until finally the drug wore off.

Later, two men came in. They asked me how I liked the food and if I drank the water. I told them I had. Then I asked if I could go to the bathroom. At first they didn't want to let me go. Then they led me to a toilet. On the way, I passed the three rooms I described before, and an office where they had books and where they took pictures of people. At the end of the building there was an office where they kept files on people. Down another hall there were about 10 cells that were about one meter wide and several meters long. I saw several people I knew.

When I returned, they sat me down, took off the handcuffs, and began questioning me again. They asked me who started CO-MADRES. Then they read from a document that stated that in 1982 someone had recruited me to one of the revolutionary organizations.* This made me laugh inside because I hadn't even met the woman they claimed had recruited me until two years later, in 1984.

"If you say I was recruited in 1982, there is nothing I can do about it." First, they accused me of being a member of the Communist Party. I said I didn't know what the Communist Party was. Then they accused me of being a member of various organizations within the FMLN. They said I was a member of the FPL (Fuerzas Populares de Liberación, Popular Liberation Forces). They asked me what the initials stood for. I said, "I don't know." They ran through all the revolutionary organizations and finally accused me of being a member of the RN (Resistencia Nacional, National Resistance).

---

* Revolutionary organizations refers to the five political-military organizations which combined in 1980 to form the FMLN.

They accused me of being a leader. They didn't know what they were accusing me of. I denied it all. I said, "No, I don't belong to any of those organizations." That's when they began the physical torture again.

The first blow hit me on the head, hard. I fell to the floor. Then they hit me from the front and from behind.

"What's wrong with you, Ma'am? Everything okay?" they asked.

"I'm fine. Just fine," I mumbled.

This made them even angrier. Every time I said no to their accusations, they belted me into the wall.

I told them that we knew who they were. "You come to our demonstrations. We watch you. We have taken pictures of you so we can identify you. You are soldiers. We know," I said to them.

"Why do you have pictures of us?" they asked. "Are you going to kill us?"

"No," I answered. "We have pictures so that we can identify you when we denounce your atrocities."

"You old bitch, don't lie to us. We know that you know things," they told me.

Then the door opened and the boss came in.

"We think she is going to talk," said my torturers. "She is important to us." They pushed my head next to the wall and began to hit my head against it. Then they hit my head on the floor. Then they grabbed me by my blouse and hit me on the head with their hands. I couldn't hear anything. I was seeing little colored lights. I couldn't concentrate on what they were saying. Then they faced me to the wall so my chest was touching it. They would hit me from behind with their open hand so that the side where my heart was would slam against the wall. They were double blows from behind and from the wall in front.

It was all a jumble in my head. They were telling me horrible things they would do to my children, and they kept repeating the accusations.

"You know where the secret houses are," they shouted. "You have safe houses in the city filled with weapons."

"CO-MADRES never has safe houses nor arms because we don't belong to the FMLN. We are a humanitarian organization, and our only weapons are the testimonies, photographs, and documents about the disappeared in our office," I replied.

They said that I had contact with a comandante from the FMLN named Quincho, whom I had helped. They said he was wounded and had stayed with me in my house. This was absurd. I did know a compañero from the FMLN, but I didn't know if he was a comandante or not. He was Violeta's son. Once I went with her to meet him in a restaurant. I sat at one table and they sat at another.

They didn't like my answer and started to torture me again. They sat me on the ground, put the handcuffs on tight, and blindfolded me again. Then they pressed on my spine as hard as they could with their knees to cut off circulation from the large artery that runs through the back. They pressed so hard I felt my circulation being cut off. They beat my spine with their knees. Then they beat my legs as well.

They said that kneeing you in the back and in the legs very hard was the only way to see if you were a guerrilla. It's this stupid idea they have. They believe that since guerrilleros get a lot of exercise they will be able to resist this punishment. If you do, that is supposed to prove you are a guerrilla.

They each grabbed one of my arms and pushed me up and down in deep knee bends. After about 25, I felt like I couldn't get off of the ground. But they pulled me up by the hair. Then they sat on my shoulders and made my chin touch my knees. I passed the rest of the day like this and part of the next.

The next day at midday they brought me food again—rice, beans, and a tortilla. I was afraid to eat, but my baby needed the food. I just ate the tortilla.

"Aren't you hungry?" they asked. "Why don't you eat? You have to eat so you won't go out of here saying that we don't give you food." They were drinking coffee and smoking.

"What do you want? Coffee? A cigarette?" they asked.

"No, thank you."

I like coffee and I smoked, but I just didn't want to take it from them. Afterwards, they took me into an office where they had photographs of men and women from the different revolutionary organizations. They had some huge photographs. They told me that they were going to show me all the pictures to see who I knew. I didn't know any of the people in those pictures.

After showing me the pictures they grabbed my left hand to take my fingerprints. "Do you know which hand this is?" they asked.

"No," I said.

"Do you know which finger we grabbed you by?" Then they hit me very hard in the chest. "We are speaking to you."

"The left hand. The left hand," I moaned.

"Yes. Because you are a leftist."

They took all my fingerprints. After that they took pictures of me from all sides. They dressed me in a black prisoner's shirt.

The accusations and the torture started again. They accused me of all the same things as before, plus more. They said that I had known comandantes and had brought them into El Salvador. That I was a student leader and had mobilized students. They mentioned all my actions for the past four months. They had clearly been following me. They told me the time I left my home and where I went. What they had done was to mix real details of my life with their false accusations to make it look like they knew everything I did. They did this to confuse me. They continued beating me on the chest and on the head. They also seated me on the floor and put my arms behind my back over a bench. They would pull up on the bench while pulling my hair. They kept asking me questions—like rain that never stops pounding on the window.

"You went to Mexico. What were you doing?"

"I was working."

"Who took you to Europe?"

"A German woman."

"Who? Who was she?"

"I don't know. I don't speak German."

"What were you doing there?"

"I was looking for solidarity and support."

And this went on and on. I finally had to use the bathroom. On the way there, when they took off my blindfold and handcuffs, I saw Violeta. There she was sitting on a bed, smoking and reading the paper, and looking pretty comfortable. She saw me looking at her. I didn't know I was going to see her. I had intended to look at whomever was in the cells and remember any details so I could share information with people if I got out.

I knew that she had been talking to them. She probably said that she and I belonged to a revolutionary organization, that she was an important person in the organization. She gave them the names of everyone she knew. That's why they didn't torture her.

When I saw her sitting there, I became furious. If they hadn't taken me away from there, I probably would have tried to attack her. I was so angry. I was so surprised and angry that I could hardly walk. Another policeman came and told me to move along. She probably heaved a big sigh of relief when I left. She saw the utter fury on my face.

I went to the bathroom. I couldn't sit down because my thighs had been so badly beaten. I sort of leaned against the wall to prop myself up. That was hard.

After I relieved myself, they started to interrogate me again in another room. There were four men in there. They said that I knew a lot of things that were of great interest to them and if I told them they wouldn't beat me anymore. They told me that I could choose between more torture or telling the truth. That's when they subjected me to the capucha.* They also seated me on the floor again putting a bench under my arms and raising it. They beat me again in the head, in the arms, and on the chest. I only remember that I repeatedly asked for spiritual help.

"Dear God, please help me to resist all this. Help me to be strong in this difficult hour. Don't let me give in." I repeated this to myself. I also thought about Monseñor Romero. I asked him to give me strength. My religious beliefs helped me a lot in this period. All the members of my family are Catholic and we believe in God. We believe that he exists and protects us when we have faith.

In this dark time during my torture, I felt an amazing sense of protection. On top of my head I felt hot. This heat might be what gave me enough life, enough force to endure the torture. I had to endure five days and nights of different tortures non-stop. They didn't beat my baby inside, but they beat me everywhere else. They were trying not to leave any permanent marks. Before, they used to leave people all swollen and purple with chemical burns and burns from electric shocks. Now they are more careful.

They told me again that they were going to kill my children and my family. They kept telling me that my family was in Cuba. I told them that my children were in Mexico.

---

* The capucha is a particularly horrible form of torture in which the prisoner's head is covered with a hood which may be coated inside with toxic chemicals. As the prisoner breathes, the hood sticks to his or her face. The more one breathes, the more it sticks. It is applied to make the person come close to suffocating. Some prisoners actually suffocate to death.

"My family isn't here. My children are in Mexico." I was afraid they would pick up my children. This had happened to many families. Not only did they pick up people's children, but they brought in the kids and tortured them in front of their parents. I didn't want this to happen.

After five days of torture, they were fed up with me. They said that they couldn't do anything with me and that there were too many people pressuring the government to release me.

"Those damn old biddies are at the president's house clamoring for your freedom. They are protesting in front of the Cathedral, demanding that we let you go."

Then someone else came to see me and said, "I feel sorry for you, you fool. No one remembers who you are. No one has asked about you. They don't know where you are. You are in trouble."

These were their tactics. They were trying to break me in a psychological war.

During this time one of the people who had captured me came to talk with me. He took off my blindfold and sat down. He was quite young.

"How do you feel Ma'am?" he inquired.

"I'm OK," I answered. "Who are you? Who are the people who captured me?"

"We are part of the military. Why do you think you were captured?" he asked.

"I don't know. If you are military authorities, why don't you identify yourselves when you detain people?" I responded.

"Because we receive orders. They tell us that we have to carry out our operations in secret and make it appear like it was done by the guerrillas. We are supposed to confuse people. That way no one will know that it was us."

I sat and talked with him for a while. He said he didn't like what he was doing, but that he was forced to do it. He was in the army because he needed work. You could see that even among the soldiers there is some level of consciousness. Unemployment is high, and a lot of young men join the military just to survive. A lot of them see the injustice committed by the military and they have deserted. We were still talking when his boss approached.

"What are you doing talking to her?" he asked.

"I was interrogating her," responded the young man. Then he started yelling at me, getting tough while his boss was watching.

"I will be back," he yelled. "When I return I want answers to all my questions." He left and I didn't see him again.

They stopped beating me. There was no longer physical torture, but the psychological pressure continued. They sent a man to see me who they called the Cuban. He was a dark man. He came on like he was your friend, liked he cared about you.

"How are you Ma'am?" he began very politely.

"I'm fine."

"How have they treated you?" he asked sympathetically.

"Badly," I replied.

"What a shame," he said. "They should be nice to women here."

"I don't know," I answered.

"If you had been with me," he said, "I wouldn't have tortured you. We could have become good friends. I wouldn't have touched a hair on your head because I can see that you are a good person. I wouldn't have let anyone beat you. And I'm not going to hit you now so don't be afraid. They call me the Cuban. I used to live in Cuba. Then I came here and they captured me. They tortured me. Didn't the same thing happen to you? But after I was here a while they told me not to be stupid. They said that I could get into the military and have a career. I resisted, but in the end they convinced me to join the police force."

He continued, "What do you want for your country? It's fine the way it is. You have food, freedom, and a job. When I lived in Cuba, it wasn't so nice. There was no food and the government only gave you one pair of shoes. You had to wear them until they were completely worn out before they would give you another pair. You got one pair of pants and one shirt, and the food was rationed. When I came here to El Salvador, things looked different to me. I said, this is where happiness and democracy can be found. I love democracy. Here you can have ten pairs of shoes. You can have a good watch and nice clothes. You should see my house here compared to what I had in Cuba."

He continued to talk to me.

"Look what happened to Violeta," he said, "Nothing." She was with me. She didn't get beaten and now she is going free. There is still time for me to help you if you will accept it. You can go free. We can talk and I will give the order for them to set you free." He was a sergeant in the National Police.

"Okay," I replied. "What are we going to talk about?"

"We will talk about a lot of things. Like the RN," he stated quietly.

"I don't know anything about the RN," I said.

"Well, Violeta knows about it," he said.

"Okay, but I don't," I replied. "If you already know so much why are you asking me?"

"I'm not a fool," he said. "I know a lot of things."

"Well, good. If you know a lot of things that's fine."

Then he left, telling me he would return. He went to see Violeta and came back. He spent a lot of time going back and forth between the two of us trying to confuse me.

During this time, they started to torture another prisoner. The sounds were terrible. He was screaming. While I was sitting outside of a room, I saw someone I knew, Renaldo from the Human Rights Commission. When they asked me, I said I didn't know him. Then they brought in another person from CREFDES (Comité de Refugiados Desplazados, The Committee for Displaced Refugees). I knew him too, but I said that I didn't. He told them about the organization's work and its supporters. They tortured him in spite of the fact that he was talking to them.

Then they brought in another young man. I think his name was Manuel. Our torturers had decided that we knew each other and belonged to the same revolutionary organization. They blindfolded me and took me to him. Then they took off the blindfold so that we were facing each other. I had never seen this young man in my life.

"I don't know this man," I said.

"I don't know her either," Manuel stated. "I've never seen this woman before."

"What?" one of the police officers yelled. "You told us that you know him."

"No, I never did," I said.

These were the kinds of things they did to try to confuse you. Just about then the Cuban came back to see me.

"Would you like a cigarette?" he asked, like he was a good friend of mine.

I didn't want to take it. I was afraid they were trying to drug me again. I always thought about the worst possibilities.

"Hey, I'm your friend," he reminded me.

"How nice," I replied.

He took out a cigarette and started to smoke it. "Don't be afraid," he said. "You think it has drugs in it. It doesn't."

He gave me the lighted cigarette. He said that because he had been a victim of torture he never tortured other people. He detained people in order to convince them to join his side. He said that he had convinced a lot of people to work with him and that they were always grateful to him afterwards for all that he had done for them. He spoke to me some more and then left.

Later that day, the director of the National Police arrived. When I saw him, I was frightened. Oh no, I thought, another torturer. I knew that he wasn't coming to see me out of the goodness of his heart. He must have seen the fear in my eyes.

"Relax, Ma'am," he said to me. "I'm not going to torture you. I only came to talk to you. I am a sergeant with the National Police." He told me his name, but I don't remember it. He took off my handcuffs and told me to sit down.

"I have come to talk with you in an official capacity," he stated. "We know that you have told people that you were captured by the National Police the first time you were picked up. And that is the truth. It was the National Police who captured and tortured you. I promise you that I am going to investigate your case and see that those who were involved will be punished."

"Listen, sir," I said. "I never identified any particular national security body. I never said that it was the National Police who captured me. You can investigate it if you like. The people who captured me were heavily armed civilians. That's different from the National Police."

"But I'm worried about this, about the disorder here in some of the units," he told me. "If they are doing things that shouldn't be done, we are going to investigate and prosecute. Now, you should answer my questions about your capture, because you saw who captured you. Tell me about them and the whole situation."

"I didn't recognize anyone," I said to him. "I didn't even know where I was."

"Okay," he said. "And how did they treat you? If you had been with us you would have been treated correctly. This has been bad. I wish you good luck, señora." And he left.

People kept coming day and night to see me and ask me questions. After about six days, people from outside the country started inquiring about me. They began to pressure the government. Later, they put me in a room with two other people, Herbert Anaya and Reina Isabel Hernández. They put us in the same room on different chairs and told us that we were going to see a very interesting video. They turned on the video and Dora Alicia Campos Segovia appeared on the screen. In the video, she made a diagram showing the organizational structure of CO-MADRES. She said she was in charge of the organization. On the chart, she indicated other leaders. Then someone else spoke. It was Violeta, the one who had turned in so many of us.

On the video she said, "My name is Dora Alicia Campos Segovia. I am known as Violeta. I am a member of a revolutionary organization and I can testify that all the people I will name are also members." Then she named all of us who were currently being held and tortured. She stated that all the humanitarian organizations in El Salvador were fronts for the FMLN. All of this surprised me because I never had any idea that she belonged to any revolutionary organizations.

Afterwards, they told us that she had made these announcements in front of the press and for some foreign diplomats. It became clear why they had shown us the video. They wanted us to make one as well—to denounce people and say we were revolutionaries. They came to me and apologized for torturing me. They said that there was still time for me to make a video with similar confessions and I would be set free. They made all kinds of proposals, offering me freedom in exchange for a confession. On June 9th, we were moved to the jail and they asked me to sign an extrajudicial declaration.

"Can I read what it says?" I asked.

"No. Just sign it if you want to leave the police headquarters."

I didn't want to sign it. But they threatened me. I finally signed it, and they took photographs of me and took me to a military doctor. He examined me and confirmed that as I left the custody of the Hacienda Police there was nothing wrong with me. He testified that I had not been tortured and was able to walk without any problems. After the doctor left, I heard a man talking into a tape recorder:

> We are making this statement on June 9th with the terrorist María Teresa Tula known as Laura Pinto, who belongs to the terrorist organization "Resistencia Nacional." We declare that we have freed her and we have no responsibility for what

happens to her once she leaves our custody. —The Hacienda Police.

They took more pictures of us from all different angles and told us that we were going to be freed any moment. Soon a woman came in to see us from the Red Cross. They didn't set us free but put three of us in handcuffs and told us that the police were going to take us to the women's prison in Ilopongo. At the same time, they were taking some men to Mariona, the men's prison.

Before we left, a representative from the government's Human Rights Commission came. He asked me how I was.

"Fine," I answered. "And what exactly is it that you do at the Human Rights Commission? Why didn't you come before? What are you doing about all the human rights violations committed by the security forces?" I knew him. We had worked together before on various human rights issues.

"The only thing we can do is support decree number 50.* If we learn that you have been detained for more than 15 days, then we can do something to get you out. That's all. If it is less than 15 days then there is nothing we can do." He did nothing to help me and left.

When I left the Hacienda Police I had been in their custody for 12 days. I spent the entire time inside in darkness, like in a deep, dark cave. When we went outside, we covered our eyes with our hands to keep out the light. It was so bright it burned our eyes.

"Why are you covering your faces?" yelled the police. "Because you know you are dangerous! Don't hide your faces. Everyone knows that you are terrorists. You can't hide."

The three of us knew that we were in danger when we were being transferred to prison. The Hacienda Police could no longer be held accountable for what happened to us. They could pretend there had been an armed confrontation with us, like they always do. They say that the guerrillas attempted to rescue the prisoners, that there was a violent

---

* Legislative decree number 50, created in the mid-1980s, allowed police to hold prisoners incomunicado for three months. This permitted many disappearances and assassinations. Once someone was officially held and acknowledged as a political prisoner for 15 days they were supposed to be brought before a judge and formally charged.

confrontation and the prisoners died in the scramble. We knew that could happen to us. There were armed men all around us. That is how we left.

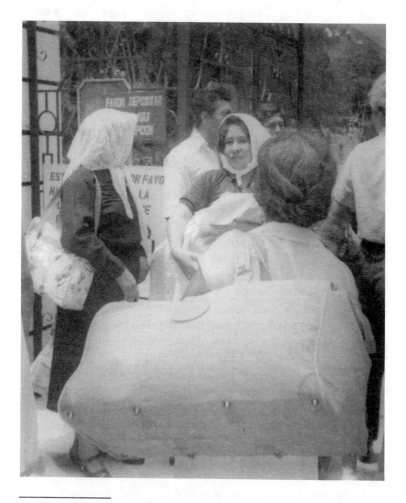

María leaving the women's prison in 1986 with her son Oscar.

CHAPTER 12

THE WOMEN'S PRISON

When we arrived at the prison, something quite amusing occurred. It seemed that the prisoners had heard that the new arrivals had betrayed all of their compañeras and were making press announcements and videos. Violeta, Michele, and Elena—the prisoners—thought we were them. The women had organized themselves to beat up these stool pigeons. They had chains and sticks ready.

They were surprised when they saw us. I had been doing work in prison so people knew me there already. They greeted us with a loud round of applause. They knew me and shouted, "There goes the compañera from CO-MADRES." I felt better because I knew the prisoners would help me. There wouldn't be so much repression there because the jail was organized.*

Within the prison there is an organization of political prisoners. COPPES has different committees for food, cleaning, health, and to take care of women who were tortured before they came to prison. Many women arrive who can't sleep. They scream and are afraid to trust anyone for fear they will be tortured again. The first day they gave me food and a sleeping pill. The next day I had to go to the prison clinic. The doctor was from the government Human Rights Commission. The women warned me about this man. They told me he was bad news. Many women

---

* Political prisoners in El Salvador's jails were among the best organized in the world. The jails were viewed by many as an important sector to organize as part of the movement toward change.

had gone to see him because they had been physically and psychologically tortured by the national security forces. Most of them were severely traumatized. But this doctor told them that the reason they acted traumatized was because they weren't getting enough sex while in prison. Can you imagine this diagnosis? What an idiot! To say this to a woman who has been tortured and raped. When I went to see him, he immediately began to question me.

"Why were you put in jail? What did you do? What happened?" he said.

"Look," I answered. "Is this a medical exam or another interrogation session?"

"No, no," he replied. "I just need this information to know what might be wrong with you. Did they torture you?"

"Yes," I said.

"Are you sure they tortured you?" he asked again.

"Yes, they tortured me," I answered.

"What's wrong with you?" he wanted to know.

"I am having trouble hearing and my spinal column is injured. I can't stand up straight and it hurts me to walk," I replied.

He just gave me some pills and told me that if I took them I would get better. That same afternoon I fell down some steps while I was on my way to a little store inside the prison to buy some coffee. I just lay on the steps and nobody helped me, even though they knew me. Maybe they were afraid. Finally, the two women I came into the prison with noticed that I hadn't returned from the store, and they came looking for me. They found me lying on the steps with a swollen foot, unable to walk, and pregnant.

The next day I had more trouble with my ears. I couldn't hear. I went to another clinic within the prison that had better doctors. There was a woman doctor everyone liked. The women from COPPES had a good relationship with her. She told me that my ear drums were severely damaged and she wasn't sure if they could be repaired. She told me that it would take time and that she would try to get a specialist in. My ear drums had become detached when they hit my head against the wall. They began to heal and reattach after about 20 days.

In prison, I met lots of young girls. Some of them weren't even 15 years old. Most of them were from peasant families. They had been captured by mistake or because their parents belonged to organizations that the government didn't like and they were kidnapped along with their parents. They were so young and scared that they didn't speak to anyone. We worried about them and tried to talk with them to make them feel better.

We women would talk to each other about all the horrible things that had happened to us. We had been tortured and raped by as many as eight or ten men, and some got pregnant as a result. That is where some of these children came from.

Some of the women were refugees who had been captured by the army. I remember one who was over 60 years old. They raped her with a flashlight over and over again. "Shove the flashlight in her vagina. See what she is hiding in there." These women suffered horrible things. It was terrible. Almost everyone had signs of torture. People had received electric shocks on their breasts, in their ears, and in their private parts. They were treated like animals, not respected like human beings. I will never forget it.

One of the most amazing things was how we were able to organize women inside jail. Some of the prisoners had no political consciousness. They had been captured and jailed and they didn't even know why. They were accused of being terrorists but they didn't even really know what a terrorist was.

Slowly, we all began to talk with one another and to communicate. The Committee for Political Prisoners was important in this work. Every weekend we would all get together. We would have a little meal together and we even danced. We borrowed a tape player to provide a little atmosphere in that dreary jail.

Through the church, we were able to start a school for the women who didn't know how to read and write. We formed a women's chorus, and there was a kindergarten for the children. In jail, children were constantly attached to their mothers. They were afraid to leave them. The kindergarten helped children become a little more independent and gave their mothers a rest.

You can imagine that all these activities provided some optimism for women in prison. When you are in jail, the normal routine is to do nothing all day long. The only program there before we organized things was to produce crafts. Women would spend all day sewing, embroidering, or making tablecloths that they could sell. They used the money they earned to buy something to eat for their children. The only food they gave us in jail was tortillas and beans. Once a week we had an egg, and maybe some macaroni and soup. The children would get one tortilla and so would their mothers. When the children were hungry the women would give up their tortillas. That's the way we mothers are. We prefer that our children eat.

While I was in prison we proposed a project to an international group called Doctors of the World. We asked them to help us set up a little farming area with an orchard, a vegetable garden, and a place to raise some animals. We argued and argued with the prison director. Finally, she gave us about 2 acres of land inside the prison. It was probably the worst land within the prison—it was filled with dead corn stalks—but there were a lot of women from the countryside who knew how to work poor soil. They were campesinas. Meanwhile, the women with small kids took turns caring for each other's children. Some women would take care of the children, others would work the soil, and others would prepare meals for everyone. It was a nice project.

We also had a psychologist who came to prison and we developed ways of educating people about family planning. We also had sessions on health and treating childhood illnesses. On Sundays, we had activities for all the visitors that would focus on why we had been detained. Many of the political prisoners' relatives didn't understand what had happened to us, or why, and they were afraid.

People began to visit me in jail. I had made friends in my travels in North America and Europe. People came to visit almost every day in delegations from countries we had visited—Australia, Norway, all over. Often they brought gifts with them, such as fruit, food, money, and clothes. I gave the donations to the Committee for Political Prisoners, which would then distribute the goods to those who were most in need.

After a while my husband's family came to visit me in jail. On the one hand, they were very happy to see me, but on the other, they were displeased with the fact that I was in prison and they came to scold me for getting arrested.

"What are you doing here?" they said. "Why did you get arrested?"

"If you came to see me, that's fine," I said. "But if you came to yell at me, just leave."

They didn't understand my work or what I was doing. They didn't know about it. At the same time, they had some of my children and were looking after them. I could understand their feelings.

"What are you doing here with these women?" they asked. They thought the place was full of criminals.

"These women are honorable," I answered. "They are very special people. They are not just anyone. If anything happens to me here they will take care of me."

"What about feeding your daughter? Is she safe here?" they asked. My youngest daughter Gisela was in prison with me when she was five and six years old.

"Won't something happen to your daughter here?" they asked.

"No." I answered quietly. "Right now she is safer in here than anywhere else she could be." After our conversation, they left.

They were the only ones from my family to visit me. My blood relatives abandoned me for all practical purposes. Only one of my aunts came to visit me twice for about ten minutes each time. I had sisters in San Salvador and two half-brothers and a sister who lived in Santa Ana. My uncles who lived in Izalco never came to visit me. It was hard for them. They were afraid. I can understand their feelings too. But I needed to have someone around to visit me. I was in prison with my youngest girl. The largest family I had was the women in CO-MADRES, the foreign solidarity workers who came to visit, and the other women in prison.

We had political activities in prison—marches and hunger strikes. Prison is another arena for struggle. We were fighting for political prisoners' rights. After being captured and tortured, you also see injustice inside the jails. These activities brought the political prisoners into a lot of contact with the regular prisoners. Many of these women supported our activities. We knew how the economic system had worked to put them in jail. We wanted to let them know about the economy and how we were fighting for change. We were tortured for our beliefs about change and a lot of people in jail didn't even know that this was going on. They lived in a different world. So we told them about our work and about the situation in the country. After a while, these women would come to us for explanations about a lot of different things.

They also watched out for us. When there was danger, they would let us know. They knew who the soldiers and the police were and they would let us know if they were coming inside. Some of the women who were security guards for the regular prisoners also came to trust us as well. We didn't have any security guards inside the political prisoners' section because they knew that we were responsible. We didn't fight with one another. There was never any problem with us. In some of the other sections the women would fight among themselves and even beat each other up.

My son Oscar was born during my first month in prison. Seven children were born within a few months of one another while I was in prison. There were 89 women political prisoners and 27 children.

When he was born, Oscar seemed fine. But after about two days he began to have all the symptoms of colic and he was very sick. He was so little and skinny. I didn't think that he would survive very long in this prison. I'll never forget some of the women who helped me out after he was born. One woman helped me a lot even though she was about to have a baby herself. Another woman named Gregoria washed my children's clothes and my clothes for me. I couldn't make it down the stairs to the sink. I was having a lot of trouble with my spinal cord, especially after the birth. She would massage my back and help me with my children. This is something that I will be grateful for until the day I die.

A couple of months later, on August 20, 1986, President Duarte announced on television that he was going to free me. He said, "I am going to go to the Central Jail to free Señora María Teresa Tula of CO-MA-DRES." He said that he had investigated the case and was going to personally set me free. Everyone was very excited for me. Some of the women were happy, and some were sad. They wanted me to leave, but at the same time wanted me to stay. I felt the same way, but I still didn't believe it.

"Listen," I said, "This is all a lie. Nothing is going to happen."

And nothing did. August 20th passed, the 21st passed, and the whole month passed by. We celebrated my daughter's sixth birthday in jail. And then on the 23rd of September, a representative of the Red Cross came to tell me that I was free.

"Hurry up," she said. "You are now free and I am supposed to take you to the residency of the president. That's the order that my chief gave me at the Hacienda Police."

"I am not going to the president's residency," I told her. "They didn't capture me there or take me there before. I'm not going."

"Okay," she said. "If you don't want to go I will rip up this letter and you can stay in here forever. If you want to leave you have to go to the president's residence so that he can question you."

"I'm not going. I'm not going there," I shouted. I was very angry. Outside, the judge who was responsible for me was talking to the people from CO-MADRES and the Committee for Political Prisoners. They told me that the women from CO-MADRES were there.

"All right. I will go, but you are responsible for anything that happens to me," I told the woman from the Red Cross. My idea was to get in the car, but to jump out at a stoplight. The women from CO-MA-DRES were riding behind me and the judge went in front of us. The judge and the woman from the "Red Cross" were speaking English in front of us so that they could plot what they were going to do with me and I wouldn't understand.

"Okay," the judge and the others said. "We will take you to the CO-MADRES office as you wish." But it didn't take long to see that they weren't heading toward the CO-MADRES office at all. We protested.

"That's right," said the woman from Red Cross. "I have to take you to the president's residency because those are my orders."

"So," I said, "you work for those animals." I was taken in a Red Cross ambulance, but she didn't let anyone else go with me because she was really from the police.

I got out in front of the president's house with my little son and holding my daughter's hand. The women from CO-MADRES were with me. The judge turned around and saw us and he came running over and grabbed me by the hair and hit me in the face very hard as we were getting out of the car. One of the women from CO-MADRES tried to get into the ambulance. But the woman from the "Red Cross" slammed the door on one of her fingers so hard that the compañera fell down.

"Go on. Get in there," she said to me.

"Come on, I'm taking you inside," shouted the judge. The men who had tortured me were there. They received me as I walked in the door.

I told the woman who was supposed to be with the Red Cross, "You took me from jail so now you have to go in with me. The women from CO-MADRES have taken down all the license plate numbers and they know who you really are. If anything happens to me, you will be responsible."

They pushed me inside the president's house. I went into the main room to sit with my children. I was incredibly angry. When I got to the main room I didn't see anything. Nothing. I could see nothing at all.

Then I remember that President Duarte rose and said, "Gentlemen of the press, as I promised, I am freeing Señora María Teresa Tula. She is here today because of the democracy and respect we have for human rights in this country. Señora María Teresa, you are free to go." Then he gestured with his hand to three seats in front of him and he held out his hand for me to shake. I didn't shake his hand.

"Sit down" he said pointing to the chair next to his. I sat down in another seat and my daughter sat in the chair he had motioned for me to sit in.

The woman who was supposedly from the Red Cross began to talk with the president, thanking him for his great humanitarian gesture. The truth is that the only reason I was set free was because of international pressure and my own innocence. Thanks to the CO-MADRES office in Washington, Amnesty International, and the solidarity efforts of many people who sent cards, letters, and telegrams—thanks to them I was freed.

While I was close to the president I presented him with a document from the women in jail. We demanded better food and living conditions. He said that he would review it.

I was talking to the president and surrounded by media, but still not really seeing anything. I was so angry with this man. Then suddenly, probably because some photographer poked his flash at me, I was able to see. At first I couldn't tell the difference between what was natural light and what came from the flashing cameras. I turned around and saw my husband's niece and his father standing there in front of me. I knew that they were forced to be there. They had been summoned by the president. When I saw them there I was afraid for them. As soon as I saw them I said, "Thank you very much gentlemen, but I have nothing more to say. If you need more information, there will be a press conference at the CO-MADRES office at two o'clock in the afternoon." And then I left.

My family left with me. They thought I was going to go home with them, but I didn't. I didn't want anything to happen to them. They were very angry that I didn't return with them. Instead, I went home with someone from CO-MADRES. I knew that if I went out alone they would pick me up again. For about a week, I was staying in a different house every night. At the end of a week I went to the CO-MADRES office, but I was afraid. I never walked alone. There were always several people with me.

This lifestyle was very difficult; it was during this time that my baby got sick. I had to take him to the emergency room. I was staying in very humble houses. It wasn't good for a newborn baby to be staying in a house with a mud floor, no water, no electricity, and a lot of animals and bugs.

During the fall of 1986, I lived in different houses. I was constantly afraid. I kept seeing the blue van that had captured me around town and it was always traumatic. Every time a car would screech in the street I would go into a panic because it reminded me of when I was picked up.

On October 12, 1986, there was a horrible earthquake in San Salvador. It destroyed a large part of the CO-MADRES office and many of our members' homes. It destroyed the house I was living in. I had just moved in a few days before and suddenly it was gone. It was a terrible time. A lot of people died and then there were aftershocks. This was kind of the final straw for me. I decided to leave El Salvador. It was just too difficult to keep living there, changing houses, always moving, always afraid.

The police were constantly looking for me as well. They would send people to places I had been staying and ask who lived there or if there was a room for rent. I was constantly pursued. I decided I should leave my country and go first to Mexico.

María with a U.S. supporter in San José, California, 1988. Photo by Jacque Gharib

CHAPTER 13

LIVING IN THE UNITED STATES

I finally was able to leave in January 1987. The women from CO-MADRES helped me to leave for Mexico. I left legally with a passport and went with an official delegation. While I was in Mexico I was sent an official invitation to visit the United States signed by about 48 congresspeople including Senator Kennedy. Armed with this letter, I went to the United States embassy in Mexico City to get a visa.

We arrived at the embassy at 4:30 in the morning so that we could get in at nine o'clock. There is always a long line for visas. When I reached the office, they looked my name up in the computer and then told me that I couldn't go to the United States. "You are a communist and a terrorist. That's what it says here. We are very sorry but this status does not allow you to enter the United States. Your request for a visa is denied."

"How is it possible?" I asked. "I have all of these letters and one is signed by all of these congresspeople. Don't you respect the wishes of your own Congress?" I said.

They told me, "That is Washington, and this is Mexico. We can do what we want here." So I never got the visa.

I stayed in Mexico and worked for a while. Then in February 1987, I started thinking again about going to the United States. I decided to go visit my sister who was in Los Angeles. I left on February 14th on a bus for Hermosillo. From there I went to Piedras Negras and then across the border to Arizona. We crossed the border on March 3rd through a desert.

We walked for five hours and then we were in Arizona. We came across with a coyote.* From there we went to Tucson.

I remembered that there were some families from Tucson who had visited me in El Salvador. They had always said that I could call if I ever needed their help. I had their telephone numbers with me and called them. I stayed with them a little while and then went to Los Angeles to look for my sister and my oldest daughter. People in Tucson helped us raise enough money to travel to Los Angeles. I was travelling with two of my children.

When I left El Salvador I brought documents and photographs with me in spite of the fact that people advised me not to. I had my passport and birth certificates for myself and my children. I also took a lot of photographs of my family. They were the only memory of them I have. I took them wherever I went. I wanted something intimate to remind me of my family and my life in El Salvador. It's very important to have some things like that when you are so far from home.

It was difficult when we got to California because I had lost my sister's phone number. I had to call a lawyer whose telephone number I had and he helped me locate my family. We looked for them for three days and finally found them. They were very surprised to see me, especially my oldest daughter. I had not seen her since 1982. I had a surprise waiting for me too. My daughter had given birth to a little girl seven months earlier. I was a grandmother and didn't even know it. My daughter was very happy to see her little brother and sister.

The whole time I travelled in the United States, I relied on people I had met in El Salvador and their friends. It was almost entirely through church networks that I had places to live and people who would help me. There were many lawyers who helped as well. They would pick me up at the airport, find me a place to stay, and give me advice.

After I stayed a while in Los Angeles, I went to New York. After 15 days I decided to ask for political asylum. I spent four or five days with lawyers, giving them my testimony. On April 4th, we went to U.S. Immigration to petition for political asylum. The lawyers told me that I could move about with a little more freedom now that I had started the

---

* Coyote is a term referring to those people who take others illegally across the United States-Mexican border. It is a profitable business commanding from $200-$400 per person.

process of trying to get legal status. They also told me not to talk to anyone about my experience because it could be dangerous.

After completing the asylum petition, I decided to go to Washington, D.C., where CO-MADRES has an office. When I arrived, I called a Salvadoran I had met at a conference in San Salvador. He had told me to call him if I ever needed a place to stay in Washington. I did and lived with him for a while.

I came to the United States with my two youngest children. Oscar was about seven or eight months old and Gisela was not quite seven years old. From the day I first set foot in this country, I saw that it was a completely different society and way of life from El Salvador. In our country, people talk about the United States as if everything is beautiful. And it *is* a beautiful country. There is a lot of solidarity here for the Salvadoran people. You can feel that on a visit. Living here is totally different. Integrating myself into American society has been really difficult. I didn't know how to get around, how to speak English, or how to do anything.

After staying with this Salvadoran friend for eight days, a woman who was friendly with the CO-MADRES board found an American family for us to stay with on 16th Street. All they had was a tiny room with beds in it for me and for my two children. I felt very sad in that room. I didn't go out because I was afraid. I was also very frustrated not to be able to communicate with the American family.

They were a good-hearted family. They had a nine-year-old daughter who became friends with my youngest daughter. This little girl made my daughter feel welcome. Later, we were able to move into a larger apartment where we lived for a year. It took some time, but I finally felt comfortable going back and forth to the office and getting around.

The CO-MADRES work in the United States consisted of holding daily press conferences about people disappearing from social movements in El Salvador. We kept in touch with Congress and the White House, trying to make information available. Most of the work was simply keeping the public informed and writing letters about what was going on in El Salvador. This was very different from what we did in El Salvador where the work was much more activist-oriented. We visited families of the disappeared and prisoners, and we held demonstrations. I was always busy. Here the work was much more low key. People told me I had to understand that work in the United States was different than in El Salvador. At one point, I was so frustrated that I wanted to go home.

Life was so hard here. For example, in El Salvador, when I needed to leave my children for an hour, a day, or even two days, I could leave them with my family without any problem. Here it was different. I had to constantly look for someone I could trust to care for my children.

Even getting used to the food took some effort. Our diet in El Salvador is very basic, but it is good. We eat rice, beans, and tortillas. I would go to the supermarket here and not only would the food be different, but if I asked for something in Spanish, no one would understand me. I missed everyone and everything—my family, my friends, CO-MADRES, the food, even the landscape.

In El Salvador, it is almost always sunny, and the sky is blue. Here it is cloudy more often. In Washington and other parts of the country, I almost always have to wear a jacket or a coat. Not in El Salvador.

I missed the beaches even though I didn't go there every day. I just knew, however, that if I wanted to go, all I had to do was get on a bus and I would be there. In just a few hours, or at most a day, you can go wherever you want in El Salvador. It is a small country. Here, I had no idea where to take my children to play. Sometimes, the family we were living with would take us to a park or a restaurant. But usually we would just stay inside the apartment.

I started to have a little more self confidence after I participated in a congressional hearing on political asylum in 1987. It was a general hearing, but my case was used as an example. At that point in time, I still hadn't heard the outcome of my petition. More than a year later, in May 1988, they denied my request for political asylum.

The State Department opinion attached to my asylum case stated that I was a terrorist, anarchist, communist, and a guerrilla fighter and that I would present a security problem for the United States. They said they didn't believe that I was captured and tortured; they said I had made it all up just to receive political asylum. The State Department also said that there was respect for human rights in El Salvador. This was their answer to my request for political asylum. Since then they have said nothing new on the case.*

---

* This was recorded in April 1991. That same year María received temporary residency due to an interim law giving Salvadoran refugees 18 months to live

After they denied my request for political asylum, I received a letter from immigration informing me that I had to be out of the country by June 1988. My lawyers told me not to leave. They wanted to study the case some more before filing an appeal. I haven't heard from immigration since I received that letter four years ago.

Nobody was surprised by what the State Department had to say about my case. One of my lawyers went to El Salvador in 1987 to collect some information. She went to the U.S. embassy with some women from CO-MADRES and asked about my case. "Well," they said, "you are defending a terrorist."

"No," she replied. "I am defending a member of a human rights organization." After that she could see how things were in El Salvador and what they thought of CO-MADRES. In 1987 and 1988, my lawyers collected information about all the threats that CO-MADRES had received.

In 1988, the CO-MADRES office was bombed and destroyed. Two people were injured. The most serious injuries were suffered by a young man who was only 15 years old. I was told by witnesses that a woman had come to the office and knocked at the door. She asked if she could use the bathroom. The mothers let her in, she went into the bathroom, and then left. About ten minutes later, the bomb went off. It seems obvious that the bomb was planted by the death squads, but the U.S. embassy stated that someone in the CO-MADRES office was making a bomb and it had gone off by accident.

One of the positive aspects of being in the United States is that I have seen all the love and support that exists here for the Salvadoran people. I have met many different kinds of people and travelled in 48 of the 50 states in the United States. I went to a lot of rallies and met people like Jesse Jackson. I also began to travel to cities where Friends of CO-MADRES organizations existed, like in Boston and Seattle. I stopped wanting to return to El Salvador when I started travelling more and could see all of the solidarity organizations that existed in the United States. I took my son with me everywhere because he was still small. I would leave my daughter with some friends.

in the United States legally. She renewed this status in 1992 and again in 1993. María is still waiting to hear on the appeal for her political asylum case entered in 1991.

After a while, people invited me to speak in their communities. They wanted to hear my testimony and about what was going on in El Salvador. When you give your testimony, you start to relive all the difficult things that have happened to you. It's very hard to constantly remember all those terrible moments. But when I think about the hundreds and thousands of people in El Salvador who have similar stories, and who never had the opportunity to tell anyone, then I feel I have to make a real effort to tell my story one more time. For them. It's really hard to hold back the tears every time I tell my story. But we decided in 1986 in El Salvador, when they made a film called "No More Tears," that we didn't have any more tears to cry. We have suffered for years and years and we are all very sensitive about what has happened, but we can't cry any more.

At one point I went to see a psychologist because I couldn't live with what had happened to me. It was harming me. I was completely depressed and I didn't want to talk about it to anyone else even though I knew it was the only way to make people understand the barbarous acts that the Salvadoran army was carrying out against its own people.

Sometimes I think, "Why am I telling my story to these people? Maybe they won't believe me." Sometimes I ask myself, "Why am I even alive to tell my story? How can I tell it another time?" But I always answer that I have to tell my story because the tortures that we received in El Salvador were sent by the United States.

We have to make people understand how men in power in El Salvador have turned into beasts who don't respect women of any age. Women from 13 to 70 have been systematically raped as part of their torture. This is the hardest thing to deal with. I feel deeply ashamed telling people that I was raped during my torture.

The reality is that the majority of women who are detained are raped. A lot of women think that rape is something that happens to someone else. Even in El Salvador. When other women would come to the office in El Salvador and talk about what happened to them in their torture, I felt like telling them, "It didn't just happen to you." Many women have been raped.

Telling my story in the United States is difficult. Maybe this isn't part of U.S. culture, but people here don't believe things until they see them. I suppose that is natural. Many people who listen to my story pay attention and are very supportive. Others don't believe it. They say they just can't imagine how it could be true. They tell me, "How can you just be sitting there talking normally about all these tortures if they really happened?" It's as if they think that I imagined it all. There have been plenty of people who have heard my story and then questioned it. After I talk, they stay after and then come up to me. They always tell me that it is only the communists that administer this kind of torture. That makes me feel bad because I'm not making this up.

People in the United States have never lived in the middle of a war. This country is always preparing for wars in other countries. Right now the war in the Middle East makes me very sad as a mother for two reasons. On the one hand, I understand the mothers of those soldiers who went to fight for U.S. interests—for oil. But the people I really feel for are those living in the middle of the war—those women and children. They are the ones who are being bombed, who are cold, who are hungry, whose houses are being destroyed. They are the ones who feel the terror of seeing their families killed and maimed by bombs. As Salvadorans we feel a great deal of affinity for those people suffering in Iraq because we are living in the middle of a war too.

I saw opposition to the war here in the United States, particularly from people who were a part of the Central America solidarity movement. I think that they feel a lot of solidarity for the victims of the war and for the families here whose children were sent to serve in the Middle East. We think a lot about the mothers of soldiers and how they must feel when they learn that their sons are going to fight overseas. Europeans have protested more against this war because they are a part of the Persian Gulf alliance. They lived through World War II and therefore they express stronger opinions against the war.

Most Americans still believe what their government tells them. They believe it when the government says, "We are going to defend an oppressed country." They think the United States is going off to help the downtrodden, like Superman. Mr. Bush says that he is ready to fight tyranny and dictatorship, and to defend democracy. But I know from my own experience, the United States doesn't always defend democracy.

It's interesting. When there are macabre crimes and murders committed in this country then people demand justice. I've seen it on television here. When someone commits a bloody crime like a rape or a murder, they can be sentenced to die in the electric chair. And yet when these same kinds of savage crimes are committed in El Salvador, no one demands justice. They don't believe what goes on in my country. Even journalists who have interviewed me use language that de-legitimates my experience. They write, María Teresa Tula "alleged" or "said" that she was tortured. The way they frame my responses makes it sound like there is some doubt about what happened or that I imagined what happened to me. This is very painful for me and anyone who gives testimony about their own torture.

Sometimes I say, "How come they don't believe me?" I'm not going to take off my clothes in public and say, "Look, here are the scars from my wounds where I was tortured." I'm not going to hold up a piece of x-ray film and say, "Here is evidence of how my spinal chord was injured during my torture." I'm not telling my story because I want pity. I don't want people to say, "Pobrecita, poor thing." We don't want people to feel sorry for us.

Often after I tell my story people are crying. But, meanwhile, they believe what their government tells them about El Salvador. They believe that U.S. aid is going to help bring democracy to El Salvador. When I see people crying during my story and then telling me this, I don't feel like telling my story anymore. It can be very discouraging.

I guess I just keep talking because we realize that it is something that the U.S. public needs to know. They have to hear people who are from what is called the "Third World" talk about the kinds of human rights abuses we suffer. These abuses are not just about torture and killing. There are many other kinds of human rights abuses as well, like the lack of education. Right now, 70 percent of Salvadorans don't know how to read and write. We don't have access to basic medicine. We have insufficient nutrition and substandard or no housing. They never talk about these conditions. They just talk about establishing democracy in our country.

Well, there is democracy in the United States. People can march in the street and talk to their senators or go to other countries at will. And even though there are poor people here, most of them have a place to live. Most of them have jobs of some sort. There is a minimum wage and some social benefits. We have none of this for the majority of Salvadorans. The only democracy we have is the word itself, spoken in the air. If we asked for the things that most U.S. citizens have, we would be run over in the street by tanks, killed, and disappeared.

Democracy has to begin with meeting basic needs. Many people don't have real houses in El Salvador. They live in dwellings made of cardboard. We have no electricity, no running water, and no sewage systems. When we talk about the crushing poverty in our country, sometimes people say, "Well, maybe they don't want to work or people don't economize or think about saving for the future."

We do think about the future and we want it to be different. We are hard working people. But the conditions are different in El Salvador than in the United States. Suppose that an enterprising family was able to find enough money to open up a tortilla factory. The problem in El Salvador is that there aren't enough people with money to buy the tortillas. So the business would fail. Farmers would like to farm, but there isn't enough available land. There isn't even land for building houses. People who can't find work in the countryside but are struggling to survive, end up coming to the cities and making their houses out of whatever they can find. They are creatively trying to eke out a living in their cardboard houses. They are trying to create some kind of future.

Personally, I don't think about my own future very much. My future is in my children. I hope they are able to take advantage of the opportunity they have here to educate themselves. I don't want them to suffer the same way I did. I don't have a profession. My job was to do domestic work for less than minimum wage. I want them to grow up in a different world. I don't want there to be war. I want there to be love, peace, and tranquility. I think what we have been through both here and in El Salvador can be an important experience for them so they understand the difference between their country and elsewhere. I hope that being in exile will ultimately be a useful experience for them and that they will feel proud of their Latino roots. I don't want them to lose their customs and their principles. I hope they will use what happened to our family as a way to educate other people. I hope that they will be "maestros de la realidad," teachers of reality.

I've been alone now for more then 10 years. I haven't been in a relationship. It's just been me and my children. I'm used to that. I don't think that I will get involved with someone because as an activist I don't have a lot of time. I don't have enough time to devote to my family as it is, and they always need a lot of love and attention. Sometimes my work affects my relationship with my children. I might come home very tired and my children want to talk to me. "Let's not talk right now," I say. "Please let me be. I'm so tired." And this makes it hard for them.

In spite of getting tired sometimes, I want to keep moving forward and fighting for social change. Right now, I am focusing on working with women in El Salvador. We have always been marginalized. People always said that we were weak and that we didn't have the capacity to do any real work or to be equal to men. They have been telling us that for a long time.

In most parts of El Salvador, women don't know how to read and write because we have our first child at age 15, and then another, and another. Once we have so many children, we are not able to go to school or learn a trade. A woman's profession is to take care of children. Girls become mothers and then they become grandmothers. They mother their children, their husbands, and then their grandchildren. In this process we never have time to think about ourselves.

More than half the women in El Salvador are single mothers. The fathers have either abandoned their children or they have been killed in the war. We have to work with these mothers. That is why we decided to support the women's movement in El Salvador. We have to change the machismo that exists. We don't blame the men personally; we blame the whole system that keeps women down.

We are all used to obeying our husbands. They can go out whenever they want, they can do whatever they want for entertainment. But not women. If women smoke, it is terrible. If a woman drinks, she is degrading her family. If a woman falls in love with another man, she is guilty. She is a prostitute. We are always the guilty ones. Men can have a relationship with two women at once because they are men. They can smoke, they can drink, they can go out and behave whichever way they like because they are men. They don't suffer any consequences for their behavior.

We don't want to get rid of men. We just want to educate them. They have to change and to listen to their compañeras. They have to learn that women have rights also. They have to learn that they can help take care of children and work in the house.

The women's movement in El Salvador is organizing around these basic issues. It is growing to include peasant women and market women; even the prostitutes are getting organized. CO-MADRES is also involved in this struggle. Because we evolved as part of a human rights movement, we have usually seen ourselves as mothers and not as women. I am a woman, but I was also a wife and mother. Now we have to unify as women. What is our struggle now? We have to fight for representation in the government. All the politicians and judges are men. There aren't any women. We want to elect some women as representatives in the assembly and to be judges so that we can have a women's platform in El Salvador. We don't just want women's bodies in these positions, but women who will represent our issues. We truly believe that women can make a big difference in the democratic future of our country.

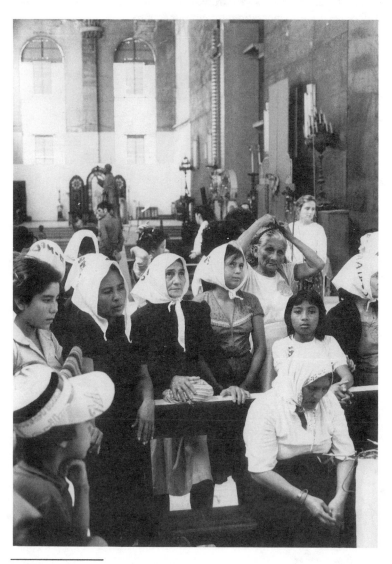

CO-MADRES members end their marches in song and prayer before the tomb of Archbishop Romero. Photo by Jacque Gharib.

CHAPTER 14

THE PEACE ACCORDS

On December 31, 1991, when the FMLN and the government agreed to sign the peace accords in El Salvador, we all felt joyous and hopeful that the situation was going to change. And on January 16th, when the peace accords were actually signed in Mexico, it was broadcast live on Spanish-speaking television. I planned to stay home to watch it. On my way home through my Salvadoran neighborhood in Mount Pleasant I could see that there were televisions and radios on everywhere—in restaurants, in bars, in stores. Everybody was interested, and waiting.

When they finally signed it, I was very moved. I could not believe that our dreams had come true. I could not believe that the FMLN and government officials signed the agreements. It was amazing to see each of them embracing and shaking hands with enemies they had been fighting for years. I felt so moved that I cried with those on the television when their voices cracked with emotion.

It was hard to believe what was happening because a few weeks earlier it looked doubtful. There was intervention from the United Nations. And we can't forget the role of the U.S. government, pressuring the president of El Salvador to sign the peace accords. Cristiani did not want to sign the agreements. And then I could see that even though the U.S. government promoted this war for so many years, they also wanted it to end. That is what we all hoped for, but certainly we don't believe that those who supported the war for so many years are going to be our best friends now.

We did have a revolution in El Salvador. In my opinion there was and still is only one revolution because there is only one Frente, only one Frente Farabundo Martí (FMLN) which has been struggling and fighting for a long time. During 12 of those years we had different revolutionary organizations. Many died in a fight for real social change, for the day when these peace accords would be signed. We think that the war situation in El Salvador was continually eroding the physical and economic condition of the country, and as the war continued these conditions got worse. We all knew the war had to end because we couldn't keep living under such inhumane conditions. We knew it wasn't going to be easy to defeat the military of El Salvador because they were very well trained due to the constant support of the U.S. government. Our best option was to negotiate. However, even though the U.S. government used all possible measures to destroy the movement and the FMLN, they failed.

We believe that we did win in the negotiations. We convinced the two sides to negotiate because people did not want war. In spite of the fact that many people said that the Frente was a bunch of ogres, that they were degenerates, the FMLN demonstrated politically and ideologically to the United States, to the government of El Salvador, and to the world that they cared about the future of a people who had suffered tremendously. Unlike the Salvadoran government, the Frente fought for the people, not for its own self-interest.

Now we have to go through a process. This year, the elections for representatives and mayors will begin. We will see if real social change is possible. We will see if free elections can be guaranteed where people can present their own candidates, as they do in the popular movement. There are a lot of capable people who can be candidates. Then, in 1994, there will be presidential elections. We will see if there can be truly free elections. Rubén Zamora is a presidential candidate for the FMLN and the Democratic Convergence.

Human rights is another concern since the peace accords were signed. The treatment of human rights in Chile and Argentina are a lesson for us. We can learn from what happened there. But this January we were at the United Nations in New York where we presented our demands to the government. We also asked the International Committee on Human Rights in the United Nations to help us by acting as intermediaries in our negotiations with the government. We want the U.N. to investigate the fate of the disappeared and not to grant immunity to those who are guilty.*

---

*   The United Nations Truth Commission for El Salvador published their report called "From Craziness to Hope: The Twelve Year War in El Salvador" in

We want the government to open their records from 1975-1992 and to
us who was captured, to tell us about the secret cemeteries we know exist
in places like El Salto del Angel at Boquerón where they would throw the
bodies. We demand that the government provide the legal means so that
the mothers can identity all the young people who died and determine
when they were killed. We want to be able to help these mothers find their
children. We will not be satisfied with amnesty for the killers.* Even if it
takes years and years we want them to be punished. Some of the them
have already been punished. Like Duarte and D'Aubuisson who died of
cancer. That was the punishment for those two criminals.

Others who committed crimes must be investigated and punished.
We want to know what happened to our young people. Why were they
persecuted? What crimes did they commit? What horrible things were
done to the disappeared? And also those who survived and are alive, no
matter what their condition is, their mothers need to find them.

I believe that the role of women in the revolutionary movement is
central. Even if some men have gained some ideological and political
consciousness, they still have a problem with women's rights. This is not
true of all men; many men have been supportive of women. But others,
even though they are revolutionaries, have their own ideas. Not long ago,
I asked one of the five comandantes who signed the peace accords about
women: "My question to the Frente is, what do you think about the
women's movement in El Salvador today?"

March 1993. The report implicated 15 top military officials and others in gross
human rights violations. Several members of the FMLN were also implicated.
The report stated, however, that 95 percent of the human rights abuses
committed during the 12-year period were caused by security forces, the
military, civil defense forces, and death squads. Five percent of the cases were
blamed on the FMLN.

* The United Nations Truth Commission recommended that the military be
  purged of officers who had committed human rights violations and that all
  individuals who had committed violations be barred from holding public office
  for ten years. The FMLN accepted these conditions, but the National Assembly
  of El Salvador voted in April 1993 for a blanket amnesty for all accused. This
  resulted in the immediate release of two military officers convicted of the
  assassination of six Jesuit priests and their two assistants at the Central
  American University in 1990. In May 1993, due to international pressure,
  Alfredo Cristiani, president of El Salvador, reluctantly agreed to purge the
  military of 15 officers.

This comandante turned to me and said, "We have to listen to the women, see what proposals they have and support them. If they have political candidates, then they should participate and we will support them."

I think that there is more support for women today. Men in the movement will no longer just tell women, "go do this" without examining the ideological and political context of what they are doing. They have made some mistakes in the past. So right now there are discussions about women's proposals. They have to take them into consideration. If they don't, they know that the women's movement may become a problem for the Frente.

This comandante told me, "We support all initiatives taken by women."

Well, I hope so. When I mentioned some of the past problems to this comandante he nodded and said, "Well, yes this is true. We made some mistakes."

For example, in the past, comandantes would give us orders, often asking people to do some very difficult things. They wouldn't listen to someone saying, "I can't do it because I have these problems or reasons that prevent me from doing it." They would just say, "You have to do it." And people would. So now they realize that they were very hard on people, on those who directly supported the Frente.

People wanted to know why the leadership was so rigid and harsh and why they didn't respect the feelings of the activists who supported them. The leadership later said that during the most difficult moments they had to be harsh. If they hadn't been so hard-nosed then we wouldn't have this peace process. We discussed these issues with the comandante.

He also talked to me about the future. He said, "I've been asking myself over and over, what am I going to do now? I won't need to walk around with a gun over my shoulder anymore. None of us will need our guns anymore. I spent all of these years fighting for these changes. I didn't have time to study or to do anything because I devoted my life to my work. But now that everything has changed we have to ask ourselves, what are we going to do? Do I want to continue doing political work, or should I prepare to live my life? All of these years I did not have a life outside of my work. I had no family, no children. Now I plan to have a family."

As he spoke, I realized that I had begun to think about some of these things two years ago. I would think, what will happen if the war ends? If a peace accord is signed? What have I done with myself? And now that moment has arrived. Everyone is asking themselves, what will happen now? Should I learn a new trade so that I can make a living when I go back to El Salvador?

My plan is to return to El Salvador. I don't know when, but I am positive that I want to return. I will continue working with CO-MADRES; today, more than ever, there is so much for us to do. We have to reconcile the entire country. We have to think about helping the mothers of the soldiers—mothers like us who were affected by the same war. We need new plans on how to help the wounded from both sides, whether they are government soldiers or soldiers from the FMLN who did not receive any medical help for years because of the conditions they lived in. We will have to work closer with communities, supporting their needs and helping all the women and mothers develop so they can survive in the future.

You know, even though there have been a lot of changes, I am still the same person. I still think about what happened. Even though we talk about the changes and reunification of families, the war is something you can never forget. The pain and suffering of the destruction of a family will always be there. At the same time, I think that mother earth is happy because there is no more war. She will not be burned or destroyed by chemicals anymore. The atmosphere will be clearer and nature will thrive after so many years of destruction. This gives me great pleasure and fills me with love and hope for a better life. However, I cannot forgive them for what they did to me and for all that happened. I cannot forgive that. I don't feel hatred, but I have pain, a deep pain that will never, never be forgotten.

Women from Nueva Candelaria gather for food distribution as part of a program sponsored by Asociación de Mujeres Salvadoreñas (AMS). Photo by Lynn Stephen

CHAPTER 15

IT'S A HARD LIFE

WOMEN IN EL SALVADOR'S

ECONOMIC HISTORY

by Kelley Ready

The historic backdrop to María Teresa Tula's life story is as volatile and dramatic as the geography that has earned El Salvador its reputation as " The Land of Lakes and Volcanos." In the land where " coffee is king," long-standing wealth and land inequities provided centuries of fodder for the civil war which took more than 80,000 lives between 1979 and 1992. Poverty is a tradition for the majority in El Salvador as are women's struggles to survive and raise families on close to nothing. In this chapter, I will outline El Salvador's economic history beginning with the rise of coffee production and following through to the end of the civil war. Large population shifts in this century from the countryside to the city, the emergence of the informal economic sector, large-scale internal migration, ever-increasing economic stratification, and the civil war's devastating effect on production, health, and family life provide some of the context for understanding women's organized struggles and María Teresa Tula's personal experiences.

The Coming of Coffee: The Struggle for Land Intensifies

As the smallest country in Central America and with the region's highest population density, land in El Salvador has been a precious and disputed resource since the Spanish conquistadors arrived in the sixteenth century. First wiping out or displacing El Salvador's indigenous population, the conquistadors launched a long history of brutality and increasingly unequal concentration of land. The landowning classes began to consolidate their power after winning independence from Spain in 1821, but the process was accelerated as international trade in coffee began to dominate the Salvadoran economy in the mid-1800s.

Hailed in government reports and newspaper articles as the key to " modernizing" the Salvadoran economy in the nineteenth century, the expansion of coffee cultivation was limited by a pattern of land ownership in which communal landholdings coexisted with individual private ownership of large estates. Much of the best coffee-growing land was claimed by indigenous subsistence farming villages that held the land communally and distributed the right to cultivate it to its members.[1] Such land could not be sold. In addition, many small farmers with privately owned subsistence plots were hesitant to take up coffee cultivation because it was so labor and capital intensive. Because it took three to five years for coffee plants to mature, few peasants could afford the high costs of starting to cultivate coffee. Only large hacienda owners who had access to credit could survive the price fluctuations in the international coffee market and reap the tremendous profits that coffee afforded.

A government survey from 1879 shows that over 25 percent of Salvadoran territory was held in communal village lands.[2] Editorials published throughout this period complained that peasants were unavailable to work as laborers for large coffee estates because they had access to land for growing their own food. This problem along with the other obstacles to " modernization" were overcome by a series of decrees passed between 1879 and 1882. Within a few years, these laws abolished communal land holdings and transformed the entire agrarian structure into one based on private property and wage labor.

Converting communal lands to the private property of individual male heads of households significantly changed the relationship of men and women to the land. The reforms severely limited women's access to the land. Many men as well as women, however, were penalized by the reforms. While peasants who had occupied or farmed communal land were supposed to receive legal title to their plots, frequently they did not. Indigenous peasants could not necessarily read the notices detailing how to make claims, and fraud, the inability to pay taxes, and debt resulted in the dislocation of many peasants from their land.[3] Hardest hit were indigenous peasants whose land was in coffee-growing territory.

Those who ended up without land were persecuted under anti-vagrancy laws. These measures required peasants without land to work a certain amount of time on large estates. While these laws had been on the books for 40 years, it wasn't until 1881 that " agricultural justices" were appointed in each village to enforce the law by keeping track of workers. Local armies, precursors to the National Guard, were set up to help enforce these policies.[4] Coffee drew El Salvador increasingly into the world market and made Salvadoran coffee workers vulnerable to fluctuations in the international price of coffee. After 1910, the United States became an important trading partner, especially after World War I. In 1922, a New York bank refinanced the Salvadoran foreign debt on the condition that repayment come directly out of customs duties. By 1931, 33 percent of Salvadoran government revenues went to service this debt.[5]

By the turn of the twentieth century, the urban economy was also expanding with small businesses, government employees, and a small industrial labor force.[6] But it was not growing at a rate sufficient to absorb the peasants who had been displaced from their land. These peasants, along with the people who had been born during a population boom that almost tripled the number of Salvadorans between 1878 and 1931, swelled the ranks of unemployed in rural and urban areas.[7] As more labor was available, wages dropped. With increasing coffee production, the cultivation of food crops decreased and food prices rose.

These pressures, along with unsatisfactory working conditions, led small groups of artisans and workers to organize urban labor unions. Unrest broke out periodically. Railroad workers struck in 1919 followed by a tailors' strike in 1920. On February 8, 1921, government troops went directly from attacking a demonstration by market women protesting monetary policies to breaking up a general strike by shoemakers.[8] The economic and social principles of modernization were not improving living conditions for most Salvadorans.

Stillborn Revolution: The *Matanza* and its Aftermath

These conditions worsened significantly during the 1929 Depression. A drastic drop in world coffee prices resulted in widespread layoffs and pay-cuts in both the private and public sectors in El Salvador. Coffee estate owners left crops rotting in the fields rather than pay workers to harvest them. When farmworkers protested, they were massacred by the National Guard which had been created in 1912 to control the rural population and protect the haciendas. [9] In response to the situation, a trade union federation, influenced by the newly established and clandestine Communist Party, organized a demonstration in San Salvador of 80,000 workers—one fifth of El Salvador's total population—on May Day 1930. [10]

In what is known as El Salvador's only free election, Arturo Araujo, was elected president in 1931 as a reform candidate. But he quickly lost popular support when he failed to keep his campaign promises. Amidst charges of corruption and financial mismanagement, Araujo was overthrown by the military at the end of 1931 and replaced by General Maximiliano Hernández Martínez. Though peasant revolts were already breaking out, particularly in coffee-growing areas of the countryside, the leaders of the Communist Party called for restraint in response to the coup. Party leaders were confident that their candidates would make significant electoral gains in the January 1932 municipal election that the military had pledged to respect. However, when it became clear that the Communists' expectations were coming true, the military reacted by suspending the elections. Party members, headed by Augustín Farabundo Martí, responded by trying to harness the spontaneous insurrectionary actions and transforming them into full-scale, organized revolt. [11]

With the collaboration of a few sympathetic members of the military, Martí and other members of the Central Committee of the Communist Party began to implement plans for a general uprising. The military discovered their plan, however, and several leaders of the revolt, including Martí, were arrested the night before the insurrection was to begin. The uprising happened anyway, though, without the coordination of the men who had called for it. Peasants armed with machetes attacked government offices and warehouses. The rebels succeeded in taking over several towns, the largest of which was Sonsonate in the heart of the country's coffee-growing region. After government troops regrouped, they took the offensive and most of the rebelling peasants were forced to pulled back to Sonzacate near the town of Izalco.[12]

Under the command of a woman known as Julia, Sonzacate became a rebel stronghold. But her 5000 troops were soon driven out by the superior firepower of two advancing army units and mowed down with machine-gun fire as they retreated.[13] An indigenous leader of the revolt, José Feliciano Amá, was captured in this retreat and publicly hanged in the plaza opposite the church in Izalco.[14] The military regained control of the country within three days and unleashed a reign of terror from which the events of this period take their name—La Matanza, The Massacre. Between 10,000 and 30,000 mostly indigenous peasants were brutally slaughtered in a matter of weeks.

The effects of La Matanza on Salvadoran politics and culture were profound and enduring. Because it was seen as an "Indian" rebellion, people were rounded up and killed solely on the basis that they appeared "Indian." Subsequently all outward signs of indigenous culture such as language, clothes, and religious practices, had to be abandoned especially by men. Because of the fear instilled in the population by the history of La Matanza, Sonsonate has been a particularly difficult region to organize, although many have carried on its proud tradition of struggle, including María Teresa Tula, who was born and raised in Izalco.[15]

General Martínez's handling of the uprising put him in good stead with both the oligarchy's agrarian faction and those interested in coffee processing and export. The emergent coalition of rebel forces, indigenous peasants, and communist trade unionists, gave the oligarchy reason enough to support a military government. Martínez remained unchallenged in office for 12 years until he began to encroach on the economic domain that the oligarchy had reserved for itself.

Martínez tried to centralize state control over economic institutions in 1942 but he failed. The anti-fascist ideology that had come into vogue when El Salvador joined the Allies in World War II provided the cement for a broad-based multi-class coalition that organized a non-violent general strike in 1944 (The "Idle Arms" strike.) While students began the strike, within days many others including teachers, secretaries, doctors, market vendors, bank officials, government employees, railroad workers, industrialists, and some members of the oligarchy shut their factories, put down their tools, failed to report to work, and demanded that Martínez step down. The coalition succeeded in ousting Martínez, but the diverse interests of the participants meant that it was short-lived; the military resumed control of the government within a year. The agro-export element of the oligarchy that had supported Martínez's ouster because he was an obstacle to the "modernization" of the economy was free to pursue their agenda.

Gender and the "Modernization" of the Salvadoran Economy

The continued "modernization" of the Salvadoran economy pursued in the years following the ouster of Martínez did little, however, to address problems that had driven the peasants and workers to rebel in 1932. Pressure on land in El Salvador continued to grow as "modernization" failed to create enough jobs to keep pace with population growth. As landlessness increased, peasant families were forced to rely more heavily on wage labor. But the combination of low wages and the part-time nature of seasonal agricultural work meant that most families continued to rely on traditional handicrafts, petty commerce, gardening on small plots, raising animals, and fishing as sources of income. While men migrated to work on plantations, women in the countryside would carry out these income-generating activities in addition to the domestic chores that rural living required. Some women also worked on coffee plantations. After the institution of a women's minimum wage in 1965 (equal to seven-ninths of that received by men), coffee-growers stopped hiring women except at harvest.[16] During harvest season, it was not uncommon for entire families to migrate temporarily to pick coffee beans. Thus women not only supplemented cash income through their subsistence activities, but also served as a reserve labor pool for the harvest.

Increased mechanization in agriculture meant fewer jobs, especially for women. Not only were women considered unsuitable for mechanized agricultural jobs, but traditional "female work" such as grinding corn by hand for tortillas was partially eliminated by electric grinding machines. As handicrafts such as pottery and handwoven hats were replaced by industrial substitutes, economic survival became more precarious for poor rural Salvadoran women. While men commonly sought temporary agricultural work or to colonize supposedly unclaimed land over the border in Honduras, women were more likely to migrate to urban areas.[17]

Many of the Salvadorans who did relocate to Honduras were displaced when the Salvadoran military attacked Honduras in the "Soccer War" of 1969. This war not only led to the expulsion of 130,000 Salvadoran peasants who had settled in Honduras, but El Salvador lost its largest market for industrial goods. Honduras closed its borders to Salvadoran products and withdrew from the Central American Common Market as a result of the war.[18] The returning peasants joined the ranks of the landless which increased from 12 percent of the population in 1961 to 41 percent by 1975.[19] Their alternative was to find employment in the already over-crowded urban sector.

According to official measures of economic activity, women's participation in the Salvadoran economy began to increase in the 1950s, and climbed rapidly in the 1960s and 1970s.[20] During that period El Salvador had one of the highest annual growth rates in Latin America. The economy grew an average of 5.6 percent per year between 1960 and 1978.[21] High coffee prices after World War II provided the Salvadoran oligarchy with profits to invest in non-agricultural sectors. Industrialization was also profitable because of the cheap cost of Salvadoran labor in the 1960s.

With the growth of the economy, Salvadoran women's official labor force participation began to change dramatically. Between 1971 and 1978, the number of economically active women more than doubled going from 252,155 to 507,042.[22] The percentage of women in the work force rose from 30.5 percent in 1978 to 37 percent in 1988. In 1990, 40 percent of Salvadoran women were estimated to be economically active. These are among the highest rates of women's official labor force participation found in Central and Latin America.[23]

Since women's increased labor force participation is usually positively correlated with their level of education, it is not surprising to find that Salvadoran women's participation in the educational system as students made slow but steady progress throughout the 1950s and 1960s, and accelerated in the 1970s. Forty-six percent of women were illiterate in 1971. By 1985, this figure was down to 30 percent.[24] Despite the cutbacks in the funding of education, women made progress at all educational levels, but particularly in the university. In 1976, women made up 34 percent of the students studying at the university level. By 1983, they represented 42 percent and in 1987, 47 percent of the student body.[25]

But these changes did not affect all Salvadoran women equally. The most striking characteristic of Salvadoran society is its extreme economic stratification. While there are no studies that measure stratification per se, a few statistics illustrate the degree of inequality that exists in Salvadoran society. In 1975, 50 percent of the total wealth of the country was controlled by just eight percent of the population. At the same time, 58 percent of the people earned no more than $9.60 per month. Less than one percent of business-owners received 60 percent of profits.[26] A 1980 study of poverty in El Salvador revealed that 68 percent of the population lived in poverty and 51 percent out of that 68 percent lived in conditions of extreme poverty.[27]

Another important factor defining the living conditions of Salvadoran women is urban or rural residency. Economic stratification in the countryside is even more pronounced than in the city. By 1971, the landholdings of six of the wealthiest families were equal to the landholdings of 80 percent of the rural population.[28] In 1980, more than 90 percent of all farms were below the minimum size needed to meet an average family's food needs.[29]

Poor women, who are part of the 57 percent of the population that lives in the countryside, spend a majority of their time engaged in subsistence tasks that enable families to live on the low wages of farmworkers. Being female limits access to land in different ways. While 70 percent of the landowners who had land taken from them under land reform were single women or women who were widowed, separated or elderly, only 10 percent of those who received titles when the land was redistributed in 1989 were women.[30] The lack of electricity and running water, especially in those regions that have been devastated by the war, assures that many hours of women's labor is devoted to carrying water, collecting firewood, and grinding corn for tortillas. Services such as health care are often not available in the countryside. Almost three quarters of the maternal deaths that occurred in the country between 1983 and 1987 were in rural areas.

Gender discrimination limits women's access to jobs in both rural and urban areas. In 1980, 76 percent of "economically active" women were in the service sector, 18.2 percent were in industry and only five percent were in agriculture.[31] These figures probably do not include the many women involved in the informal sector where it is estimated that as much as 63 percent of women's labor is located.[32] A majority of women in the so-called informal sector work watching children, cooking and selling food, and cleaning for wages. Many relocated to the city when they found diminished employment opportunities in the countryside. As real income shrunk during the 1980s, the informal market exploded drastically. The central market area in San Salvador grows each year. The rickety stalls—overwhelmingly staffed by women—line the sidewalks, obscuring the storefronts, and forcing pedestrians to walk in the streets. As the numbers of MacDonald's, Pizza Huts, and Pollo Camperos (the Central American equivalent to Kentucky Fried Chicken) have increased, so have the stalls of women selling every conceivable item that block their entrances. Workers in the informal sector are estimated to have salaries one-third of the already inadequate 1993 minimum wage of approximately $3.00 per day.

The Economic Impact of the Civil War on Women

The dramatic growth rate of the Salvadoran economy slowed significantly with the outbreak of civil war, going from an average 5.6 percent growth between 1960 and 1978 to negative 6.7 percent growth by 1982.[33] As economic growth declined, official unemployment increased from 3.65 percent in 1981 to 33 percent in 1985.[34] The feminization of unemployment occurring in El Salvador during this period was even more dramatic than the feminization of the workforce. The number of women working rose seven percent between 1980 and 1985 from 442,000 to 472,000, however, the official number of unemployed women during this same period rose 37 percent from 111,000 to 152,000. While women were 28 percent of the unemployed in 1978, by 1985, they were 54 percent.[35] Underemployment statistics are not available, but it is likely that a majority of the Salvadoran population were underemployed during the war.

As unemployment increased and the civil war raged on, international migration for economic and political reasons increased steadily starting in the late seventies.[36] By 1985, as many as 750,000 Salvadorans had left the country for Mexico, the United States, and Canada. By 1990 more than 1 million Salvadorans were outside their country. In the beginning, men made up a higher percentage of the migrants, but by the mid-1980s the number of females who had migrated exceeded the number of males.[37]

Forced to leave the country because of the political and economic situation, these migrants have been the salvation of the Salvadoran economy. The quantity of money being sent back from the United States increased 10-fold between 1980 and 1989, rising to approximately $760 million.[38] With the real purchasing power of a minimum salary in 1990 at 64.5 percent of what it was in 1980, this figure represents a significant contribution to family income. But the money sent from abroad is not going to the poorest part of the population. Usually only lower-middle-class families can afford the expense of sending a family member to the United States.[39] Households receiving money from the United States are also almost one and a half times more likely to be female-headed than those in the general population.[40] Family remittances from the United States equaled the $1.5 million per day in aid that the U.S. government sent to the Salvadoran government during the war.[41]

While male migration accounted in part for the feminization of the Salvadoran workforce, it was not the only drain on the male population during the 1980s. The civil war pulled large numbers of men into the military of both government and guerrilla forces. The Salvadoran armed forces increased from 7,000 in 1977 to over 51,000 in 1985. The FMLN is estimated to have had between 10,000 and 20,000 troops during the course of the war.[42] While many women participated in the guerrilla forces and made up a large percentage of their "rear guard," combatants were primarily male. In addition, men made up the majority of the 80,000 killed and 8,000 disappeared.

This drain on the male population not only transformed the workforce, but also affected family structures. While female heads of households were not a new development in El Salvador, the war forced women to bear an even heavier burden within the family. Before the war, men were absent from the home because they had migrated to find work. The constant search for work clearly strained the ties that men had with their families. However, until the intensification of political repression, these kinds of extended absences did not necessarily imply that male family members would never return. But with the rising masculine mortality rate, high rates of male emigration to the United States, and growth of the guerrilla forces and army, the absence of males in the household became more permanent by the 1980s. In 1978, 26 percent of women were reported as heads of households. By 1989, the figure had almost doubled to 51 percent.[43] As women have had to take on more responsibility for maintaining their children alone, they are bearing the invisible costs of the war and the economic adjustment that has accompanied it.

In the 1990s, many more Salvadoran children are being raised in poverty than before the war began. By 1989, 80 percent of Salvadoran families were living in poverty.[44] In 1988, more than half of the urban families living in extreme poverty had no running water, one third lived in dirt floor shacks and close to half were in overcrowded conditions.[45] Shantytowns are scattered throughout San Salvador located on whatever vacant lot or riverbank can be claimed. The residents of the *champas* (shacks made from cardboard or other previously discarded materials) may be peasants who fled the countryside because of the war or *damnificados* (victims of the 1986 earthquake who never recovered from their losses).

These types of living conditions result in significant health problems. While the infant mortality rate has decreased at a rate of three percent per year in the 1980s, it is still high: 60 out of 1000 live births. The maternal mortality rate, 140 to 200 out of 100,000 live births, is one of the highest in Latin America.[46] El Salvador has only one public maternity hospital. Because of the risks associated with maternity, women are more sensitive to the deterioration of the health system that has accompanied the war. Thirty percent of the Salvadoran hospital beds were destroyed between 1981 and 1987.[47] In addition, the percentage of the national budget for health care has declined steadily from 10 percent in 1978 to seven and a half percent in 1987. Defense spending rose dramatically during this period. In 1980, defense spending was nine percent of the budget; by 1986, it was 25 percent.[48]

The reallocation of resources in El Salvador brought on by the civil war added to women's already heavy burden. While women's level of economic activity expanded, their responsibilities within their families multiplied as a result of the increased absence of men. For all mothers, but especially those raising children alone, carrying out those roles was harder with the deteriorating economic situation and its accompanying crisis in health and education. Nonetheless it was the vital contribution of many of these very same women, like María Teresa Tula, that challenged the conditions that created the crisis in El Salvador and without whose participation, change would not have been possible. What is perhaps most amazing about Salvadoran women is that in the midst of the economic and emotional havoc of the war, they were able to create one of the strongest networks of grassroots organizations found in Latin America.

Notes

1. David Browning, *El Salvador: Landscape and Society* (Oxford: Clarendon Press, 197), 171.

2. Jenny Pearce, *Promised Land: Peasant Rebellion in Chalatenango El Salvador* (London: Latin American Bureau, 1985), 20

3. Browning, *El Salvador*, 217.

4. Browning, *El Salvador*, 217 and Pearce, *Promised Land*, 21

5. Patricia Parkman, *Nonviolent Insurrection in El Salvador* (Tucson: The University of Arizona Press, 1988), 15.

6. Parkman, *Nonviolent Insurrection in El Salvador*, 10-14.

7. Browning, *El Salvador*, 171.

8. Roque Dalton, *Miguel Mármol: Los sucesos de 1932 en El Salvador* (San Jose, Costa Rica: EDUCA, 1982), 96-97.

9. Dalton, *Miguel Mármol*, 224 and Pearce, *Promised Land*, 82.

10. CAMINO (Central America Information Office), *El Salvador: Background to the Crisis* (Cambridge: CAMINO, 1982), 13.

11. Dalton, *Miguel Mármol*, 223-240.

12. Thomas Anderson, *Matanza: El Salvador's First Communist Revolt of 1932* (Lincoln: University of Nebraska Press, 1971), 120.

13. Anderson, *Matanza*, 124.

14. CAMINO, *El Salvador*, 33.

15. Phillip Berryman, *The Religious Roots of Rebellion: Christians in Central American Revolution* (Maryknoll, NY: Orbis Books, 1984), 95.

16. CAMINO, *El Salvador*, 50.

17. Isabel Nieves, "Household Arrangements and Multiple Jobs in San Salvador," *Signs: A Journal of Women in Culture and Society* 5,1 (Spring 1979):139 and Alastair White, *El Salvador* (London: E. Benn, 1973), 146.

18. Anderson, *Matanza*, 141.

19. Martin Diskin and Kenneth Sharpe, *The Impact of U.S. Policy in El Salvador, 1979-1985* (Berkeley, CA: Institute of International Studies, 1985), 5.

20. Ana Isabel García and Enrique Gomariz, eds., *Mujeres centroamericanas, Vol 1* (San Jose, Costa Rica: FLACSO, 1989), and Emma Esther Castro de Pinzón, "Informe final sobre la situación de la mujer campesina frente a la legislación" (San Salvador: Organización de las Naciónes Unidas para la Agricultura y la Alimentación, 1989), 14.

21. United Nations, *Statistical Yearbook for Latin America and the Caribbean* (New York: United Nations, 1991), 70.

22. María de la Paz Muñoz Guardado, "La mujer y el trabajo en la industria manufacturera-Sector San Salvador, Periodo: 1984-1988," Thesis for Licenciatura in Sociology. (University of Central America-Jose Simeon Cañas, San Salvador, 1989),89.

23. García, *Mujeres centroamericanas*, 24.

24. García, *Mujeres centroamericanas*, 122.

25. García, *Mujeres centroamericanas*, 180 and Castro de Pinzón, "Informe sobre la situación de la mujer campesina," 14.

26. Tom Barry, *Roots of Rebellion: Land and Hunger in Central America* (Boston: South End Press, 1987), 56.

27. García, *Mujeres centroamericanas*, 108.

28. Harold Jung, "Class Struggle and Civil War in El Salvador," in *El Salvador: Central American in the New Cold War*, Martin Gettleman et al. eds., (New York: Grove, 1981), 65.

29. CAMINO, *El Salvador*, 40.

30. Castro de Pinzón, "Informe final sobre la situación de la mujer campesina," 86-87.

31. Interamerican Development Bank, *Economic and Social Progress in Latin America* (Washington, D.C.: Inter-American Development Bank, 1990), 224.

32. Castro de Pinzón, "Informe final sobre la situación de la mujer campesina," 17.

33. United Nations, *Statistical Yearbook*, 70.

34. United Nations, *Statistical Yearbook*, 11.

35. García, *Mujeres centroamericanas*, 120.

36. William Deane Stanley "Economic Migrants or Refugees from Violence? A Time-Series Analysis of Salvadoran Migration to the United States," *Latin America Research Review* 23,1 (Spring 1987):135.

37. García, *Mujeres centroamericanas*, 114.

38. CEPAL (Comisión Económica para América Latina y el Caribe) "Remesas y economia familiar en El Salvador, Guatemala, y Nicaragua."(United Nations, Santiago, Chile, CEPAL, 1991), 12.

39. CEPAL, "Remesas y economia familiar," 20.

40. CEPAL, "Remesas y economia familiar," 19.

41. CEPAL, "Remesas y economia familiar," 19.

42. García, *Mujeres centroamericanas*, 115.

43. Castro de Pinzón, "Informe final sobre la situación de la mujer campesina," 10.

44. García, *Mujeres centroamericanas*, 108.

45. UNICEF, " Análisis de la situación actual de la mujer en El Salvador" (San Salvador: Unicef, 1991), 60.

46. UNICEF, " Análisis de la situación actual de la mujer," 3.

47. García, *Mujeres centroamericanas*, 128.

48. García, *Mujeres centroamericanas*, 128.

CHAPTER 16

MARÍA'S COMPAÑERAS

WOMEN'S GRASSROOTS ORGANIZING IN

EL SALVADOR, 1970-1991.*

Introduction

Of all the Central American countries, El Salvador has provided perhaps the most complex terrain for women's struggles. Beginning with the re-emergence of popular organizations and the FMLN's armed struggle in the late 1970s, Salvadoran women have achieved an impressive track record in organizing. While many were initially mobilized to organize around survival issues or class struggle in the 1970s, over 15 years of experience within mixed movements and organizations has resulted in a wide range of women's or women-dominated organizations that deal with gender-specific concerns. Women's economic struggles as wives and mothers, their health concerns, rape, battering, and legislative discrimination are now a part of the Salvadoran political spectrum, thanks to the relentless persistence of women activists.[1]

* The author gratefully acknowledges the collaboration of the following women whose willingness to be interviewed and to share their insights were critical in writing this chapter: Gudelia Abrego, Cecilia Masín, Pasita Rosales, Susana Rodríguez, Gloria Castañeda, Margarita Jímenez, Alba América Guirola Zelaya, Mercedes Cañas, Alicia Panameño de García, Sofía Escamillas, and Oralia de Rivas. Interviews were carried out in September 1991. Some of these

While this chapter is not a comprehensive guide, it does provide a context for understanding women's grassroots organizing in El Salvador during the past 25 years. I will look at a sampling of organizations that have emerged since the 1970s and ask several questions about the fundamental strategic and political issues they face.

- What are gender ideologies found in women's grassroots movements and how do they compete with and contradict one another?
- How have these ideologies, especially feminism, been adapted by working-class and poor women to fit their own life situations?
- What strategies of growth and change have Salvadoran women's organizations had in recent years?
- How have women's organizations influenced larger movements and organizations such as human rights groups, labor unions, and political parties?

Before moving on to address these specific questions, let's look at some of the background to women's organizing.

Many political analysts believe that the 1970s marked the breakdown of El Salvador's political order with widespread electoral fraud, extreme repression, and human rights violations.[2] The 1970s was also characterized by a resurgence of popular organizations—community-based, peasant, student, urban poor, and labor unions—which responded to a faltering economy and army repression by increasing their demands and public presence. The obvious electoral fraud of 1972 in which Napoleon

women no longer work with the organizations they were associated with at the time of the interviews. Organizations included in interviews in 1991 were Centro de Estudios de la Mujer "Norma Virginia Guirola de Herrera" (CEMUJER), Asociación de Mujeres Salvadoreñas (AMS), Comité de Madres y Familiares de Presos Políticos, Detenidos, y Asasinados de El Salvador "Monseñor Romero" (CO-MADRES), Instituto Para Investigación, Capacitación, y Desarrollo de la Mujer (IMU), Asociación de Mujeres Salvadoreñas (ADEMUSA), Comité Femenino de la Federación Nacional de Trabajadores Salvadoreños (CO-FENESTRAS), Mujeres por La Dignidad y La Vida, Rompamos el Silencio (DIGNAS), Comité Femenino de la Unión de Desplazados de El Salvador (COFEUNADES), Coordinadora Nacional de la Mujer Salvadoreña (CONAMUS), and Mujeres Universitarias de El Salvador (MUES).

Duarte and Guillermo Ungo were robbed of a clear victory, beaten, and exiled, called into question the process for achieving democracy in El Salvador.[3]

During the 1970s, the armed left also began to emerge in El Salvador. Three important guerrilla groups (FPL-FM, ERP, and FARN) dedicated to achieving profound socio-economic and political transformations were formed in the first half of the decade.* PCS (Partido Comunista Salvadoreño, Salvadoran Communist Party), founded in 1930 and banned in 1932, did not support armed resistance until 1980. Another small armed group, PRTC (Partido Revolucionario de Trabajadores Centroamericanos, Revolutionary Party of Central American Workers), was formed in 1979. In 1980, a coalition of the four guerrilla groups and the Salvadoran Communist Party formed the FMLN (Frente Farabundo Martí para la Liberación Nacional, Farabundo Martí National Liberation Front). Meanwhile, all mass organizations opposed to the government united under the name FDR (Frente Democrático Revolucionario, Democratic Revolutionary Front). It recognized and supported the FMLN, the joint military command of the insurrection.[4] After the FDR dissolved in 1988, its political functions were filled by the Convergencia Democrática, Democratic Convergence, incorporating three center-left parties. The emergence of the National Committee for Permanent Debate in 1988, which joined together over 100 popular organizations, has also played an important political role in recent years. Since the signing of the Peace Accords in January 1992, the FMLN has become a legal political party and ran candidates in the 1994 elections for president, legislature, and local municipal posts in conjunction with the Democratic Convergence. Grassroots electoral work was a political priority in 1993 and 1994.

The popular church was also an important political actor during the 1970s. In response to the 1968 Bishops' Conference in Medellín, the progressive Salvadoran Catholic Church began to define poverty and

---

*   The FPL-FM (Fuerzas Populares de Liberación-Farabundo Martí, Popular Forces of Liberation "Farabundo Martí") was formed in 1970 from a radical wing of the Salvadoran Communist Party; the ERP (Ejercito Revolucionario del Pueblo, the People's Revolutionary Army) was formed in 1971 by dissident christian democrats and other leftists; and FARN (Fuerzas Armadas de Resistencia Nacional, the Armed Forces of National Resistance) was formed in 1975 from a faction of the ERP.

oppression of the masses as a sin, "the most profound contradiction to Christian faith."[5] The organization of hundreds of Christian base communities that discussed and organized around the problems of poverty in relation to biblical teaching politicized both the rural and the urban poor. Priests, along with peasant leaders, union leaders, and others labeled "subversives," were arrested, tortured, and disappeared.

Without a doubt, one of the foundations of women's organizing and political experience in El Salvador is the popular church philosophy of liberation theology. It is here that women found their participation was not only welcomed, but encouraged. The popular church also offered women some of their first institutionalized leadership roles by naming them "delegates of the word." Much of their political experience came through their participation in Christian base communities in both rural and urban areas.

In 1969, a group of European priests began setting up ecclesiastic communities in the slums of San Salvador. The communities grew over the next 10 years, but by the end of the 1970s, persecution had become so severe that the priests were obliged to leave the capital.[6] Women were deeply involved in these communities and many remember them as the source of their political activism. Alicia Panameño de García, one of the founding members of CO-MADRES, remembers the Christian base communities of Zacamil (a poor neighborhood of San Salvador) as the first place she questioned gender relations within the family.

> A lot of families didn't have very good internal relations. In the Christian communities we talked a lot about the participation of everyone—husbands, wives, and children—in family decisions and about sharing costs. We received a kind of social education in a different way of living. And a lot of mothers in CO-MADRES came out of these communities. A lot of their children were cooperativists and catequists who were captured or assassinated for this work. CO-MADRES was very much a part of these communities.

Because of the severe repression against Christian base communities, many women first became politicized around human rights issues. In the Zacamil Christian base communities, over 600 people have been murdered since their formation.[7]

Christian base communities and organizations also proliferated in the liberated zones controlled by the FMLN and in Honduran refugee camps during the 1980s. Here, women acted as lay religious practitioners who could do everything a priest did except administer confession, communion, baptism, and marriage. As so-called " delegates of the word," these women carried out weekly celebrations and acted as councilors and deacons. The concept of the delegate not only facilitates the growth of the church by incorporating more leaders into it, but also diffuses the power of priests in the Catholic hierarchy. For women, standing up in front of their communities in public leadership roles was an important step toward political activism. According to staff in refugee camps in Honduras, women made up over 60 percent of the delegates of the word in camps such as in Colomoncagua which had 8,500 residents at its peak in the mid-1980s.* Women took on active leadership roles in camp organizational structure and in some cases transferred this leadership to repopulated communities. Their first experiences as leaders in the popular church were critical in this process.

In eastern El Salvador, many of the founders of AMS (Asociación de Mujeres Salvadoreñas, Salvadoran Women's Association) an organization of peasant women from Morazán, San Miguel, San Vicente, and Usulután began their political work in Christian mother's groups. From these groups, they went on to assume leadership roles in the church and to form a women's organization. Ultimately, they separated from the church because they felt their demands were limited by biblical interpretations.

In addition, Christian base communities' educational programs promoted egalitarian relations within the family.[8] Later in the 1980s, urban and rural trade unions also began to encourage women's participation, often at the urging of popular church officials. When a second wave of women's organizations surfaced in the mid-1980s, many of them had received their political baptism and training through work with the church.

---

* Personal communication, Sara Shannon, January 1992.

Patterns in the Development of Women's Organizations

From the mid-1970s through the early 1990s, Salvadoran women's organizing can be divided into three distinct periods. First, following the creation of the revolutionary parties in the late 1970s, a few affiliated women's organizations were formed. Women's active participation in Christian base communities is associated with this period as well. Women also emerged as important activists in the arena of human rights. Second, following a period of severe repression from 1979 to 1981 when all popular organizations went underground, another wave of women's organizations emerged in the mid-1980s, coinciding with a general resurfacing and restructuring of the popular movement. Third, in the late 1980s and early 1990s, a small women's movement began to emerge and several organizations took on a more explicitly feminist agenda, which had not been possible earlier.

The 1970s was marked by the formation of several significant organizations in El Salvador. AMPES (Asociación de Mujeres Progresistas de El Salvador, the Association of Progressive Women of El Salvador) was founded in 1975. AMPES originally focused on women workers and collaborated closely with trade unions. In 1978, when CUTS (Confederación Unitaria de Trabajadores Salvadoreños, United Confederation of Salvadoran Workers) was formed, it established a Department of Women's Affairs that terminated the need for AMPES as a separate organization.[9] In 1978, the CUTS offices were bombed and many women who worked with AMPES moved out to the liberated zones. In 1981, AMPES was refounded, but in an FMLN-controlled zone.

AMES (Asociación de Mujeres de El Salvador, the Association of Women of El Salvador), founded in 1979, was one of the largest Salvadoran women's organizations formed during the 1970s.* Its initial work was directed toward women in the informal sector, called "marginadas," such as market vendors, maids, and urban slum-dwellers. Both AMES and AMPES had to go underground from 1979-1981. They resurfaced in the early 1980s, but eventually disbanded.

---

* AMES is often confused with AMS, founded in 1987. They are two different organizations.

Women were also active during the 1970s in the area of human rights. Formed principally by women but including some other family members, CO-MADRES was one of the few popular organizations that continued functioning openly throughout the 1970s and 1980s. It is perhaps the oldest and longest surviving organization of women in recent Salvadoran history. (See the Introduction for more on the history of CO-MADRES.)

In the mid-1980s, popular organizations, including those made up of women, began to re-emerge. This was probably due to pressure on then President Napoleon Duarte to appear as a tolerant "centrist," as well as to the fact that popular organizations had to come out from underground in order to grow and gather strength. The public CO-MADRES demonstrations and the highly visible repopulated communities were important in opening up political space for other groups in the mid-1980s. During this period, a number of significant women's groups were formed.

Founded in 1986 by a well known Salvadoran feminist, IMU (Instituto para la Investigación, Capacitación, y Desarrollo de la Mujer; Institute for Research, Training, and Development of Women) initially functioned as a non-governmental organization (NGO), providing support to grassroots women's organizations in the areas of communication, legal rights, and education. They modeled their programs on the educational ideology of Paulo Freire, actively involving people in their own education. In 1989, IMU's offices were broken into. Shortly thereafter, the director, Norma Virginia Guirola de Herrera, was assassinated. IMU is currently housed in a residential home purchased with international solidarity money. In 1990 and 1991, it began to develop its own organizational projects, primarily with urban women, rather than only supporting other organizations.

In 1990, family members of Guirola de Herrera established a center in her memory now known as CEMUJER (Centro de Estudios de la Mujer, "Norma Virginia Guirola de Herrera," Center for Women's Studies, "Norma Virginia Guirola de Herrera"). Never tentative about its feminist leanings, CEMUJER has always been clear about its agenda to improve conditions for Salvadoran women. The Center provides technical assistance and training for grassroots organizations and has also done important legal work in reforming the Salvadoran family code to improve women's rights. Rape law was an area of particular interest to the Center.

One of the first groups to identify itself as feminist emerged in 1986. During its first two years, CONAMUS (Coodinadora Nacional de Mujeres Salvadoreñas, National Coordinating Committee of Salvadoran Women) was primarily an educational and informational clearinghouse for other organizations. In 1987, they began to create their own bases of organization working primarily with women in the marginal zones of San Salvador. In 1988, CONAMUS opened a health clinic for women, the only one in the city. Through their experience in the clinic, organizers realized that there was a need for further programming and facilities to deal with violence against women. In 1989, CONAMUS opened El Salvador's first battered women's shelter. They have continued to work with other groups on issues of battering, sexuality, health, and economics.

In the labor sector, FENASTRAS (Federación Nacional de Trabajadores Salvadoreños, Salvadoran National Worker's Federation) began working with women factory workers as early as 1981, particularly in the textile industry, which primarily employed women. In 1986, a women's committee—CO-FENASTRAS (Comité Femenino, Women's Committee of FENASTRAS)—was created to provide popular education for its 5,000 women members. Their projects included opening a child care center and medical clinics, providing strike support for women workers, countering domestic violence, and denouncing human rights violations. In 1991, there were seven other women's committees within unions affiliated with FENASTRAS.

In the countryside, AMS (Asociación de Mujeres Salvadoreñas, Salvadoran Women's Association) was founded in 1987 at the initiative of several religiously based women's committees in the eastern part of El Salvador and Christian mothers' committees in the north of Morazán and San Miguel. Rural women found they were unable to farm due to the fact that their fields were constantly under military attack, and they wanted to move beyond the passive stance of the church and begin actively protesting their dire economic situation. By 1988, AMS had organized over 4,000 women in 43 rural communities.[10] Recent projects include economic self-sufficiency programs in the countryside such as sewing cooperatives, health workshops for mothers and infants, and education on sexuality and family life.

During the 1980s, these organizations suffered repeated break-ins, arrests, detention, tortures, and disappearances of their leaders. Beyond this external repression, they have also had ideological and organizational conflicts with the political parties they work with. While founded specifically to integrate women into revolutionary party structures and their supporting organizations (peasant federations, labor unions, student organizations, teachers unions, and urban shantytown associations), the ability of women's organizations to be autonomous and participate in coalitions was often constrained because of competition between parties and a prioritization of class struggle over women's oppression.

The period from 1989 to 1991 was marked by a revitalization of women's organizations after the FMLN's November 1989 offensive. While many women's groups were harassed, had their offices destroyed and leaders detained during and after the offensive, they have since recovered and suffered fewer setbacks. One of the most outspoken new women's organizations emerged in 1990. DIGNAS (Mujeres por la Dignidad y la Vida "Rompamos el Silencio," Women for Dignity and Life "We are Breaking the Silence") worked to consolidate women's organizations from various sectors and parts of the country into one movement. DIGNAS functions as both a support organization to existing women's groups through providing training, education, and skills exchanges and as a grassroots organization. They were one of the first groups to organize workshops focused exclusively on gender. They also have their own community organizing projects located primarily in rural areas, which include community bakeries, egg hatcheries, community stores, clinics, and day care centers. DIGNAS has had contact with other Latin American feminist organizations and have brought organizers from Mexico and Nicaragua to conduct gender workshops in El Salvador. In 1993 they were one of the key players in trying to orchestrate a broader political coalition of women's groups.

In 1991, over 100 women's organizations existed at the local, regional, and national level in El Salvador, many of them organized into larger coalitions. The factionalism and vertical control that once was prevalent in many popular organizations is being challenged by women's efforts to achieve political autonomy and to democratize their organizations. While discussions of how to democratize popular organizations and parties are occurring in many sectors in El Salvador, women's organizations appear to be taking a leading role in this process as they seek to establish their independence in the political future of El Salvador. For women, this often means confronting the men they work with in larger mixed organizations and in political parties about altering the political culture of the popular movement. In 1991, the "Concertación de Mujeres" (Women's Coalition) was formed. It included women's groups from a variety of parties and sectors that had not previously worked together in a sustained manner.

The Role of Feminism and Marxism

Many Salvadoran women have been taught that feminism is equivalent to man-hating, lesbianism, and bourgeois mentality. While these stereotypes have inhibited women from using the term to identify themselves, there have been a number of counter-influences, including international exposure at women's meetings and support, education, and training offered by non-governmental organizations, some of them from outside of El Salvador. While many supporting NGOs for women's movements and organizations are reluctant to call themselves feminists, much of the material they teach with and disseminate suggests that male and female gender roles should be more equal.

Some women's organizations in El Salvador such as CEMUJER, and DIGNAS use explicitly feminist terminology in current popular education work. Gloria Castañeda de Zamora, one of DIGNAS' foremost spokeswomen, is an example of someone who has, over time, made integrating women's concerns into the popular movement a primary concern.

> When I first heard the word feminism, it was like speaking about the devil. I didn't know what it was about, but they had told me that it was bad... Now we have been learning that there are different currents of feminism and that feminism is simply the revindication of women... It's still very hard for us women to have the ability to speak openly about ourselves. It's a process. There are still a lot of individual interests, political interests, party interests...One of the objectives we have is to incorporate the perspective of gender into the popular movement, into the project of revolutionary democracy.

IMU, which has conducted support work and training for other organizations such as the labor-based CO-FENASTRAS and ADEMUSA, has also begun to use feminist terminology in its education work. IMU's training programs were originally focused primarily on economic issues related to women's responsibilities as wives, daughters, and mothers. However, as María Teresa Tula testified, simply participating in organizations is enough to produce a difficult domestic situation for women in El Salvador. As women become more involved in activities such as workshops, demonstrations, and meetings, they often cannot fulfill their duties as full-time domestic workers. They frequently have to ask their husbands and families to begin taking on some household responsibilities. Attempts to even slightly alter the traditional division of labor within the household can result in strong reactions from men and other women as well, such as mothers-in-law. Nora García discussed the evolving role of gender issues and feminism in IMU organizing in 1991.

> When women began to participate in organizing they usually had to fight their husbands at home. Men are terrified of losing power at home, which they will. The resistance is natural, they will lose a lot... While we didn't initially, now we talk about gender issues, about feminism. When we say the word feminism, men say that we are lesbians and prostitutes. Eight years ago you couldn't even say the word feminism. Now it's beginning to be discussed...People shouldn't be afraid of it. At the beginning we couldn't call ourselves feminists because the concept didn't have any meaning for us. But now that we have clarified the concept and given it our own content, we can use it.

Organizers from IMU, CEMUJER, DIGNAS, and other organizations have attended a variety of international women's and explicitly feminist meetings as well as inviting feminist organizers to give workshops for grassroots organizations they support. Brazilian organizers have come to IMU to give courses on women and culture in which domestic violence, unequal divisions of child care between men and women, and the marginalization of women in leftist organizations. IMU, CO-FENASTRAS, and ADEMUSA representatives attended the Sixth Latin American and Caribbean Feminist Conference held in Argentina in 1991. DIGNAS has sponsored workshops with Mexican activists on sexuality, women, and democracy, and on the recent experience of the national women's association in Nicaragua. Women interviewed in several organizations in 1991 were extremely impressed by this workshop on Nicaragua, and were busy discussing ways that women's organizations in El Salvador could avoid being marginalized in the formal political process if a settlement were reached between the government and the FMLN. Many Salvadoran women's groups prepared for and participated in the Seventh Latin American and Caribbean Feminist Conference held in El Salvador in October 1993.

While feminists in grassroots organizations have garnered some support from NGOs, they still face formidable challenges from the men they work with in larger organizations and political parties. In many cases, the discussion boils down to the prioritization of class conflict over all others. Gloria Castañeda de Zamora of DIGNAS says of her efforts to discuss women's oppression with men:

> The men say, yes, we understand what you are trying to do. Everything you say is true about inequality. But this is for later. When the contradictions of class have been resolved then all of the problems of women's subordination will also be resolved at the same time.

Many women activists also find it difficult to initiate and continue their work under pressure from male colleagues. Mercedes Cañas, a young activist with CONAMUS who staffed the only battered women's shelter in El Salvador in 1991, stated:

> It is very hard to be an activist in two sectors simultaneously, which is what a lot of women had to do to maintain their political credibility. You have to meet the responsibilities of participating in a larger popular organization and in a women's organization as well. A lot of male leaders pressure women not to work with women and to keep working for the larger organization such as a labor union or a cooperative.

Key Issues for Grassroots Feminists: Women's Work and Violence

In El Salvador, the fact that women came into their own organizations largely from organizations and parties built on class-based concerns is reflected in the trajectory of their political agendas and programs. Many women's organizations that began working with poor urban and rural populations focused on recognizing women's productive contributions and creating small economic projects that would contribute to household income and subsistence. These organizations also protested military repression. While CONAMUS was one of the first women's organizations to deal with health and reproduction, their earlier campaigns also focused heavily on women's involvement in productive labor and the "double shift" of Salvadoran women. A 1988 educational brochure describes the double day for women:

> Society expects that after a tiring day as a wage worker, women will return to their homes to carry out their domestic chores and meet their obligations as mothers and wives. In other words, besides contributing to family income, they should administer household money so that it sufficiently covers household necessities and beyond this they should provide affection, understanding and a clean and healthy environment. [11]

Other grassroots organizations such as AMS produced bulletins in 1988 and early 1989, emphasizing the need for women to organize around survival issues such as hunger, and the need for housing, electricity, social services, and education. Their focus is on mobilizing women to support general demands of survival and human rights, not gender-specific issues. [12] For example, in 1991 AMS organized a series of productive projects such as sewing cooperatives, which will help generate income for women.

Violence against women—everything from battering to rape at the hands of the military—has become a greater priority for women's organizations in El Salvador. Many of these issues came to light in the context of the civil war, particularly rape—a form of torture used by the military against a majority of its female prisoners. While this has been common knowledge among activists for the past 10 years, the issue has only recently been openly discussed in a systematic manner. Says Alicia Panameño de García, a founding member of CO-MADRES who was herself raped:

> In 1980 and 1981 when the death squads publicly surfaced, they began to systematically implement raping women who

were considered to be subversives. There were old women, young women who were raped. Here in El Salvador there isn't one woman who has been captured and detained who hasn't been raped. This is psychologically very difficult for women. And our own culture here still requires women to be virgins when they are married...some of this has changed in Christian base communities as sexuality was discussed. Some of these ideas have entered our work as well, in education about sexuality.

Through their denunciations of torture and detention, CO-MADRES and other human rights groups composed primarily of women raised the issue of rape for public discussion. This has benefitted women who are now beginning to question legal codes that give rape victims no rights. It has also brought out the issue of men who were raped while under military detention but are even more reluctant to talk about it than women. Says Alicia Panameño de García of CO-MADRES:

> We began to realize that it wasn't just women who were raped by the military. It was happening to men too. First we saw it with one boy who had been badly beaten. Then when I worked in the hospital there were a lot of boys who arrived, many of whom had been raped. It was happening to men too. It was a form of torture used to lower people's morale, men and women...The men would never talk about it. We just knew because we were nurses. I had to take care of them.

Denunciations of rape as a military tactic have expanded into discussions of women's general lack of control over their sexuality. For example, many CO-MADRES members report that they have never felt sexual pleasure, or discussed sexual relationships or their own rapes. Alicia describes how some women "have many children and they [still] have never felt satisfied in a sexual relationship. The man just arrived, did what he wanted, and then left... At first it was difficult for some women to talk about this. They were very embarrassed... But some of them discovered that it was good to talk about it because it's part of nature."

Meanwhile, CONAMUS learned through its experience opening a health clinic that women had other problems at home. According to Mercedes Cañas, "Women would come to our clinic with bruises from being beaten. We didn't have anything to offer them except the clinic. We discovered that we needed more so we created the shelter." Getting men within mixed grassroots organizations to take domestic violence seriously has been a major problem for women in CONAMUS and other organizations. Cañas stated,

> Men within the popular movement like their privileges as men. There is plenty of marital violence on the left. We can't take people from the left to jail or try to deal with them in the court system. We can't collaborate with the police. It requires a lot of work.

Women from CO-FENASTRAS reported similar situations within their own labor federation where women activists were victims of domestic violence by their male partners who were also union leaders.

Strategies for Growth and Change

1991 in El Salvador was punctuated by a contradictory reality that profoundly influenced women's organizations. The entire country was talking of possible peace settlements between the Cristiani government and the FMLN while the army intensified its counter-insurgency war in the countryside trying to shrink the territory controlled by the FMLN. As the army sought to undercut the geographic control of the FMLN, popular organizations developed organizing strategies for broadening their political constituencies. Their strategy was timely. At the stroke of midnight on December 31, 1991, a formal peace accord was reached between President Alfredo Cristiani and the FMLN setting the scene for a permanent cease fire, a restructuring of the military and national police, and widespread participation in the formal political arena.

Women's organizations played a key role in reaching out to new sectors of the population. Peasant-based organizations such as AMS were beginning projects in the urban shantytowns of El Salvador, San Salvador-based CO-MADRES was beginning community projects in the countryside, and educational organizations such as IMU were taking on a grassroots character. CO-MADRES, for example, had 49 different groups organized in a wide range of urban and rural communities in 1991. The programs involve groups of four to five activists whose job it is to educate and train more rural organizers. By maintaining organizers in a wide range of communities, CO-MADRES hopes to maintain its highly visible human rights work.

During this period, women's organizations were not only trying to increase their constituencies so that they could better influence the formal electoral process in 1994, they were also broadening their basis for claiming autonomy from their affiliate organizations. The larger their constituencies, the more political clout they were likely to have within the general popular movement. Their increased autonomy might also allow them to address issues of movement democracy. As Gloria Castañeda de Zamora from Mujeres Para La Dignidad y La Vida recounts,

> Some of us participate in other political organizations. We proposed democratic elections for determining representation in these organizations and they told us to get lost. They didn't listen to our proposals. That was at the beginning of this year. One compañero told us that "democracy comes from top to bottom." This felt like a contradiction to us. It was a very vertical way of thinking and also paternalistic and patriarchal—the idea that power comes top to bottom, from the father to son. That isn't democracy...So we decided to try and work on the issue of democracy and power and control within our own movement, the women's movement...By asserting our own agenda, we are also making some small steps towards autonomy, determining our own agenda.

Autonomy, however, is not possible for everyone. One young organizer from CO-FENASTRAS is sure that "if the women's committee of FENASTRAS were to propose that we become autonomous from the organization, they [FENASTRAS] would throw us out."

For many women's organizations formally affiliated with mixed organizations, such as CO-FENASTRAS, the best political strategy is to strengthen their numbers from within in order to wield political force within the larger organizations. Preparation for participation in a more open political system requires women's groups to maintain a double-edged strategy. They must continue to push political parties and mixed organizations to address their gendered demands yet also maintain a well organized constituency that is willing to back larger political platforms in exchange for concessions on women's issues.

Salvadoran Women: Beyond the "Ladies Auxiliary"

The presence of organized women in El Salvador since the 1970s has had a clear impact on popular movements. Women have emerged in positions of leadership within some of the popular organizations such as FENASTRAS (which has several women in its national leadership). They have redefined significant areas of political terrain such as human rights to include gender issues and sexuality, and are now seen by political parties as an important constituency. In San Salvador, a coalition of over 18 women's groups formed in 1991 first to celebrate International Women's Day (March 8th) and then to discuss the meaning of gender and structure a political platform for 1994. All of these changes indicate that women are taking themselves seriously as political subjects and are pushing men to do the same.

Many activists are developing a political vision that brings together gender equality with democracy, human rights, and economic justice. Women represent a major portion, if not a majority, of participants in popular organizations, particularly those in urban areas. While most leaders of mixed organizations are still men, with women's leadership confined to women's sectors or committees, their organizational presence and experience resulted in increasingly bolder demands that men seriously consider gender issues. In some organizations such as CO-MADRES, men and women have begun to participate together in workshops that deal with issues such as sexuality and marital relations. In other organizations such as AMS, men are organized simultaneously with women to facilitate their support of women's productive projects.

In order to survive the civil war in El Salvador, many people had to either organize or leave the country. Women organized for protection, to provide material and emotional support for one another, and to create basic institutional supports in the areas of health, work, and child-raising. Becoming activists and at the same time taking on larger proportions of productive work, helped women gain self-confidence and begin to use their political skills to overcome their own subordination. They are now a formidable political force, and the possibility of free elections in 1994 has opened up a whole new arena for women's organizing.

Salvadoran women's organizing in the 1990s is distinguished from that of the previous decade through the formation of broad-based coalitions such as the Concertación de Mujeres. This coalition appears to be the foundation for what could be called a Salvadoran women's movement, as opposed to the existence of individual organizations linked to popular organizations and revolutionary parties. The 18 or so member organizations of the "Concertación" prepared a platform of issues to discuss with other Central American women in a regional meeting. The articulation of the "Concertación" with similar coalitions in other Central American countries also strengthens its credibility within El Salvador. An even broader Salvadoran Coalition of women's groups, founded in 1993, brought together the Concertación with the COM (Coordinación de Organismos de Mujeres). Called Mujeres '94 (Women of 1994), it represents 34 organizations. The goal of Mujeres '94 is to provide a public space for women to participate in the political life of El Salvador and to create a platform for the 1994 elections. They held a series of open debates in 1993 on a wide range of topics including violence against women, women in the informal sector, women's place in land reform, women and ecology, sexuality, education, legal issues, and political participation. In August 1993 they published a platform that included the following points:

- an end to incest, rape, and sexual harassment;
- land, credit, and technical assistance for women;
- adequate housing with ownership for women;
- worker training, more places in the workforce, and equal salaries to men;
- stop the rising costs of basic wage goods;
- equal opportunity for girls in schools;
- coordinated medical attention for women in more and better hospitals;
- consistent sexual education and the expression of women's sexuality without prejudices;
- free and voluntary motherhood;
- responsible fatherhood and an increase in food rations;
- respect for the environment and a better quality of life for women;
- development policies that take care of women's needs;
- laws that don't discriminate against women;
- women should hold 50 percent of the positions of power.

In September 1993, the FMLN put out a proposed resolution for its first national convention that called for supporting the Platform of "Mujeres 94" and other representatives of women in social movements. In this resolution they recognized the strength shown by Salvadoran women in "the fight for peace and democratization of society expressed by their integration with the clandestine struggle, the guerrilla forces, in their work for the freedom of political prisoners, and the disappeared, in political work and in the jails, in the peasant struggle, in labor struggles and among students...without their participation we never would have gotten as far as we have." A national discussion document for a platform circulated by the FMLN in September 1993 contained the 14 points of the "Mujeres 94" platform almost verbatim. This coalition had clearly influenced the left.

Confirmation of the degree of their influence on the left and on politics in general came in October 1993 shortly before the Sixth Latin American and Caribbean Feminist Conference was to take place in Costa del Sol, El Salvador. Women from "Mujeres 94" and from other Salvadoran women's groups were part of the regional committee preparing for the arrival of 1500 women from 26 countries. The Salvadoran right began a systematic campaign to shut down the conference, claiming that all of the women coming were linked to the FMLN and they were seeking to create spaces where lesbians and homosexuals could express themselves. A new right-wing magazine called "Gente" ran a four-page expose of CISPES (Committee in Solidarity with the People of El Salvador) sponsorship of a gay and lesbian delegation to the conference and published the names, addresses, and phone numbers of all organizers involved. Hotel and restaurant owners on the Costa del Sol were threatened by phone that their establishments would be bombed and their property destroyed if they served any of the women attending the conference.[13] The regional committee denied links to the FMLN and said they could not take responsibility for the delegation sent by CISPES stating that "this is a conference for women whose sexual preference is not the defining basis for their participation.[14] Shortly before the conference, five women on the regional planning committee received death threats. Despite these difficult circumstances, the conference went forward, and over 1500 women participated.

The larger message in the threats from the right was to fracture the political effectiveness of large coalitions such as "Mujeres 94." While the

FMLN is still trying to work out internal squabbles, a wide range of women from a broad political spectrum have succeeded in remaining united. This presents an ominous political threat to the right, particularly if a significant percentage of Salvadoran women are persuaded to vote for the FMLN, which has endorsed the platform of "Mujeres 94." In late 1993, this coalition was probably the most politically unified and effective part of the FMLN electoral effort.

The embryonic discussion of democratic, participatory political culture that also begun within "Mujeres 94" and other women's groups and coalitions is beginning to be replicated within the Salvadoran left as cooperation becomes a political necessity within the context of a formal peace accord and elections. The personal and political struggle of Salvadoran women activists within the popular movement—as they have slowly achieved a significant degree of independence and autonomy since the 1970s—is an important potential source of democratic culture and decentralization of political power within Salvadoran society.

Notes

1. Similar issues are discussed in the following works on Latin American women and social movements: Sonia E. Alvarez, *Engendering Democracy in Brazil: Women's Movements in Transition Politics* (Princeton: Princeton University Press, 1990); Norma Stoltz Chinchilla, "Revolutionary Popular Feminism in Nicaragua: Articulating Class, Gender, and National Sovereignty," *Gender and Society* 4, 3 (Fall 1990): 370-397; Jane Jaquette, ed., *The Women's Movement in Latin America: Feminism and the Transition to Democracy* (Boston: Unwin Hyman, 1990); Elizabeth Jelin, ed., *Women and Social Change in Latin America*, (London: Zed Books Ltd., 1990); Themma Kaplan, "Community and Resistance in Women's Political Cultures," *Dialectical Anthropology* 15, 2-3 (Spring-Summer 1990): 259-264; Amy Conger Lind, 1992 "Power, Gender, and Development: Popular Women's Organizations and the Politics of Needs in Ecuador," in *The Making of Social Movements in Latin America: Identity, Strategy, and Democracy*, ed. Arturo Escobar and Sonia E. Alvarez (Boulder: Westview, 1992); Maxine Molyneux, "Mobilization Without Emancipation? Women's Interests, State, and Revolution," in *Transition and Development: Problems of Third World Socialism*, eds. Richard Fagen, Carmen Diana Deere, and José Luis Coraggio (New York: Monthly Review Press; Berkeley, California: Center for the Study of the Americas, 1986); June Nash and

Helen Safa, eds., *Women and Change in Latin America* (South Hadley: Bergin & Garvey Publishers, Inc, 1986); Helen Safa, "Women's Social Movements in Latin America," *Gender and Society* 4,3 (summer 1990):355-269; Lynn Stephen, "Women in Mexico's Popular Movements: Survival Strategies for Ecological and Economic Impoverishment," *Latin American Perspectives* 20,1, (Winter 1992):73-96; Lynn Stephen, "Challenging Gender Inequality: Grassroots Organizing Among Women Rural Workers in Brazil and Chile," *Critique of Anthropology* 13,1 (March, 1993):33-56.

2. Cynthia Arnson, *El Salvador: A Revolution Confronts The United States* (Washington D.C.: The Institute for Policy Studies, 1982) 15 and CAMINO (Central America Information Office), *El Salvador: Background to the Crisis* (Cambridge: CAMINO, 1982) 15.

3. Arnson, *El Salvador*, 27.

4. CAMINO, *El Salvador*, 123.

5. Phillip Berryman, "What Happened at Puebla" in *Churches and Politics in Latin America*, ed. Daniel H. Levine, (Beverly Hills: Sage Publications, 1979),84.

6. Pamela Hussey, *Free From Fear: Women in El Salvador's Church* (London: Catholic Institute for International Relations, 1989),45.

7. Hussey, *Free From Fear*, 45.

8. Marilyn Thomsen, *Women of El Salvador: the Price of Freedom* (Philadelphia: Institute for the Study of Human Issues, 1986),50.

9. Thomsen, *Women of El Salvador*, 99.

10. New Americas Press, *A Dream Compels Us: Voices of Salvadoran Women* (Boston: South End Press, 1989),76.

11. Coordinadora Nacional de la Mujer Salvadoreña (CONAMUS), "La doble jornada," Brochure (San Salvador, 1988).

12. AMS (Asociación de Mujeres Salvadoreñas) "Editorial, La mujer en acción," *Nueva Sociedad*, No. 2 (September-October, 1988); "Editorial, Hambre, miseria y opresión," *Nueva Sociedad*, No. 3 (November, December, 1988); "Editorial, La alternativa de la mujer," *Nueva Sociedad*, No. 4 (January, 1989); "Editorial, Hambre y lucha del pueblo salvadoreño," *Nueva Sociedad*, No. 5 (January, 1989); "Editorial, Mujeres participan para su desarollo," *Nueva Sociedad*, no. 13-14 (July-August, 1990); "Primer seminario de orientación económico a la problemática de la mujer," Brochure (August, 1991).

13. Sara Lovera, "Intentan cancelar en El Salvador el encuentro feminista de AL," *La Jornada* (10 October 1993), 15.

14. Lovera, "Intentan cancelar en El Salvador," 15.

María Teresa Tula and Miguel Mármol.

CHAPTER 17

THE POLITICS AND PRACTICE OF TESTIMONIAL LITERATURE

Testimonials today occupy an intermediate position between literature, the "new" ethnography in anthropology and sociology, personal narrative, and political biography. Because testimonials give voice to people whose experiences have been misrepresented or neglected they promise to convey a unique authenticity, authority, and truth. Yet testimonial creation, production, and consumption is also an inherently political process connecting a wide range of people across national, racial, ethnic, and class boundaries. What is this process actually like? What light can testimonials shed on social science, feminist theory, and political practice? What does it mean that testimonials of Latin American activists have been marketed largely to a middle-class western audience in the U.S. and Europe?

Origins of Latin American Testimonials

In the United States, testimonials have a history within Native American culture, African-American slave narratives, and family oral histories. Testimonials from Latin America have their origins in revolutionary movements. The notion of "testimony" expresses urgency, a story that must be told because of the struggles it represents. Disseminating revolutionary and opposition voices is the central mission of most testimonial publications and it is therefore not surprising that Latin American testimonials first emerged when Cuba's Casa de las Américas cultural center offered a literary prize in this genre in 1970. Other mobilizing influences have included non-fictional narrative texts in Latin American literature such as the chronicles of Bolivar and Martí, life histories used by anthropologists such as Oscar Lewis (1963), and Che Guevara's (1968) *Reminiscences of the Cuban Revolutionary War.*[1]

Salvadoran Testimonials

El Salvador's premier testimonial is Roque Dalton's *Miguel Mármol* (1982) The book covers Mármol's life story from 1905-1954.[2] Mármol died in 1993. Dalton's conviction that revelation of events after 1955 could endanger people still in El Salvador and in exile offers insight into the politics of testimonial writing that hold true not only for his work with Mármol, but for all testimonial collaborations. The introduction discusses writing testimonials as well as Miguel Mármol's political education. The book offers detailed descriptions of key events in Salvadoran history including the 1932 massacre at Izalco, the civil-military rebellion of April 1944, and the history of several Salvadoran governments. Most dramatic is Mármol's description of surviving his own execution. During the 1932 massacre, Mármol was turned in by a police informer along with other Communist Party organizers. He was briefly jailed and lined up in front of a firing squad for execution. He was fired upon several times. Left for dead because the brains of a comrade shot beside him were splattered on his head wounds, he got up and walked away. He was taken in by a group of sympathetic peasants who nursed him back to health. The theme of repeated survival against great odds so characteristic of Mármol, is found in María's story as well. She describes surviving neglect as a child, abuse by her brother, and two rounds of arrest, torture, detention, and rape.

Two other testimonials appeared in El Salvador during the 1970s, both written by leaders of the FMLN. The first, *Sequestro y capucha en un país del "mundo libre"* (1979), was written by the late Salvador Cayetano Carpio, founder of the FPL (Fuerzas Populares de Liberación-Farabundo Martí, Popular Liberation Forces), which split from the Salvadoran Communist Party in 1970. It deals primarily with Carpio's experience as a political prisoner during the 1950s.[3] In *Las cárceles clandestinas de El Salvador* (1979), Ana Guadalupe Martínez, a military leader of the ERP (Ejército Revolucionario del Pueblo, Revolutionary Army of the People), founded in 1972 by radicalized Christians and students, details her own and others' experiences as political prisoners.[4] These themes also appear in María's story with a strong focus on torture and detention, political prisoners, and work on behalf of the disappeared and assassinated.

Several recent Salvadoran testimonials also anticipate María's story. *El quinto piso de la alegría: tres años con la guerrilla* (1988) by Belgian internationalist and activist Karin Lievens, focuses on organizing peasants, life in guerrilla camps, and down-to-earth activism.[5] So too does Claribel Alegría's *No me agarrán viva: La mujer salvadoreña en la lucha* (1983).[6] The story of a guerrilla comandante, Eugenia, *No me agarrán viva* focuses on the personal and ideological transformation of a guerrilla commander. *Nunca estuve sola* (1986) by Nidia Díaz, a leader of the PRTC (Partido Revolucionario de los Trabajadores Centroamericanos, Central American Workers Revolutionary Party), formed in 1979, focuses on guerrilla life.[7]

Testimonials and Feminism

María's story also illustrates how closely Latin American women's testimonials are linked with feminist theory and method. In the stories of Rigoberta Menchú (1984), Domitila Barrios (1978), and Elvia Alvarado (1987) (only a few of the women's testimonials produced during the 1970s and 1980s, but available in English) the gendered perspective of their authors is revealed through a collective voice that speaks for a plural subject: woman, peasant/worker, indigenous/mestiza/ladina, Latin American, and political activist.[8] Their stories also emphasize women's roles in political organizing, home life, and forms of repressions and torture; a motivation for political activism through female experiences as daughters, wives, and mothers; and in the case of Alvarado, an awareness of women's oppression and discussion of machismo.

Women's testimonials integrate the personal with the political. Narratives typically begin with female socialization as girls and young women, and stories of their family and marital relationships are treated as an intimate part of their political experience. They do not usually begin from the viewpoint of a political party, revolutionary movement, or specific grassroots organization, but from their own personal history. María's story begins this way as well: through the detention and assassination of her husband, a trade union activist, María first becomes politically involved. The political impetus for her and others in CO-MADRES is the disappearance, detention, or assassination of a family member, usually defined through a relationship of wife, daughter, or mother. What make's María's story different from other women's testimonials is that she directly reflects both on feminism and on the marginalization and oppression of women in Salvadoran society and in the popular movements of the left. She has met many feminists in her international speaking career and incorporates feminist elements into her political analysis, even going so far as to challenge the FMLN leaders in New York about what they will do for women, on the eve of the signing of the Salvadoran Peace Accords. Her perspective exemplifies the ideas of "feminismo popular," or grassroots feminism, articulated by increasing numbers of women's organizations in Latin America. Such a feminism integrates commitment to basic survival for women and their children—access to housing, food, land, and medical care—with a challenge to women's subordination to men—battering, rape, reproductive control and sexuality, and political participation.

In the past, analyses of women's movements in Latin America and discussions at international meetings of women in Latin America were often divided on whether or not particular movements could accurately be labeled "feminist" or not. Organizations such as CO-MADRES that initially emphasized motherhood were sometimes labelled non-feminist because observers did not see a challenge to traditional gender norms. Acceptance of culturally defined gender roles (such as mother) and the assertion of rights based on them was counterposed against a critique of gender subordination. Movements were categorized as one or the other—not both. In the 1990s, however, movements themselves as well as analyses of them have increasingly integrated these two types of demands. María's story illustrates this important trend.

The testimonial genre discourages either/or typologies by revealing in detail the politicizing process that a woman goes through. The blending of personal identity with political activism underscores how different and conflicting pieces of individual identity interact with structural conditions to influence the evolution of political commitment and strategy. María's initial identity as a rural, part-indigenous, poor, uneducated woman accompanied her through the experience of civil war, detention, and torture, migration, and international travel and speaking tours. Who she was when she began and how she became what she is today are both visible in her story.

The testimonial form captures the reality of multiple identities in ever-changing structural conditions far more effectively than any abstract attempt at theorizing the same process because the testimonial contains personal perspective, information about transformation, and analysis all in one. For this reason, testimonials offer an important model for feminist analysis. Testimonials are integrative. They include and validate many aspects of women's identity simultaneously and also make visible women's roles in empowering themselves and others without diminishing the structural and institutional impediments to this empowering process.

Women's testimonials are also created by collaboration between two people, most often two women. This teamwork also provides a model of non- or less-hierarchical research and writing that is consistent with principles of feminist research—at least less hierarchical than traditional social science with its objective "experts" and "research subjects." During the process of making this book, for example, my own socialization as a social scientist was repeatedly challenged despite the fact that I have engaged in several collaborative research projects in the past. María read, commented on, and suggested changes for every part of this book, resulting in many interesting and animated discussions. We had to keep talking until we came to agreement about how contested parts should read. We discussed and scrutinized each other's work, learning a great deal about each other and our visions of the world in the process. The end product is not just a book, but evidence of an enduring working relationship and friendship.

Collective History

As a literary genre, testimonials offer a uniquely collective, rather than individual perspective on history and current events. If there is one hallmark of testimonial literature, it has to be the eschewing of the personal pronoun. Numerous testimonials state explicitly that the story is not just that of one individual, but of many, of a community, of collective memory. Testimonials differ significantly from autobiographies in this respect. A significant part of their authenticity and credibility is bound up in the idea of representing a collective truth, one typically marginalized through centuries-long processes of class domination, and racial, ethnic, and gender oppression. In testimonials, the voices of poor, indigenous, working-class women in Latin America boom back at us from the far corners of history to which they have been banished, broadcasting a new version of history from the margins.

What testimonial literature offers is a concrete avenue for the reconstruction of history and a chance for "marginalized subjects" to be heard. Through the claims they make to historical representation, testimonials become equivalent to the official and often repressive histories they are challenging. Roque Dalton, an early participant in the testimonial genre, wrote the following about the importance of Miguel Mármol's story as a corrective to published accounts of Salvadoran history:

> I believe that in very few published materials of El Salvador and Central America the magnitude of the historical crimes caused by the capitalist system in our country is as manifest as in this "incriminating testimony." And not only through these terrible *frescoes,* in which Mármol tremulously narrates the huge collective massacres, but also in that everyday form of dying, which is the life of the workers and cities of Central America and which is embodied in the day-to-day existence of Mármol to secure bread for his children and for himself, to secure basic rights, the minimal conditions of human existence.[9]

Testimonial literature is a form of writing that allows ordinary people to wage a struggle for access to media of public communication. They alter the power of cultural gate-keeping and cultural production.

Truth Claims

The truth claims of the testimonial are staked on the identity and credibility of the testimonial giver. If a testimonial giver is a trusted individual who can establish a legitimate identity in the eyes of the reader, then what he or she says is usually believed. But how representative are the authors of testimonials? Some people have pointed out that Rigoberta Menchú, for example, is an unusual individual.[10] She was the child of community elders, was a committed peasant activist, and has had an unusual degree of contact with the organized left. "There is the question of whether she represents more than herself, more than her family, a sector of her group, the Guatemalan Mayans, and so on".[11] Anthropologist David Stoll has questioned the interpretation that most people give to Menchú's story. He states that while Rigoberta's descriptions of high levels of militancy might be true for the Mayan refugee population in Mexico,

> among the 90 percent of the Ixl population under army control, a population reputed to have been a revolutionary stronghold in the early 1980s, the expectations raised by *I, Rigoberta Menchú* are sure to be disappointed. Most Ixils have chosen a very different strategy for survival. They have decided to cooperate with the stronger side—the Guatemalan army.[12]

Stoll has indirectly taken Menchú to task for not representing the objective truth as he saw it during his one year in Nebaj, almost eight years after Menchú fled.

Measuring testimonials against empirically oriented anthropology is not the most useful way to evaluate them. The search for the truth value of testimonials is complex. Because testimonials are often the documents of survivors, they may contain survival strategies that conflict with readers' notions of "the whole truth." Rigoberta Menchú's story, for example, contains numerous instances of secrets that cannot be revealed to Elizabeth Burgos-DeBray, the translator and editor, and hence the reader as well. "I'm still keeping secret what I think no one should know. Not even anthropologists or intellectuals, no matter how many books they have, can find out all our secrets".[13] María often reminded me that there were many aspects of her life left out of our book. The secrets kept out of testimonials are perhaps more obvious than those kept from anthropologists. Just as those who choose to tell their stories in testimonials omit certain parts of their story, so-called "informants" inevitably do the same with anthropologists, even if the anthropologists have been living in their communities for long periods of time. The omissions in published anthropological texts may not be so obvious because quotations and interviews are usually embedded in "objective" prose funneled through the supposedly value-free filter of the anthropologist's mind. Rather than judging testimonials against journalism and social science, they should be valued for the vision and experience they represent and respected for the survival strategies that their tellers have woven into them. Without these characteristics, testimonials might not exist.

Production and Consumption of Testimonials

Testimonials invoke collaboration between the story-giver and the interviewer-editor-translator who turns the story into a publishable form. At first glance, the power dynamics of this relationship may appear to reproduce the class, race, and ethnic hierarchies that are often a part of testimonial stories, but it is important to note how much of a stake story-givers have in testimonials. Political activists like Rigoberta Menchú and María Teresa Tula are interested in having their stories and perspectives reach international audiences, a goal reflected in the roles they have taken on in their respective organizations—Rigoberta as an indigenous human rights activist and peasant organizer speaking around the world on behalf of the Committee for Peasant Unity, CUC (now even more since she won the 1992 Nobel Peace Prize) and María representing CO-MADRES in the United States and in other parts of the world. They are intellectuals going about their work, organic intellectuals whose testimonials build a sense of solidarity and understanding that increases their likelihood of survival and success. While often recognized as intellectuals, they can also be romanticized as representing "the exotic other" by people who seek to demonstrate their commitment to alternative viewpoints. Treating people such as Rigoberta Menchú and María Teresa Tula as symbols for an oppressed majority diminishes their individual achievements and political work.

Producing testimonials is entirely consistent with their political work. The ability to tell one's own story, family history, and community political history is the hallmark of an intellectual in many parts of the world and that is how María Teresa Tula and Rigoberta Menchú are recognized by the movement organizations they work with. To claim that all of the power in a testimonial collaboration resides with the editor is to underestimate the skill of people such as María who use oral testimony as a political tool.

Roque Dalton, for example, points out that Mármol's version of events has been filtered through his own intellectual formation and political experience. He explains the type of Marxist education Mármol had along with his organizing experience in the Communist Party of El Salvador (PCS) to provide a guide for Mármol's interpretation of historic events. He does not offer Mármols' testimony of past events as unadulterated truth, but Marmol's perception of the truth:

> ...it is necessary to understand that Miguel Mármol gave me his life testimony (in which, as we've said, the most important events happened around 1932) as recently as 1966, which implies the elaboration of a viewpoint on those earlier problems by means of a process that has been developing ever since. Miguel Mármol tells us about the events of the '20s, 1932 or 1944 through the political thought he possesses in 1968.[14]

The validity of Mármol's testimony comes from his unique perspective, not from the fact that he will tell an objective truth. Dalton exhibited a high level of awareness of the ways in which testimonials are constructed both by the teller of the testimonial and by the editor, each with perspectives, experience, and agendas that influence the outcome.

People in a day-to-day struggle for survival have neither the resources nor the leisure to produce their own texts.[15] They also don't always have the money to purchase them, or the time or capacity to read them. By and large, testimonials are produced for a middle-class, educated audience. Sometimes published in English first (as with Elvia Alvarado's and Medea Benjamin's *Don't Be Afraid Gringo),* their audience is angloamerican. If published in Spanish, they will reach primarily educated and middle-class Latin Americans.

More than anything, testimonials are designed as bridges of solidarity and understanding, yet they still replicate the political economy of United States-Latin American relations of production and consumption. Testimonials are consumed by people who want a version of history legitimized as authentic because it is told by a Latin American. A major part of their appeal lies in the differences between the lives of those in the stories and the lives of those who read them. This is part of what makes the testimonial genre different from traditions of oral history where the story is generally consumed by those who share a cultural and historical background with the teller. In testimonial literature, the communication from teller to reader is based primarily on difference.

For activists such as María Teresa Tula, these differences are precisely why it is so important to tell her story. Building solidarity links to the United States is a major piece of her political work, particularly since the Fall of 1992 when the press and former President Bush declared that the war in El Salvador was over and freedom and democratic elections were at hand. Rebuilding from the devastating effects of war will take longer and require more resources than did surviving during the war itself. María hopes that her testimonial will move Americans to continue their support for popular movements in El Salvador. While the audience for the testimonial requires that its form be bounded by the conventions of publishing and book selling, its content represents a dialogue of solidarity that has long existed between the people of the United States and those engaged in grassroots struggles throughout Latin America.

Notes

1. Oscar, Lewis, *The Children of Sanchez* (New York: Random House, 1963 and Che Guevara, *Reminiscences of the Cuban Revolutionary War*, translated by Victoria Ortiz (New York: Monthly Review Press, 1968). John Beverly and Marc Zimmerman provide an excellent discussion on the origins of the testimonial genre on a country by country basis in Central America in their book *Literature and Politics in the Central American Revolutions* (Austin: University of Texas Press, 1990).

2. Roque Dalton, *Miguel Mármol,* translated by Kathleen Ross and Richard Schaaf (New York: Curbstone Press, 1987). The Costa Rican Editorial Universitaria Centroamerica (EDUCA) published the original edition of the book in Spanish in 1982.

3. Salvador Cayetano Carpio, *Secuestro y capucha en un país del "mundo libre"* (San Jose: EDUCA, 1979).

4. Ana Guadalupe Martínez, *Las cárceles clandestinas de El Salvador* (Mexico: Casa El Salvador, 1979).

5. Karen Lievens, *El quinto piso de la alegría. Tres años con la guerrilla* (San Salvador: Ediciones Sistema Radio Venceremos, 1988).

6. Claribel Alegría, *No me agarrán viva: La mujer salvadoreña en la lucha* (Mexico: ERA, 1983).

7. Nidia Díaz, *Nunca estuve sola* (San Salvador: UCA, 1986).

8. Elvia Alvarado, *Don't Be Afraid Gringo. A Honduran Woman Speaks From the Heart,* translated and edited by Medea Benjamin (San Francisco: Institute for Food and Development Policy, 1987); Domitila Barrios de Chungara with Moema Viezzer, *Let Me Speak! Testimony of Domitila, a Woman of the Bolivian Mines,* translated by Victoria Ortiz (New York: Monthly Review Press, 1978); Rigoberta Menchú with Elisabeth Burgos-Debray, *I, Rigoberta Menchú: An Indian Woman in Guatemala,* translated by Anne Wright (London: Verso, 1984).

9. Dalton, *Miguel Mármol*, 40.

10. David, Zimmerman, "Testimonio in Guatemala: Payeras, Rigoberta, and Beyond," *Latin American Perspectives* 18,4 (Fall, 1991):22-47.

11. Zimmerman, Testimonio in Guatemala, 31.

12. David Stoll, "The Land No Longer Gives: Land Reform in Nebaj, Guatemala," *Cultural Survival Quarterly* 14,4 (Fall, 1990:4-5).

13. Menchú, *I, Rigoberta Menchú,* 247. Doris Sommer has an excellent discussion on Rigoberta's use of secrets as a way of controlling information and protecting cultural knowledge in "Rigoberta's Secrets," *Latin American Perspectives* 18,3 (Summer 1991):32-50.

14. Dalton, *Miguel Mármol*, 26.

15. Lynda Marín, "Speaking Out Together: Testimonials of Latin American Women," *Latin American Perspectives* 18,3 (Summer 1991):51-68.

Epilogue

One year ago we Salvadorans had faith that the just peace we had so long awaited had finally arrived. Peace was declared, but human rights abuses have continued. Death squads are still threatening people's lives. We hope that little by little the signed Peace Accords move from paper to reality as the Salvadoran people keep on pressuring for peace in our country. The signing of the Peace Accords has forced some concessions, such as the dissolution of some of the most criminal elite battalions trained in the United States.

I am worried that many Salvadorans are leaving the country to become refugees or to look for new lives and new horizons in the United States. Sadly, the U.S. government won't accept cases of political asylum. The U.S. government didn't accept these cases in the 1980s, in spite of the fact that the majority of applicants had suffered persecution. Many had received threats from death squads for belonging to social movements. The U.S. government is using the signing of the Peace Accords as an excuse to reject salvadorans' request for political asylum. People in El Salvador however, are still afraid to say what they think, to speak out in public about social conditions or their political ideas.

Things will change in our country, little by little. Change is always a slow process. It's hard for me to say this, but some of our leaders who signed the Peace Accords are behind the times, even though they are politically and ideologically capable. Hopefully we will see peace become a reality. There have been changes in the structure of the military, but the same people are still in power. This is like changing an old pair of shoes for a new one. The feet are still there underneath. I hope that the feet of

El Salvador can take on the shape of peace and become part of a new body that will carry us into the future with justice.

The process of writing this book has been a long one. I wanted to tell my personal story and also let people know about the women's movement in El Salvador. I wanted to tell people, nationally and internationally, about my life: how a woman came to be politically active because she lost her husband.

I grew up in a very poor family and never had big dreams like the ones I have now. I never imagined that I would travel all over the world, come to the United States, and have a book published about my life. I had to tell my story because there are thousands of women like me who are telling their stories and living lives just like mine. I hope that this book serves as an example not of me, but of all of the women in the world who are not afraid to stand up for themselves and who are capable of doing incredible things when they put their minds to it.

María Teresa Tula
Washington, D.C.
December, 1993

Glossary

abuela	grandmother
alcaldía	the town hall
ADEMUSA	Asociación de Mujeres Salvadoreñas, The Association of Salvadoran Women
AMES	Asociación de Mujeres de El Salvador, The Association of Women in El Salvador
AMPES	Asociación de Mujeres Progresistas de El Salvador, Association of Progressive Women of El Salvador
AMS	Asociación de Mujeres Salvadoreñas, Salvadoran Women's Association
animalero	a colloquialism used to describe violent, animalistic behavior by members of the military, usually implying indiscriminate slaughter
barrios marginales	shantytown neighborhoods
cabrón	a rough Spanish equivalent to the English expression "son of a bitch" or "ass hole"
campesino	peasant
capucha	a form of torture in which the prisoner's head is covered with a hood (usually the inside of the hood is coated with toxic chemicals). As the prisoner breathes, the hood sticks to his or her face, resulting in suffocation
CEMUJER	Centro de Estudios de la Mujer "Norma Virginia Guirola de Herrera," Women's Studies Center "Norma Virginia Guirola de Herrera"
CDHES	Comisión de Derechos Humanos de El Salvador, Human Rights Commission of El Salvador, nongovernmental
CO-FENASTRAS	Comité Femenino de la Federación Nacional de Trabajadores Salvadoreños, Women's Committee of FENASTRAS

CONAMUS	Coordinadora Nacional de Mujeres Salvadoreñas, National Coordinating Committee of Salvadoran Women
champas	shacks made from cardboard or other previously discarded materials
chicha	alcoholic drink made from fermented corn and brown sugar
cofradías	religious brotherhoods responsible for sponsoring festivities for the cult celebrations of community saints
colones	Salvadoran currency
CO-MADRES	Comité de Madres y Familiares de Presos, Desaparecidos y Asesinados de El Salvador "Monseñor Romero." Committee of Mothers and Relatives of Political Prisoners, Disappeared, and Assassinated of El Salvador "Monseñor Romero"
comandante	commander
COM	Coordinadora de Organizaciones de Mujeres, Council of Women's Organizations
compañero	friend, comrade, partner
Convergencia Democrática	Democratic Convergence
COPPES	Comité de Presos Políticos de El Salvador, Committee of Political Prisoners of El Salvador
coyote	person taking others illegally across the United States-Mexico border
CREFDES	Comité de Refugiados Desplazados, The Committee for Displaced Refugees
cuñada	sister-in-law
CUTS	Confederación Unitaria de Trabajadores Salvadoreños, United Confederation of Salvadoran Workers
damnificados	victims of a natural disaster, in this book referring to the victims of the 1986 earthquake, who never recovered from their losses
DIGNAS	Mujeres por la Dignidad y la Vida "Rompamos el silencio," Women for Dignity and Life "Breaking the Silence".

enfrentamiento	an armed confrontation often feigned by the military to justify the assassination of people viewed as subversives
ERP	Ejército Revolucionario Del Pueblo, The People's Revolutionary Army, formed in 1971 by dissident christian democrats and other leftists
FARN (RN)	Fuerzas Populares Armadas de Resistencia Nacional, The Armed Forces of National Resistance, formed in 1975 by a faction of the ERP
FEDEFAM	Federación Latinoamericana de Familiares de Detenidos y Desaparecidos, Federation of Relatives of the Disappeared and Detained in Latin America
FDR	Frente Democrático Revolucionario, Democratic Revolutionary Front, united all mass organizations opposed to the government from 1980-1988
FENASTRAS	Federación Nacional de Trabajadores Salvadoreños, National Federation of Salvadoran Workers
FMLN	Frente Farabundo Martí para la Liberación Nacional, Farabundo Martí National Liberation Front
FPL-FM	Fuerzas Populares De Liberación-Farabundo Martí, The Popular Forces for Liberation "Farabundo Martí," a radical wing of the Salvadoran Communist Party
fulano	the Spanish equivalent to the English expression "Joe Schmo"—a generic anyone
FUSS	Federación Unitaria Sindical Salvadoreña, Salvadoran Unitary Trade Union Federation
guerrillero	guerrilla fighter
hija	daughter
hijillo	evil eye, evil wind or bad karma causing illness in children
IMU	Instituto para la Investigación, Capacitación y Desarrollo de la Mujer, Institute for Research, Training, and Development of Women
LP-28	Ligas Populares "28 De Febrero," a popular revolutionary organization whose small membership was heavily influenced by student militants. The organization is named after the day in 1977 when

	the armed forces killed over 100 people demonstrating against the fraudulent election of General Romero
madrecita	affectionate term meaning "little mother"
MNR	Movimiento Nacional Revolucionario, National Revolutionary Movement
MPSC	Movimiento Popular Social Cristiano, Popular Social Christian Movement
Mujeres '94	Women of 1994
patrulla cantonal	local police, also called the barefoot police
pergamanato	a vaginal suppository used for its contraceptive properties
PCS	Partido Communista Salvadoreño, Salvadoran Communist Party
PRTC	Partido Revolucionario de Trabajadores Centroamericanos, Central American Workers Party
pupusa	a thick corn tortilla filled with meat, cheese, or vegetables. One of the staples of the Salvadoran diet
refresco	refreshment; a cool, often carbonated drink
RN	Resistencia Nacional, National Resistance
sisana	in the context of this book, men making hissing noises to get a woman's attention
SLES	Sindicato de la Luz Electrica de Sonsonate, Electrical Workers Union of Sonsonate
STECEL	Sindicato de Trabajadores de la Empresa Comisión Ejecutiva del Río Lempa, Río Lempa Electrical Company Workers' Trade Union
usted	the formal version of "you," used to connote distance or respect. It is contrasted with "tu," the familiar form
yuca	Starchy root crop that is a popular fast food and street food in El Salvador. Yucca, cassava or manioc